contents

Vol. 12: Fall 2008

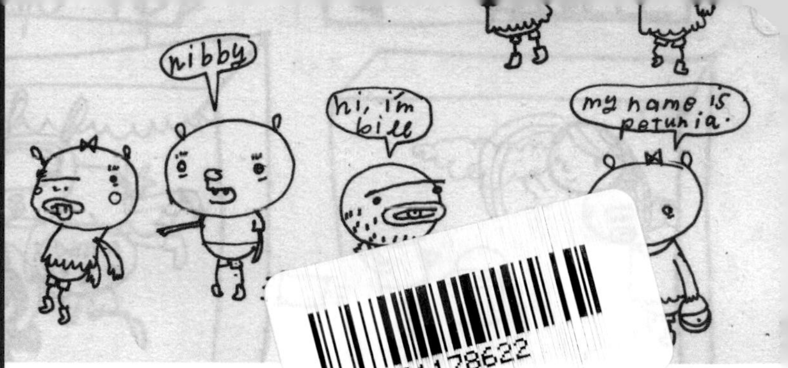
nibby
hi, i'm bill
my name is petunia.

Cover images by Olivier Sc… …ranam

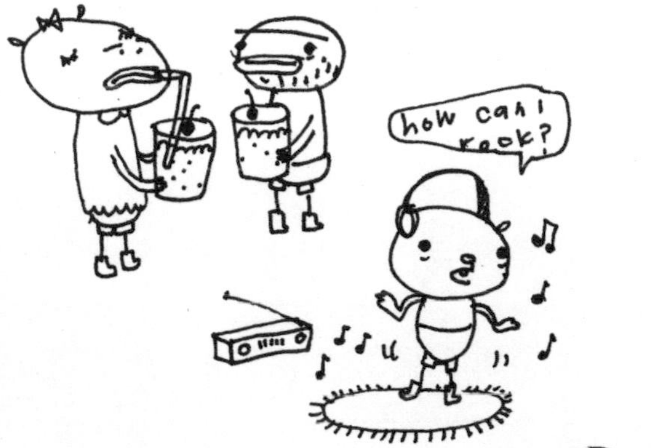
how can i rook?

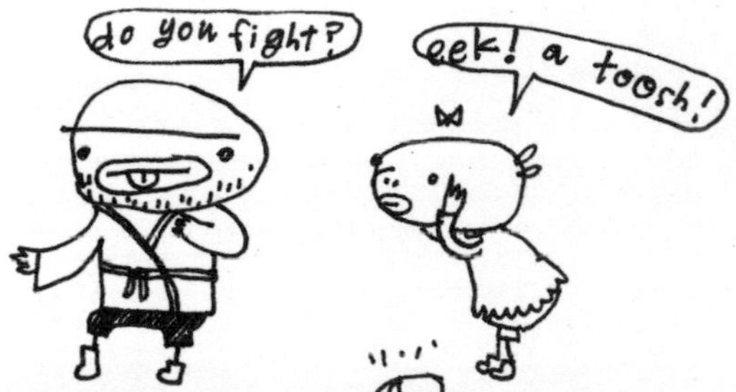
do you fight?
eek! a toosh!
ew. bwown.
my poise!
it's bwown.

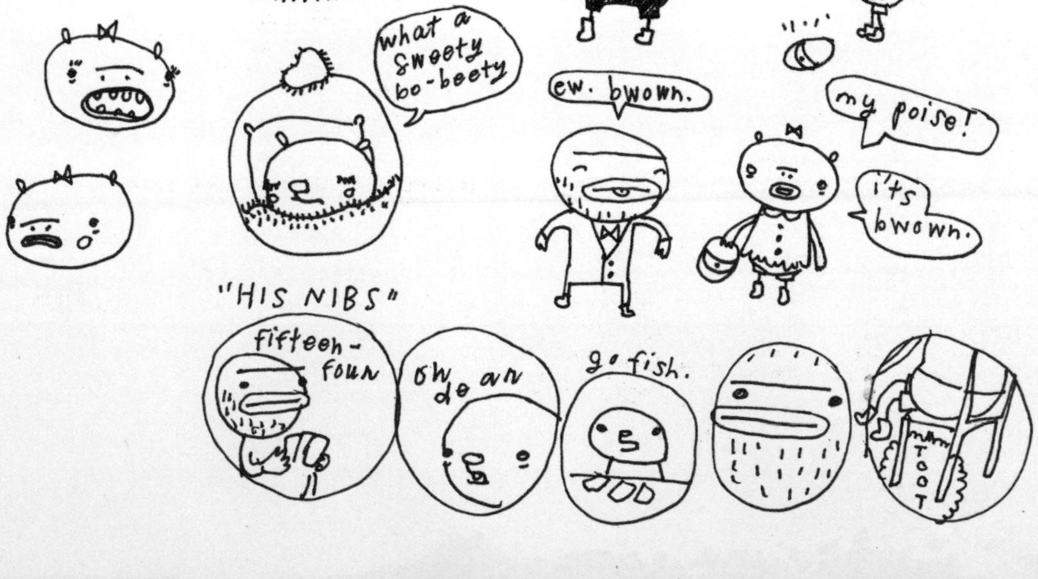
what a sweety bo-beety
"HIS NIBS"
go fish.
TOOT

particulars

Indicia / information

MOME 12: FALL 2008

Published by Fantagraphics Books, 7563 Lake City Way Northeast, Seattle, Washington, 98115. MOME is copyright © 2008 Fantagraphics Books. Individual stories and images are copyright © 2008 the respective artist. All rights reserved. Permission to reproduce material from this book, except for purposes of review and/or notice, must be obtained by the publisher. Edited by Eric Reynolds and Gary Groth. Art direction by Adam Grano. Original MOME design by Jordan Crane.

First edition: July 2008
ISBN 978-1-56097-930-2
Printed in Singapore

VISIT THE FANTAGRAPHICS BOOKSTORE & GALLERY:
1201 S. Vale St. (at Airport Way) in the Georgetown neighborhood of Seattle, Washington.

FOR A FREE CATALOG OF COMICS AND CARTOONING:
Please telephone 1-800-657-1100 or consult www.fantagraphics.com.

NOTES FROM THE EDITORS:

- This volume, we welcome five new contributors to *Mome*: Olivier Schrauwen, Sara Edward-Corbett, Jon Vermilyea, Derek Van Gieson, and Kaela Graham.
- We first discovered Mr. Schrauwen's work through his collection *Mon Fiston* (Editions de l'an 2, 2006) and fell in love immediately. We contacted him last year, inviting him to contribute and he generously agreed: his brilliant 13-page story this issue was created exclusively for *Mome*, and marks his first work created in English.
- Mr. Vermilyea was our favorite "discovery" at San Diego's Comicon last summer, where we were seduced by his phenomenal *Masters of the Universe* prints (we're not joking) and came home with his incredible comics from Picturebox (one of our favorite publishers). His *Cold Heat Special* (in collaboration with Frank Santoro) and *Princes of Time* are must-haves. May this is the first of many more "Breakfast Crew" stories for *Mome*.
- Mr. Van Gieson was introduced to us through our colleague Emily Gordon of *Print* magazine (she also introduced us to Ray Fenwick, as a matter of fact). If Mr. Van Gieson's style looks familiar, it's because you've quite probably seen his illustration work in the pages of *The New Yorker* and elsewhere, but you've likely not seen his comics before. Enjoy them. Absorb them.
- Ms. Edward-Corbett was introduced to us via an archaic communication device your parents may remember as the "U.S.P.S." This inefficient delivery system yields extremely slow, tentative transmissions in which one's "friendship status" can remain unclear until long after the relationship begins. Remarkably, our tenacious desire to bring you her work was able to overcome the vagaries of this strange social network. Ms. Edward-Corbett is probably best known for her *See-Saw* strip that ran in *The New York Press*.
- Congratulations to Lewis Trondheim and Émile Bravo, who were nominated in the "Best Short Story" category of the 2008 Eisner Awards (Mr. Trondheim for "At Loose Ends" from Vols. 6-8 and Mr. Bravo for "Young Americans" in Vol. 8). *Mome* was also nominated for "Best Anthology," alongside *The Best American Comics 2007* (Houghton Mifflin), which includes several pieces selected from *Mome*; no other anthology nominee can make such a claim, oddly.
- "The Drum Who Fell in Love" and "Dirty Family Laundry" were both translated from the French by Kim Thompson. "The Drum" originally appeared *Le Jardin Arme: Et Autres Histories* (Futuropolis, 2006). "Dirty Family Laundry" originally appeared in *Lapin* magazine (L'Association).
- The color separations for "Invasion" were provided by Jon Adams of citycyclops.com.
- We enjoy your letters of comment. Please write us at fbicomix@fantagraphics.com and include "MOME MAIL" in the subject line.

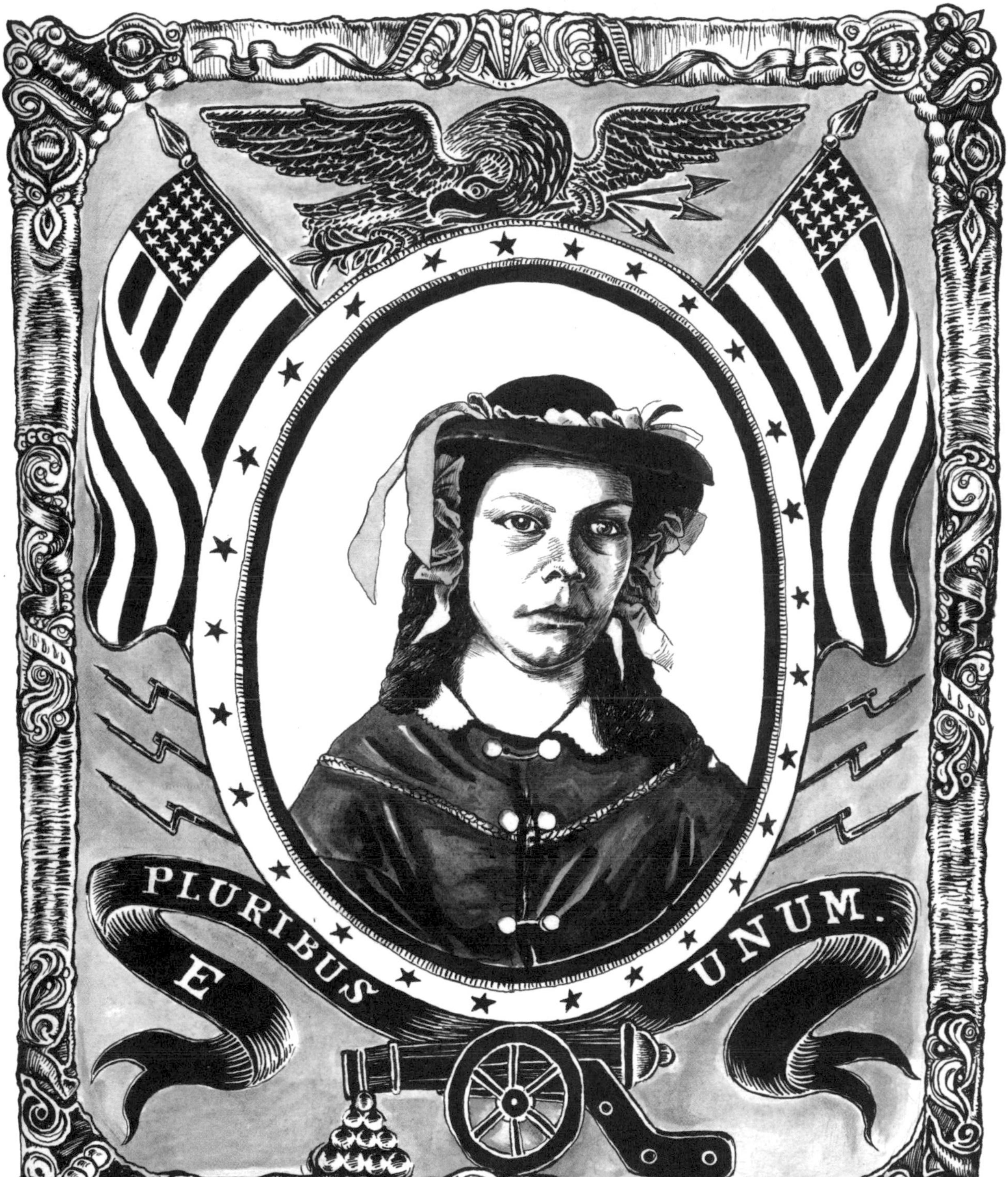
PLURIBUS
E
UNUM.

AGNES FREEMAN, HER STOLID PORTRAIT IN AN ORNATE CIVIL WAR FRAME, WENT WEST IN 1865. TIRELESS, SHE RAN HER HUSBAND'S NEBRASKA RANCH, REARED SEVEN CHILDREN, OPENED A SCHOOL AND PRACTICED MEDICINE.

TAKEN FROM A COLLECTION OF OLD WEST BOOKS "TIME-LIFE BOOKS/THE OLD WEST."

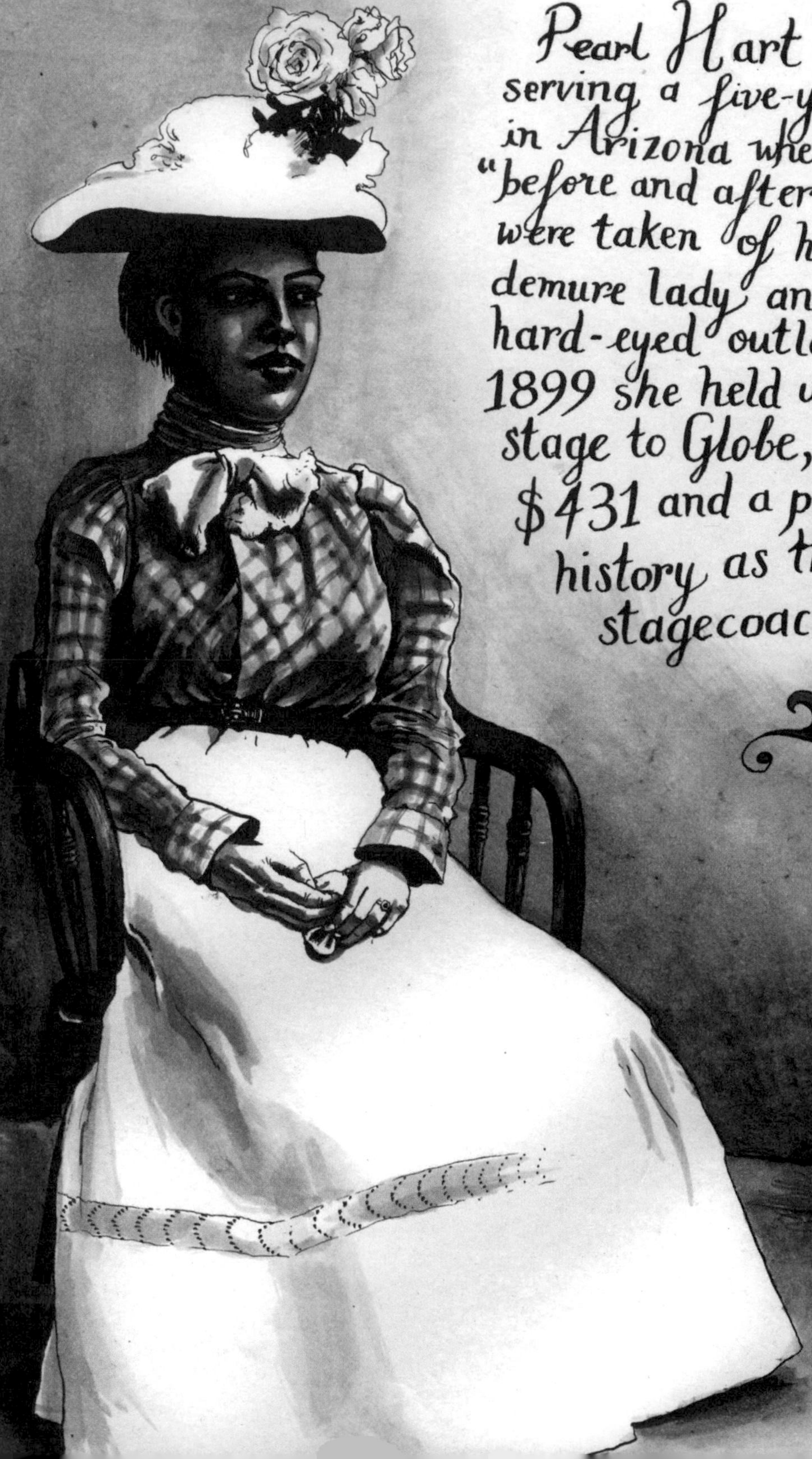

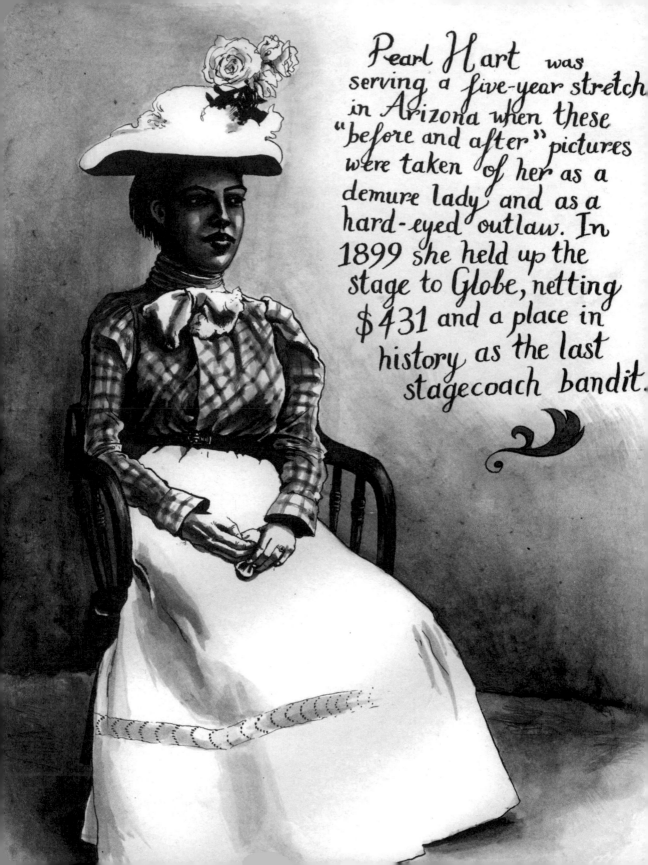

Pearl Hart was serving a five-year stretch in Arizona when these "before and after" pictures were taken of her as a demure lady and as a hard-eyed outlaw. In 1899 she held up the stage to Globe, netting $431 and a place in history as the last stagecoach bandit.

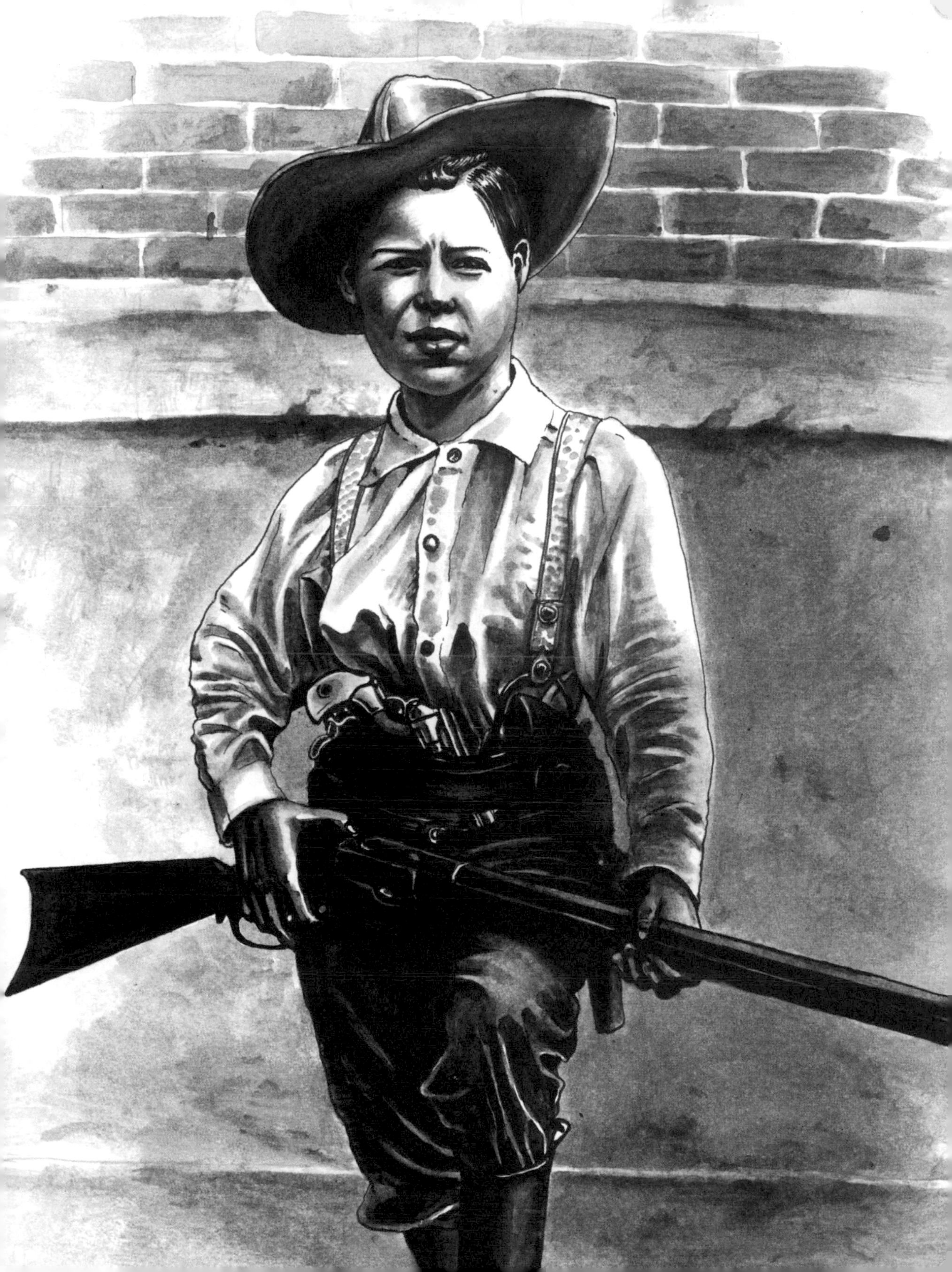

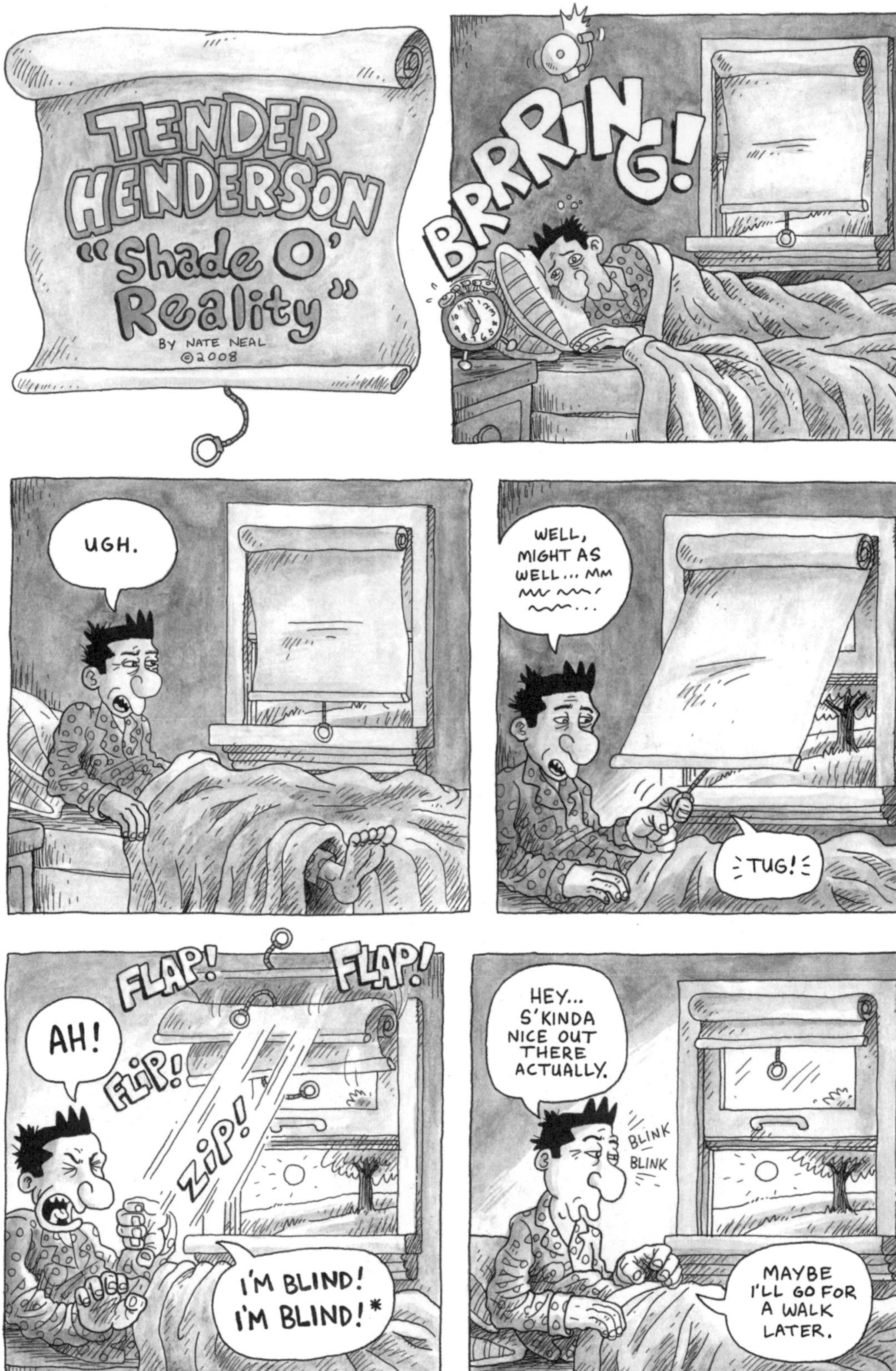
TENDER HENDERSON
"Shade O' Reality"
BY NATE NEAL
©2008
BRRRING!
UGH.
WELL, MIGHT AS WELL... MM ~~ ~~' ~~...
TUG!
FLAP!
FLAP!
AH!
FLIP!
ZIP!
I'M BLIND! I'M BLIND!*
HEY... S'KINDA NICE OUT THERE ACTUALLY.
BLINK
BLINK
MAYBE I'LL GO FOR A WALK LATER.

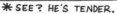

* SEE? HE'S TENDER.

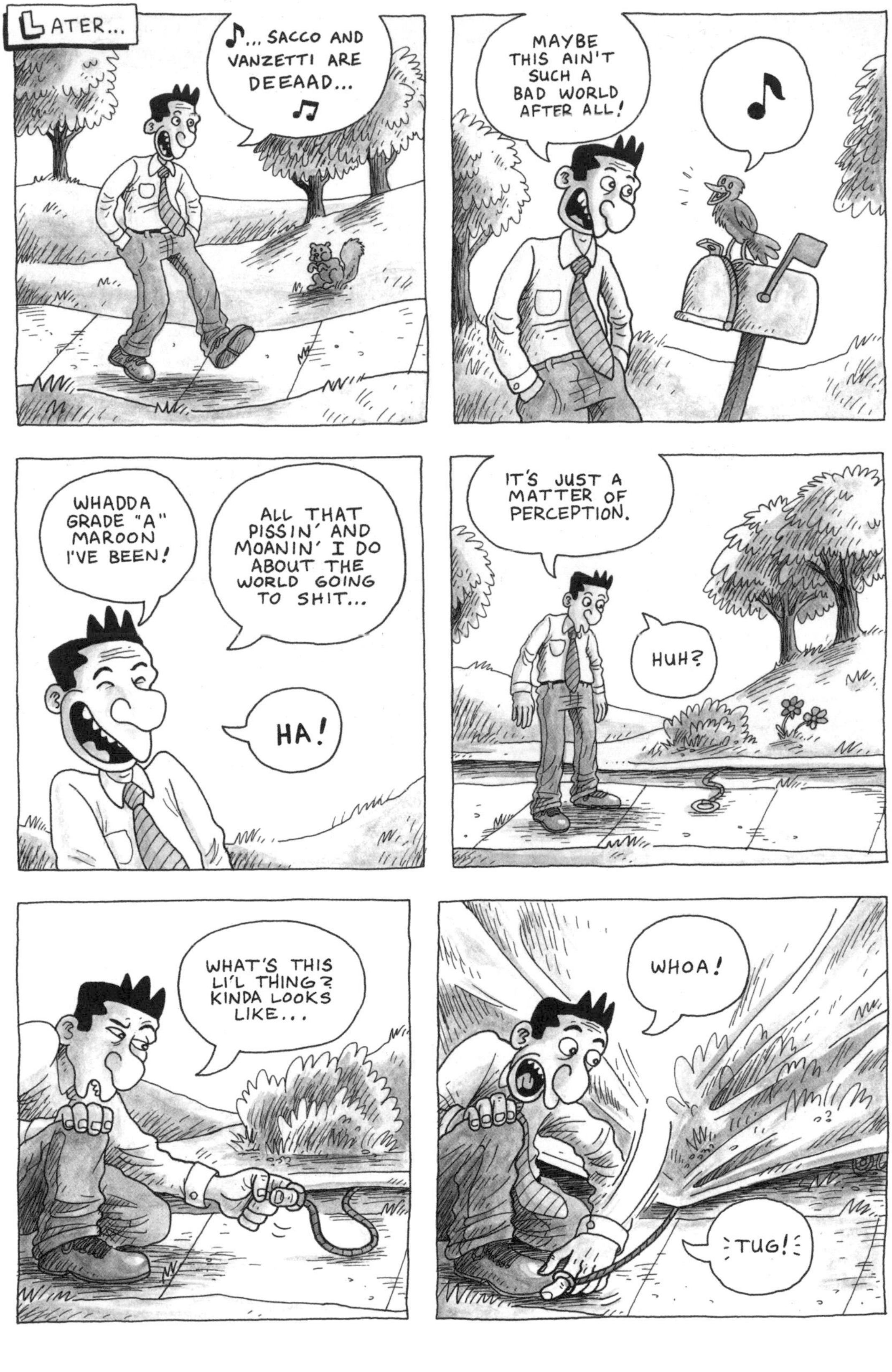
LATER...
♪... SACCO AND VANZETTI ARE DEEAAD... ♫
MAYBE THIS AIN'T SUCH A BAD WORLD AFTER ALL!
♪
WHADDA GRADE "A" MAROON I'VE BEEN!
ALL THAT PISSIN' AND MOANIN' I DO ABOUT THE WORLD GOING TO SHIT...
HA!
IT'S JUST A MATTER OF PERCEPTION.
HUH?
WHAT'S THIS LI'L THING? KINDA LOOKS LIKE...
WHOA!
TUG!

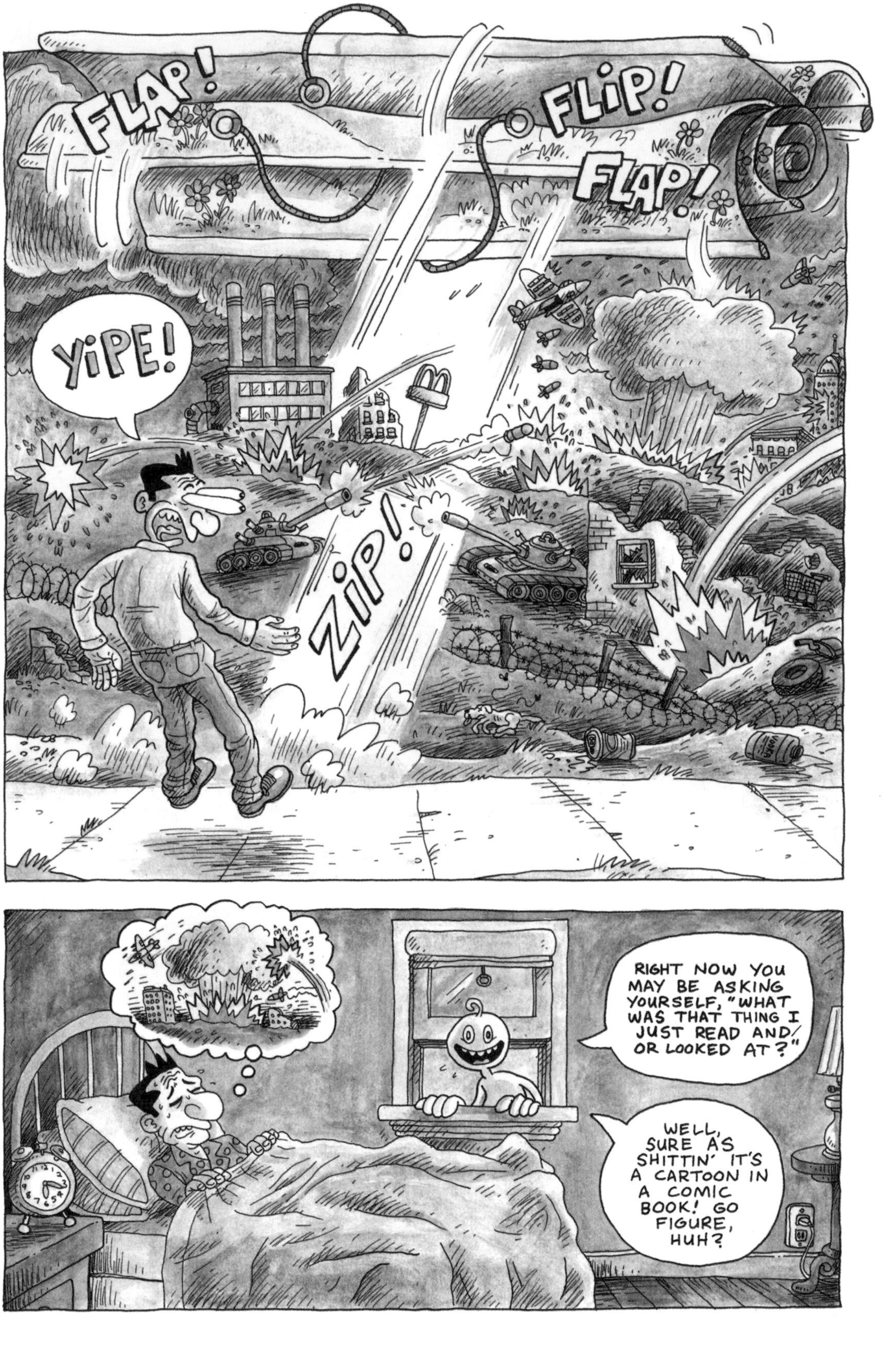
FLAP!
FLIP!
FLAP!
YIPE!
ZIP!
RIGHT NOW YOU MAY BE ASKING YOURSELF, "WHAT WAS THAT THING I JUST READ AND/OR LOOKED AT?"
WELL, SURE AS SHITTIN' IT'S A CARTOON IN A COMIC BOOK! GO FIGURE, HUH?

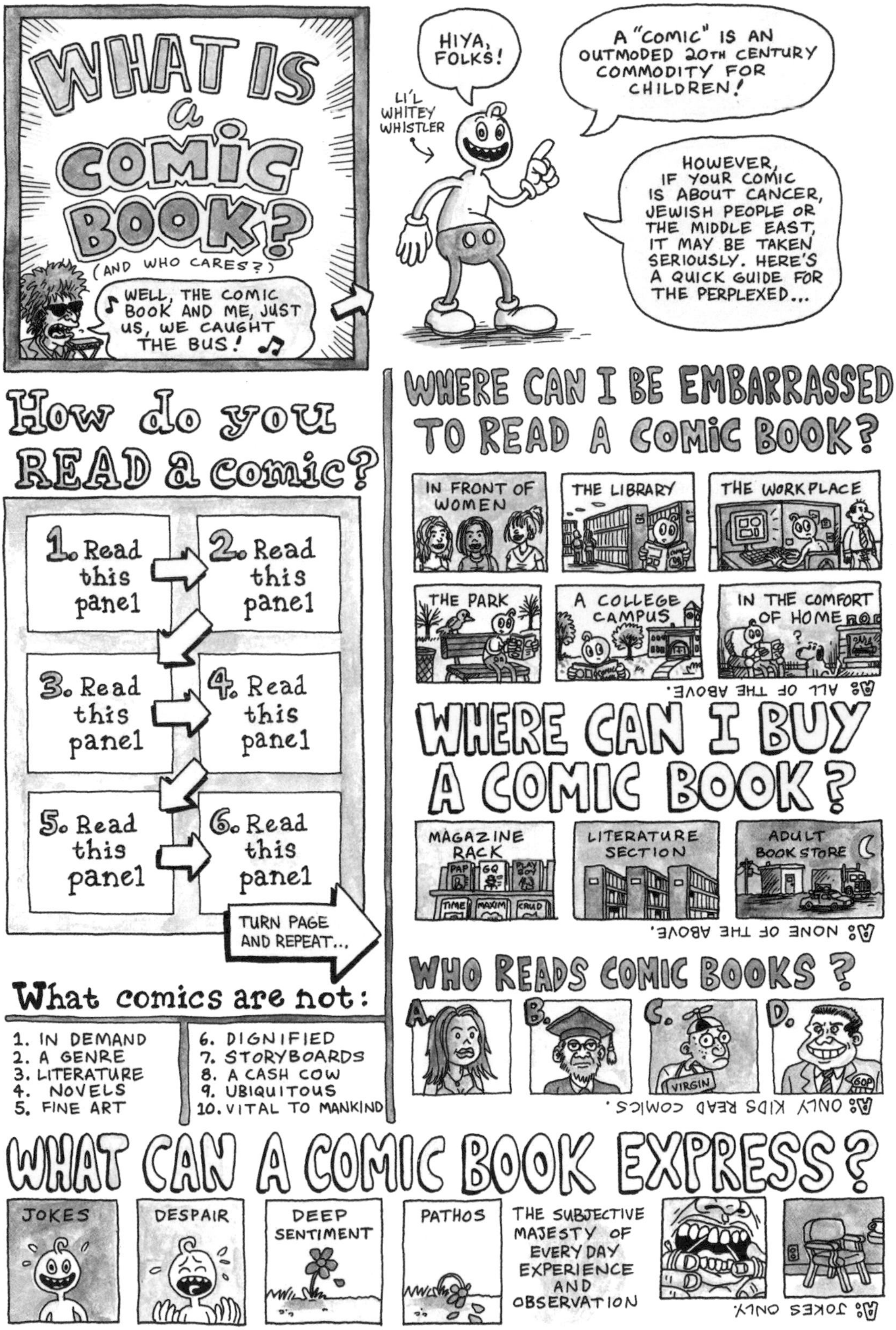
WHAT IS a COMIC BOOK?
(AND WHO CARES?)
WELL, THE COMIC BOOK AND ME, JUST US, WE CAUGHT THE BUS!
HIYA, FOLKS!
LI'L WHITEY WHISTLER
A "COMIC" IS AN OUTMODED 20TH CENTURY COMMODITY FOR CHILDREN!
HOWEVER, IF YOUR COMIC IS ABOUT CANCER, JEWISH PEOPLE OR THE MIDDLE EAST, IT MAY BE TAKEN SERIOUSLY. HERE'S A QUICK GUIDE FOR THE PERPLEXED...
How do you READ a comic?
1. Read this panel
2. Read this panel
3. Read this panel
4. Read this panel
5. Read this panel
6. Read this panel
TURN PAGE AND REPEAT...
What comics are not:
1. IN DEMAND
2. A GENRE
3. LITERATURE
4. NOVELS
5. FINE ART
6. DIGNIFIED
7. STORYBOARDS
8. A CASH COW
9. UBIQUITOUS
10. VITAL TO MANKIND
WHERE CAN I BE EMBARRASSED TO READ A COMIC BOOK?
IN FRONT OF WOMEN
THE LIBRARY
THE WORKPLACE
THE PARK
A COLLEGE CAMPUS
IN THE COMFORT OF HOME
A: ALL OF THE ABOVE.
WHERE CAN I BUY A COMIC BOOK?
MAGAZINE RACK
PAP
GQ
PLAYBOY
TIME
MAXIM
CRUD
LITERATURE SECTION
ADULT BOOK STORE
A: NONE OF THE ABOVE.
WHO READS COMIC BOOKS?
A.
B.
C.
VIRGIN
D.
GOP
A: ONLY KIDS READ COMICS.
WHAT CAN A COMIC BOOK EXPRESS?
JOKES
DESPAIR
DEEP SENTIMENT
PATHOS
THE SUBJECTIVE MAJESTY OF EVERYDAY EXPERIENCE AND OBSERVATION
A: JOKES ONLY.

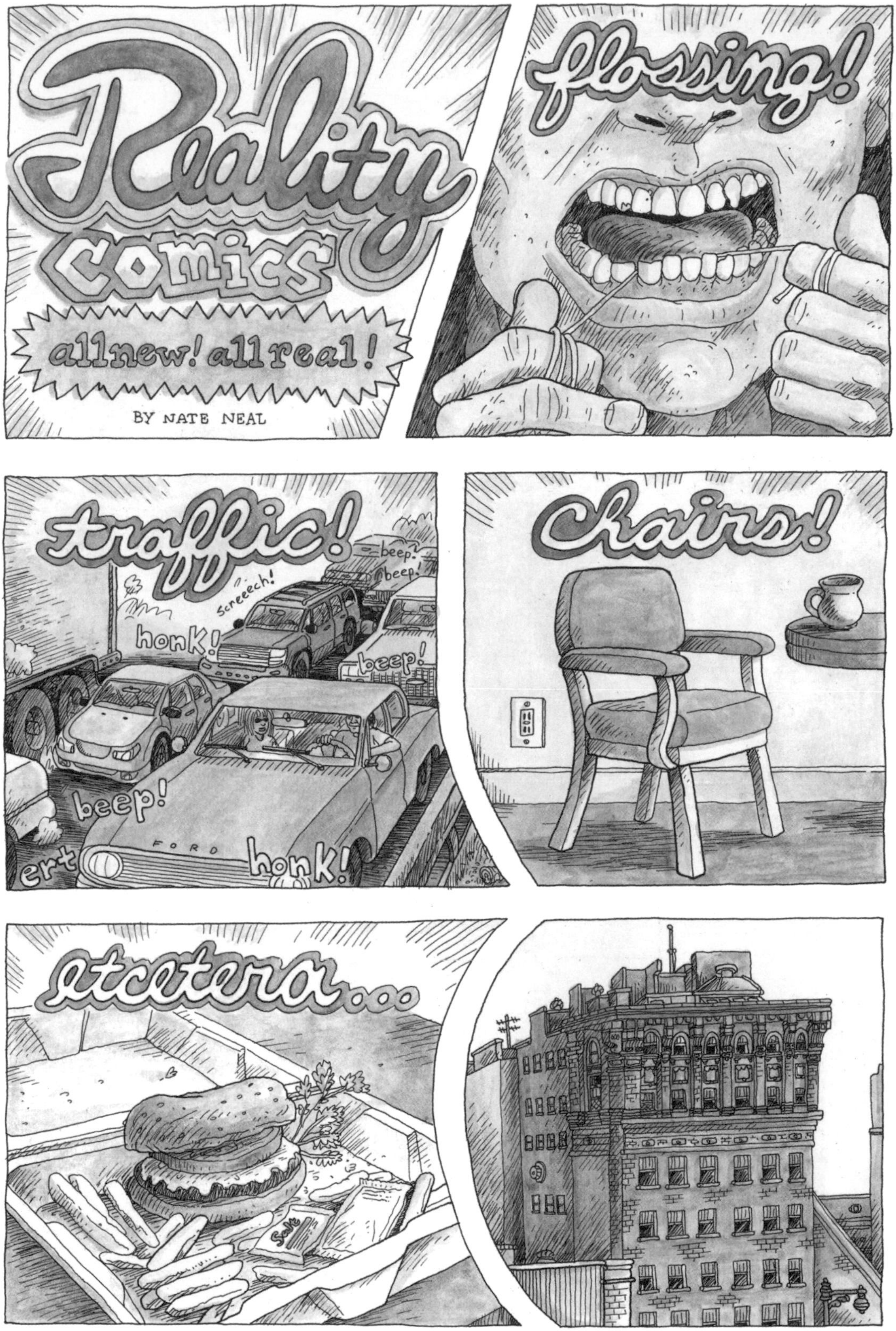
Reality comics
all new! all real!
BY NATE NEAL
flossing!
traffic!
beep!
beep!
screeech!
honk!
beep!
beep!
FORD
honk!
ert
chairs!
etcetera...
Salt

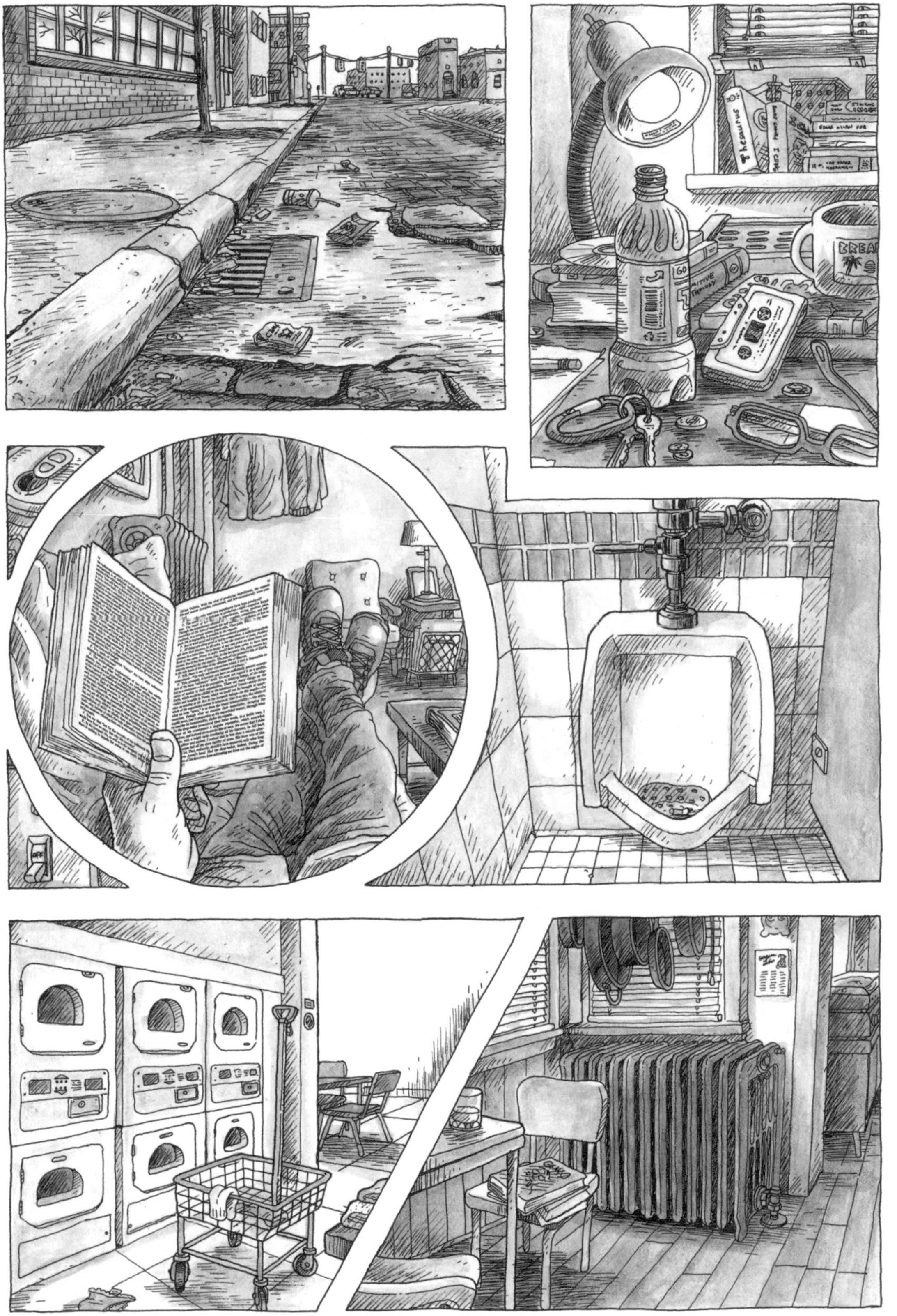
Thesaurus
EDGAR ALLAN POE
OFF

He held the door open for her at the library
and in   ffee with him.
Sh   yed with

A Reality Apart

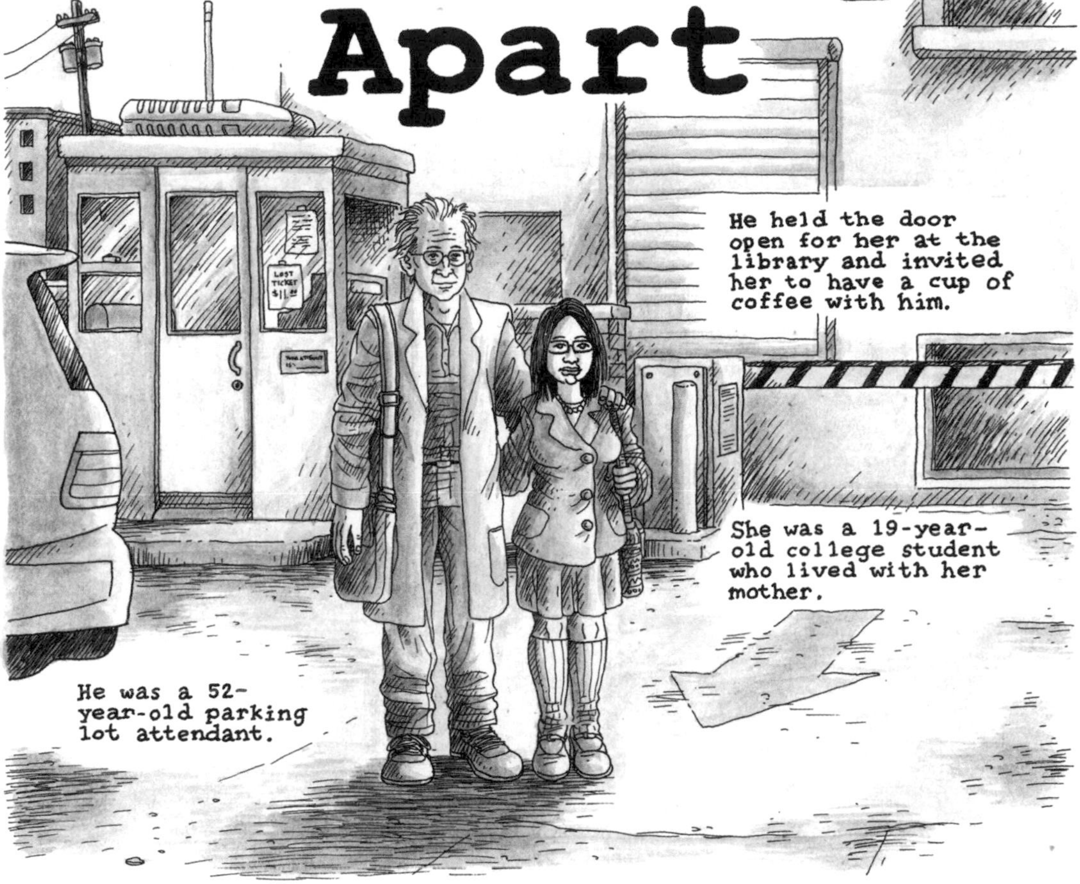
He held the door open for her at the library and invited her to have a cup of coffee with him.
LOST TICKET $11.00
She was a 19-year-old college student who lived with her mother.
He was a 52-year-old parking lot attendant.

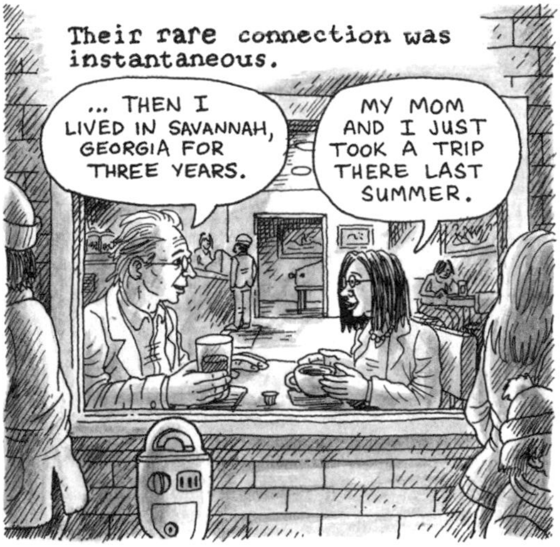
Their rare connection was instantaneous.
... THEN I LIVED IN SAVANNAH, GEORGIA FOR THREE YEARS.
MY MOM AND I JUST TOOK A TRIP THERE LAST SUMMER.

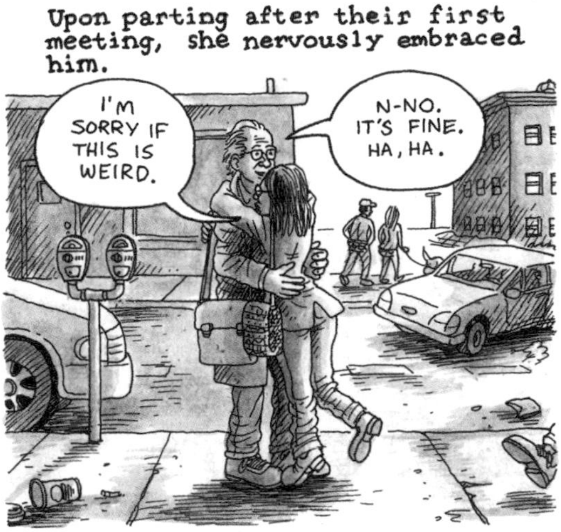
Upon parting after their first meeting, she nervously embraced him.
I'M SORRY IF THIS IS WEIRD.
N-NO. IT'S FINE. HA, HA.

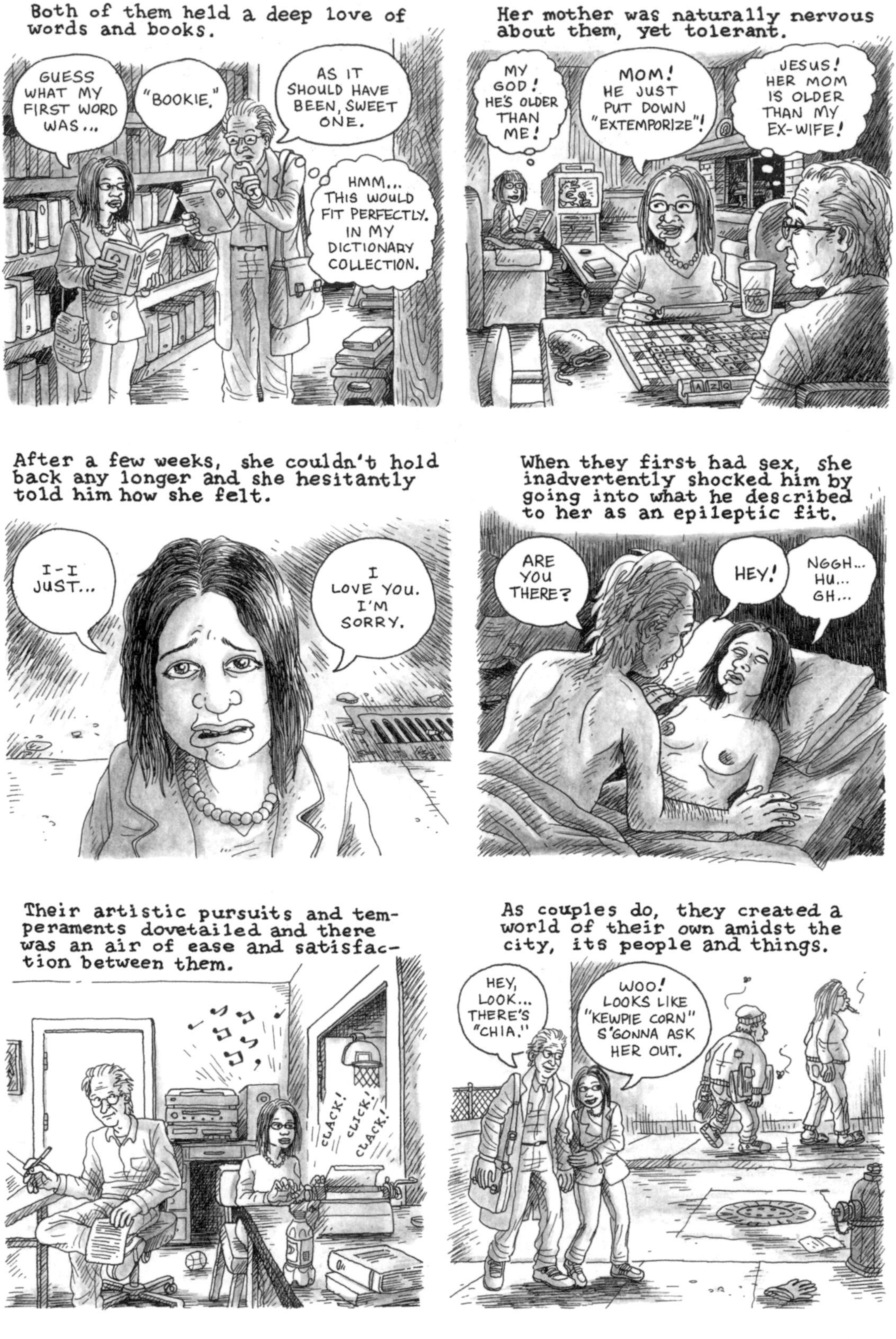
Both of them held a deep love of words and books.
GUESS WHAT MY FIRST WORD WAS...
"BOOKIE."
AS IT SHOULD HAVE BEEN, SWEET ONE.
HMM... THIS WOULD FIT PERFECTLY. IN MY DICTIONARY COLLECTION.
Her mother was naturally nervous about them, yet tolerant.
MY GOD! HE'S OLDER THAN ME!
MOM! HE JUST PUT DOWN "EXTEMPORIZE"!
JESUS! HER MOM IS OLDER THAN MY EX-WIFE!
After a few weeks, she couldn't hold back any longer and she hesitantly told him how she felt.
I-I JUST...
I LOVE YOU. I'M SORRY.
When they first had sex, she inadvertently shocked him by going into what he described to her as an epileptic fit.
ARE YOU THERE?
HEY!
NGGH... HU... GH...
Their artistic pursuits and temperaments dovetailed and there was an air of ease and satisfaction between them.
CLACK! CLICK! CLACK!
As couples do, they created a world of their own amidst the city, its people and things.
HEY, LOOK... THERE'S "CHIA."
WOO! LOOKS LIKE "KEWPIE CORN" S'GONNA ASK HER OUT.

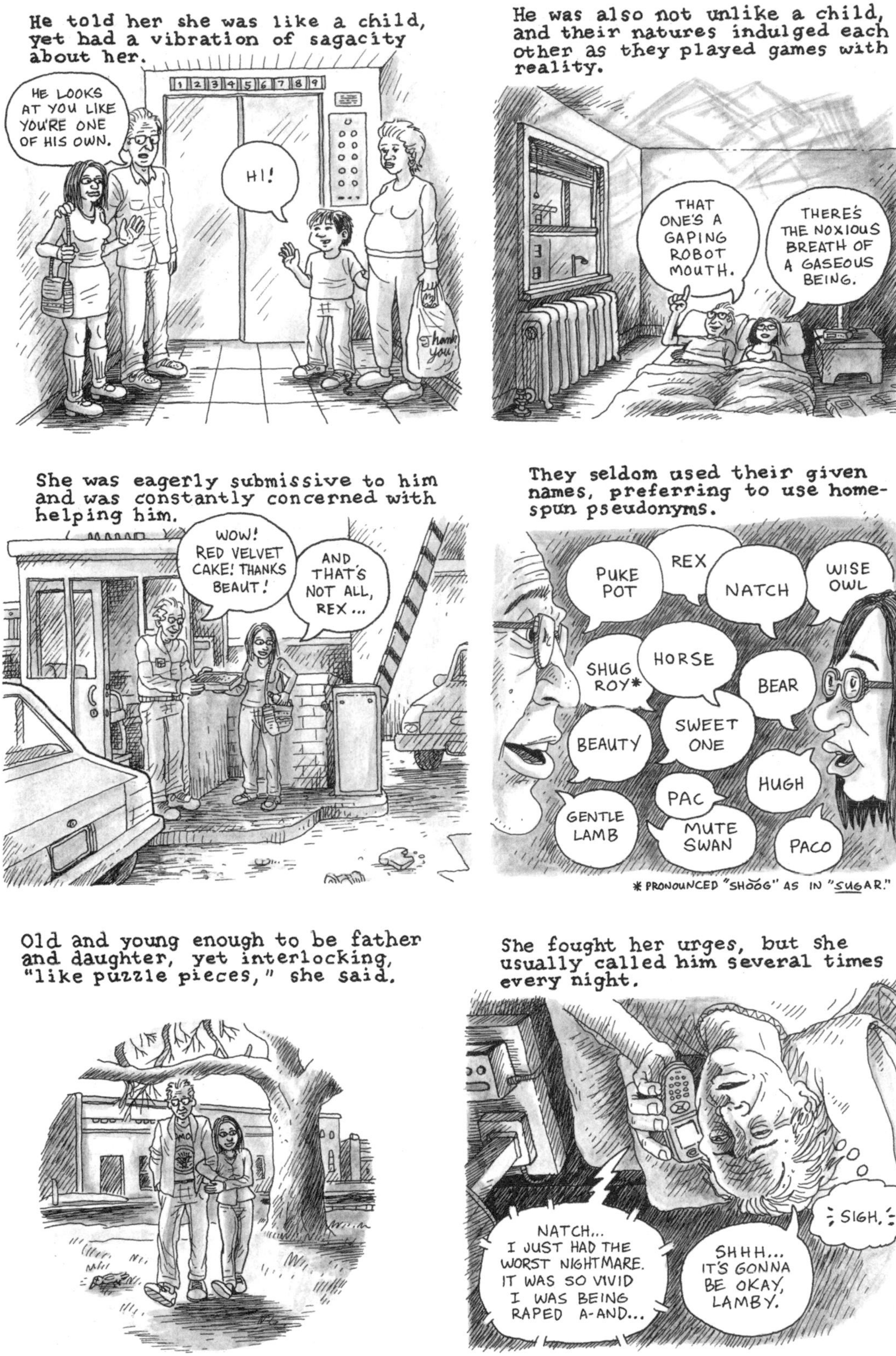
He told her she was like a child, yet had a vibration of sagacity about her.
HE LOOKS AT YOU LIKE YOU'RE ONE OF HIS OWN.
HI!
He was also not unlike a child, and their natures indulged each other as they played games with reality.
THAT ONE'S A GAPING ROBOT MOUTH.
THERE'S THE NOXIOUS BREATH OF A GASEOUS BEING.
She was eagerly submissive to him and was constantly concerned with helping him.
WOW! RED VELVET CAKE! THANKS BEAUT!
AND THAT'S NOT ALL, REX...
They seldom used their given names, preferring to use home-spun pseudonyms.
PUKE POT
REX
NATCH
WISE OWL
SHUG ROY*
HORSE
BEAR
BEAUTY
SWEET ONE
HUGH
PAC
GENTLE LAMB
MUTE SWAN
PACO
* PRONOUNCED "SHOOG" AS IN "SUGAR."
Old and young enough to be father and daughter, yet interlocking, "like puzzle pieces," she said.
She fought her urges, but she usually called him several times every night.
SIGH.
NATCH... I JUST HAD THE WORST NIGHTMARE. IT WAS SO VIVID I WAS BEING RAPED A-AND...
SHHH... IT'S GONNA BE OKAY, LAMBY.

After her father died, when she was 18-years-old, her doctors put her on Prozac and a powerful amphetamine.

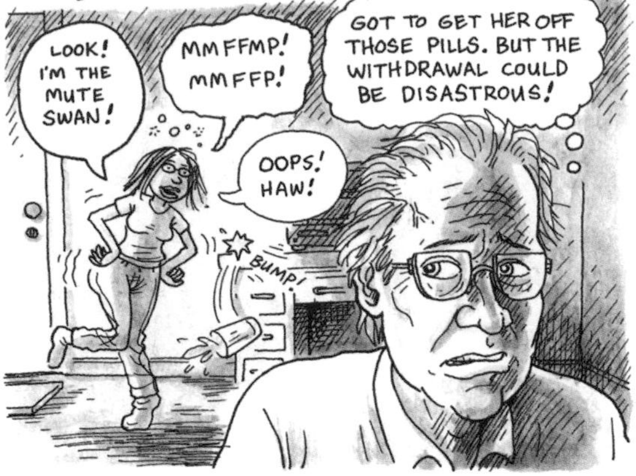
LOOK! I'M THE MUTE SWAN!
MMFFMP! MMFFP!
OOPS! HAW!
BUMP!
GOT TO GET HER OFF THOSE PILLS. BUT THE WITHDRAWAL COULD BE DISASTROUS!

Her mother refused to allow her to stay overnight at his apartment, so they developed schemes to spend the night together.

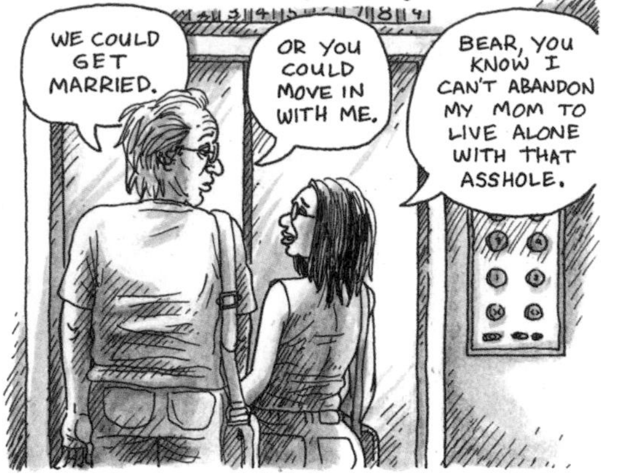
WE COULD GET MARRIED.
OR YOU COULD MOVE IN WITH ME.
BEAR, YOU KNOW I CAN'T ABANDON MY MOM TO LIVE ALONE WITH THAT ASSHOLE.

The situation between her mother and her stepfather was indeed volatile.

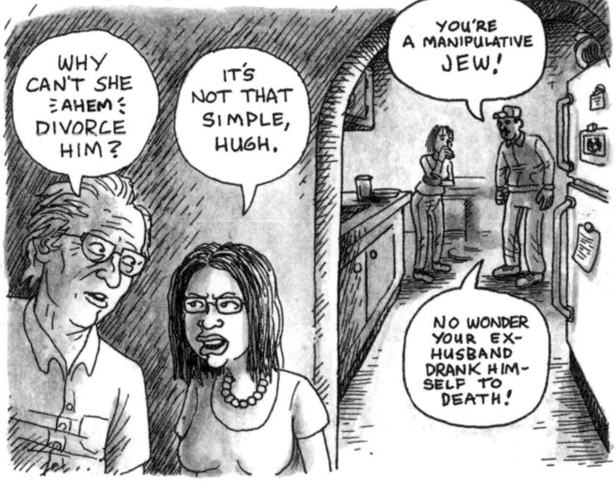
WHY CAN'T SHE AHEM DIVORCE HIM?
IT'S NOT THAT SIMPLE, HUGH.
YOU'RE A MANIPULATIVE JEW!
NO WONDER YOUR EX-HUSBAND DRANK HIMSELF TO DEATH!

He told her he felt his own marriage had been doomed during a trip to France after he refused to give money to a gypsy.

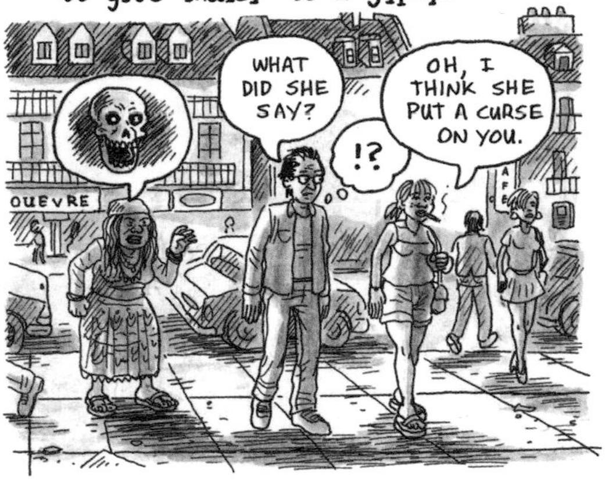
OUEVRE
WHAT DID SHE SAY?
!?
OH, I THINK SHE PUT A CURSE ON YOU.

She wouldn't talk much about her father or his death, except mentioning that he had died of cirrhosis and that she didn't recognize him the last time she saw him.

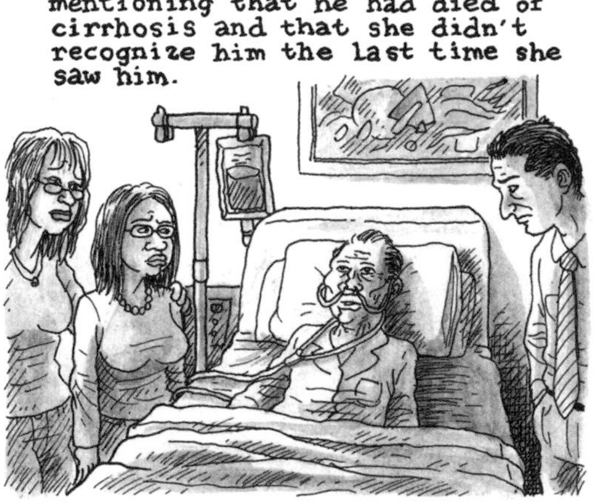

Being with him, it was almost as if she had her dad back.

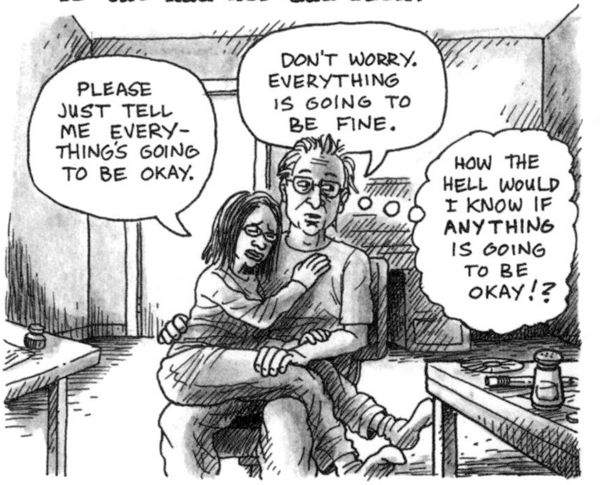
PLEASE JUST TELL ME EVERYTHING'S GOING TO BE OKAY.
DON'T WORRY. EVERYTHING IS GOING TO BE FINE.
HOW THE HELL WOULD I KNOW IF ANYTHING IS GOING TO BE OKAY!?

The more she tried to capture his attention, the more he seemed to ignore her.

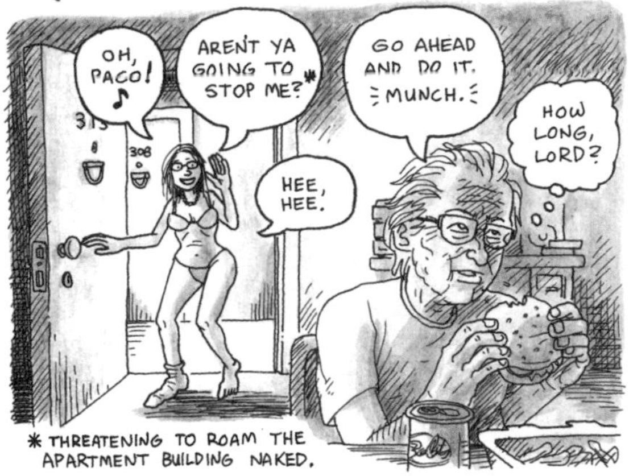
OH, PACO! ♪
AREN'T YA GOING TO STOP ME?*
HEE, HEE.
GO AHEAD AND DO IT. MUNCH.
HOW LONG, LORD?
* THREATENING TO ROAM THE APARTMENT BUILDING NAKED.

On occasion, her fears and stresses overwhelmed her with brief periods of illness.

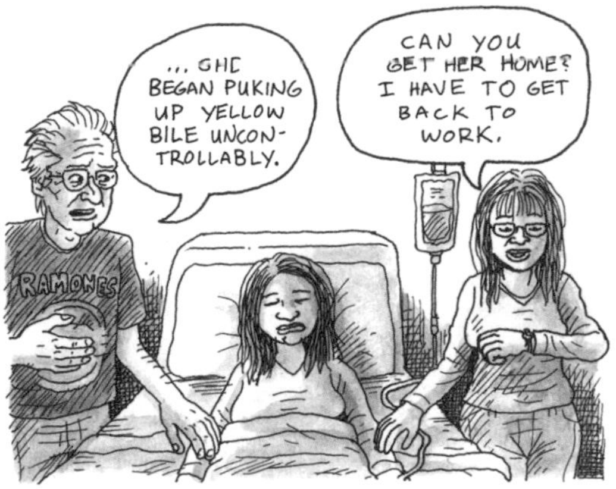
... SHE BEGAN PUKING UP YELLOW BILE UNCONTROLLABLY.
CAN YOU GET HER HOME? I HAVE TO GET BACK TO WORK.
RAMONES

The monotony of his job plagued him. Later, she attributed this as a possible factor in the rift that suddenly developed in their world.

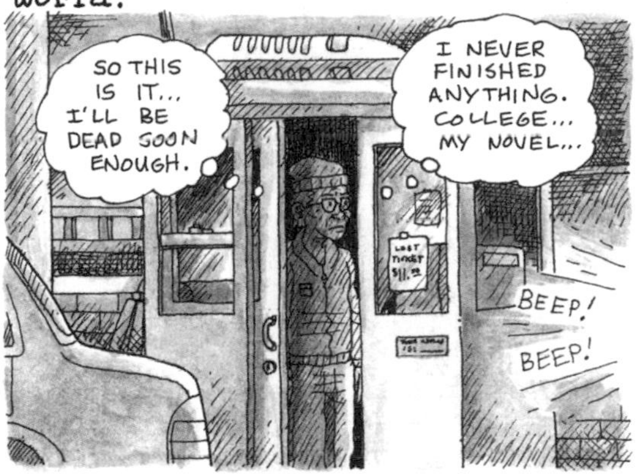
SO THIS IS IT... I'LL BE DEAD SOON ENOUGH.
I NEVER FINISHED ANYTHING. COLLEGE... MY NOVEL...
BEEP!
BEEP!

She was waiting for him to come home one night when she saw him with another woman. She had believed that he was the most honest person she knew.

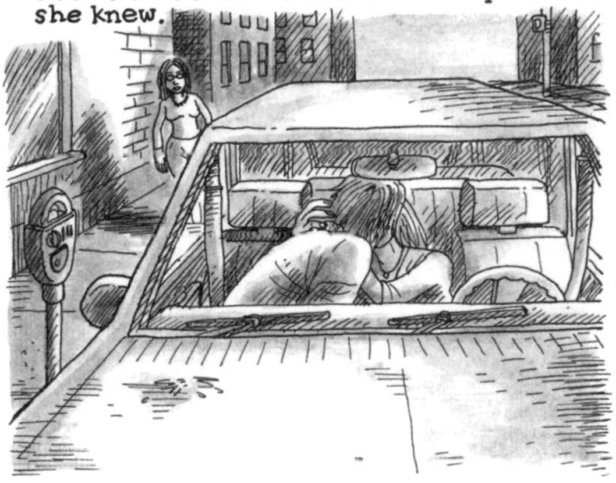

It was the anniversary of the night her father died. She hadn't urinated all day and her bladder felt as if it was going to burst.

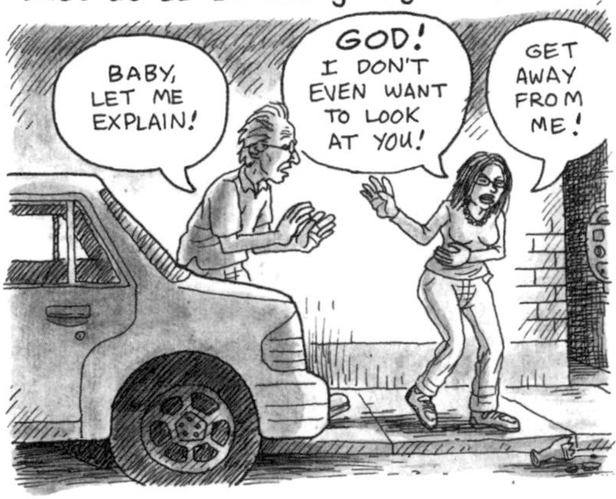
BABY, LET ME EXPLAIN!
GOD! I DON'T EVEN WANT TO LOOK AT YOU!
GET AWAY FROM ME!

Sometimes things between people are so close that all it takes is one thing to taint everything and the pieces can never be put back together.

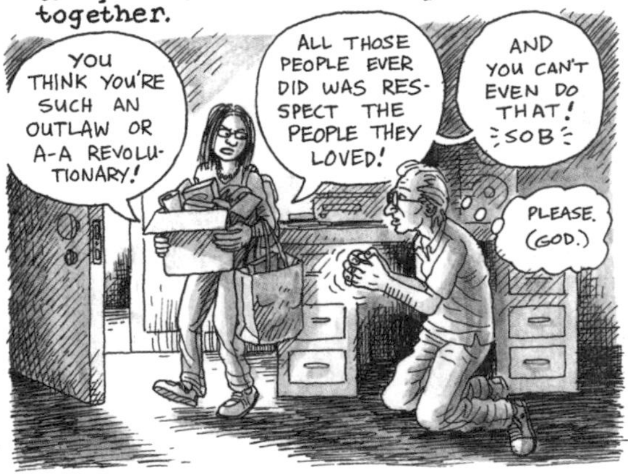
YOU THINK YOU'RE SUCH AN OUTLAW OR A-A REVOLUTIONARY!
ALL THOSE PEOPLE EVER DID WAS RESPECT THE PEOPLE THEY LOVED!
AND YOU CAN'T EVEN DO THAT! SOB
PLEASE. (GOD.)

Somehow, he convinced her to forgive him, but compelled, he claimed, beyond his understanding he destroyed everything again.

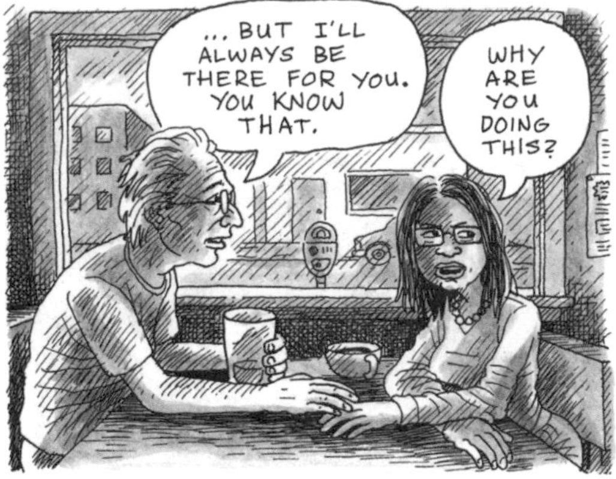
... BUT I'LL ALWAYS BE THERE FOR YOU. YOU KNOW THAT.
WHY ARE YOU DOING THIS?

She began seeing a fellow student and even began taking him to her synagogue.

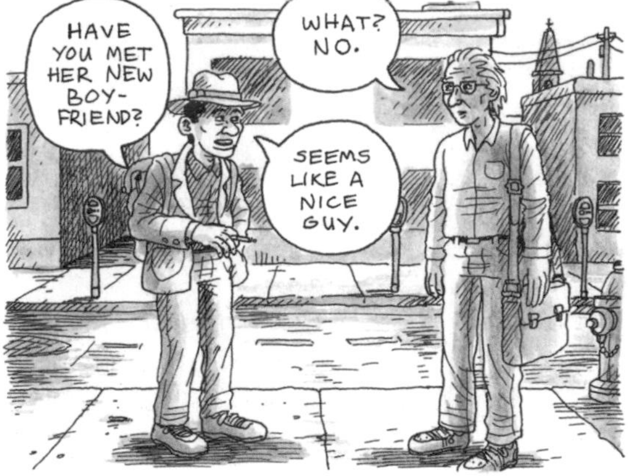
HAVE YOU MET HER NEW BOY-FRIEND?
WHAT? NO.
SEEMS LIKE A NICE GUY.

She told herself that she was better off. She hated herself when the thought arose that maybe he would've been dead by the time she was in her 40's.

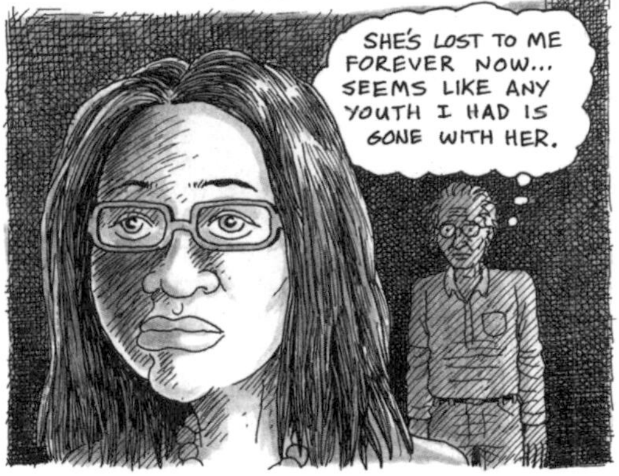
SHE'S LOST TO ME FOREVER NOW... SEEMS LIKE ANY YOUTH I HAD IS GONE WITH HER.

She heard from a mutual acquaintance (the guy with the fedora who attended her synagogue) that he was cohabitating with a middle-aged librarian.

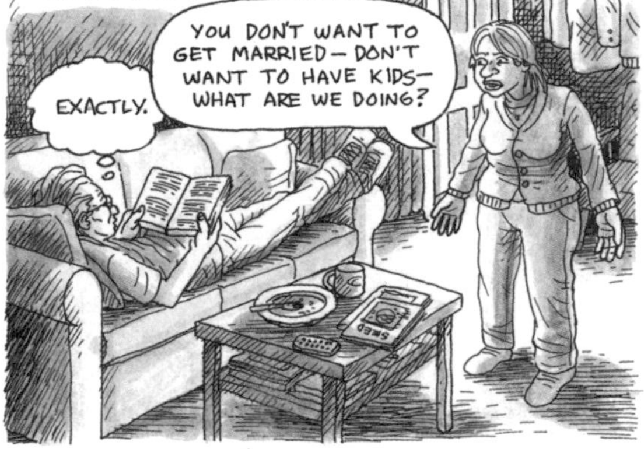
YOU DON'T WANT TO GET MARRIED — DON'T WANT TO HAVE KIDS — WHAT ARE WE DOING?
EXACTLY.

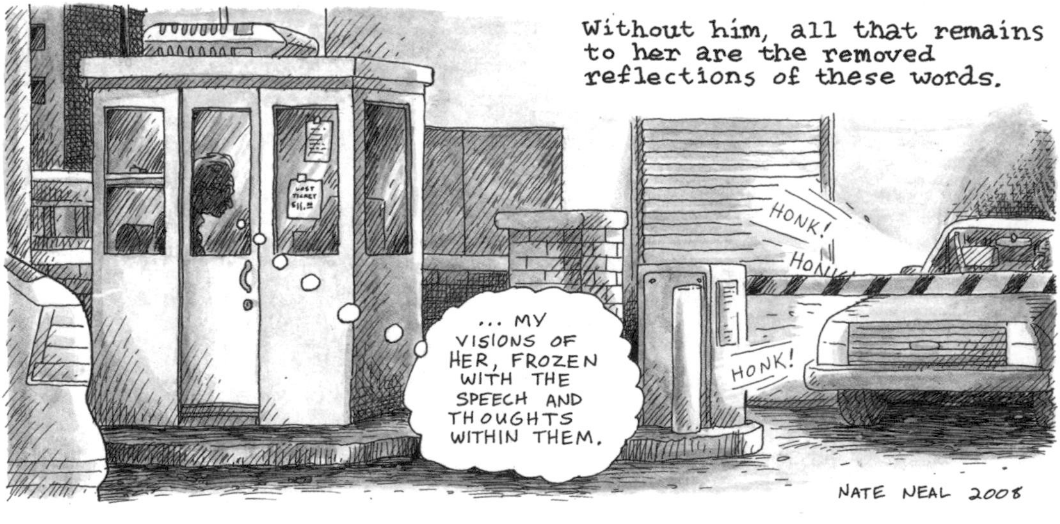
Without him, all that remains to her are the removed reflections of these words.
HONK!
HONK
HONK!
... MY VISIONS OF HER, FROZEN WITH THE SPEECH AND THOUGHTS WITHIN THEM.

NATE NEAL 2008

Continued from our previous volume...

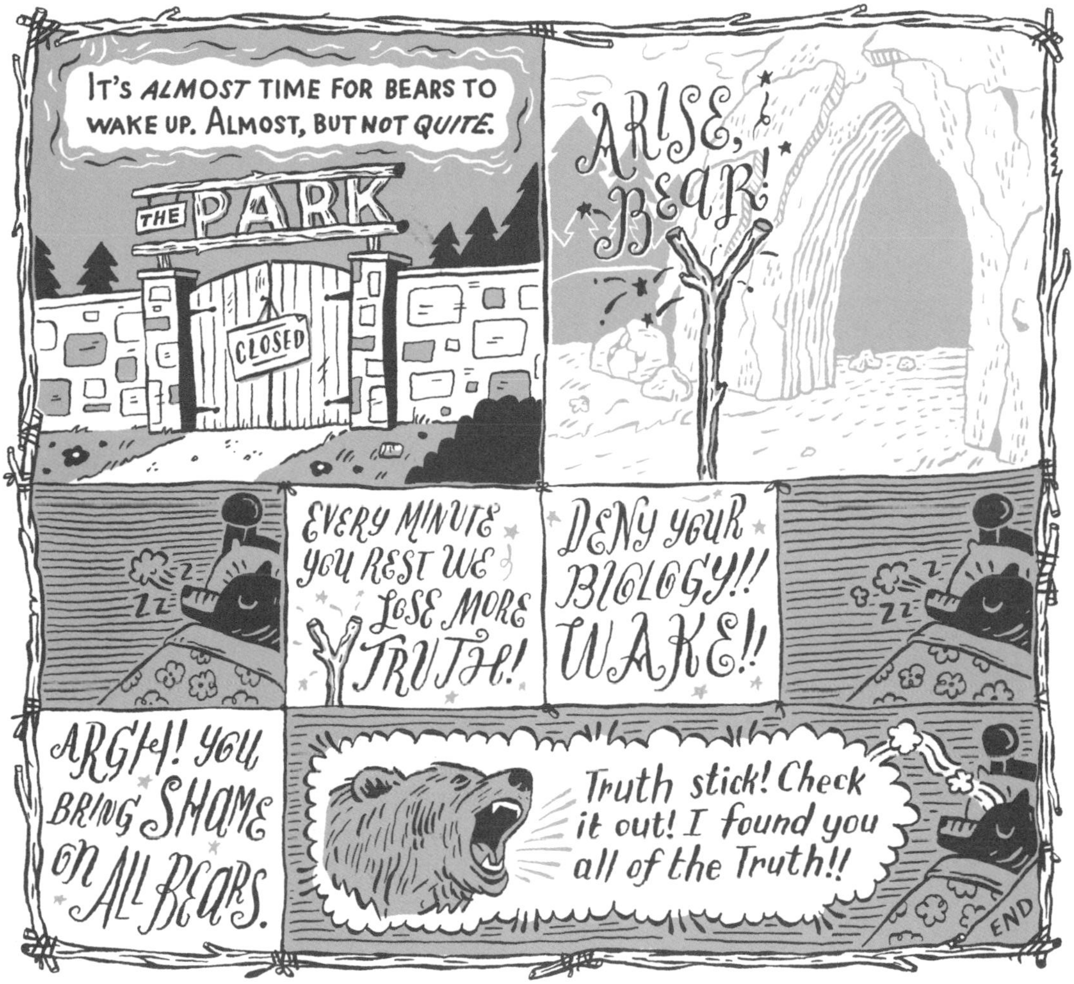
It's *almost* time for bears to wake up. Almost, but not *quite.*
THE PARK
CLOSED
Arise, Bear!
Every minute you rest we lose more truth!
Deny your biology!! Wake!!
Argh! You bring shame on all bears.
Truth stick! Check it out! I found you all of the Truth!!
END

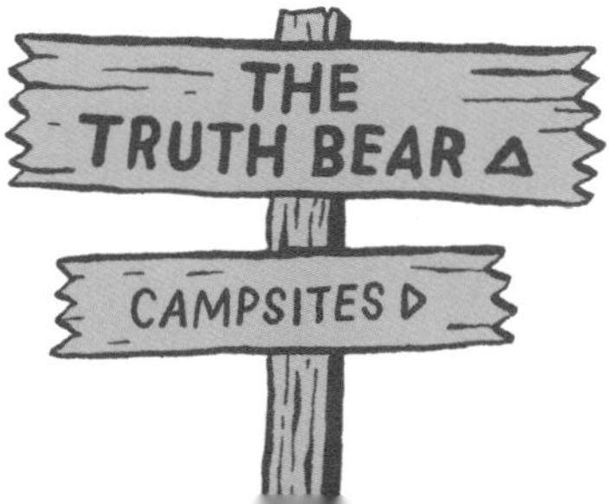
THE TRUTH BEAR
CAMPSITES

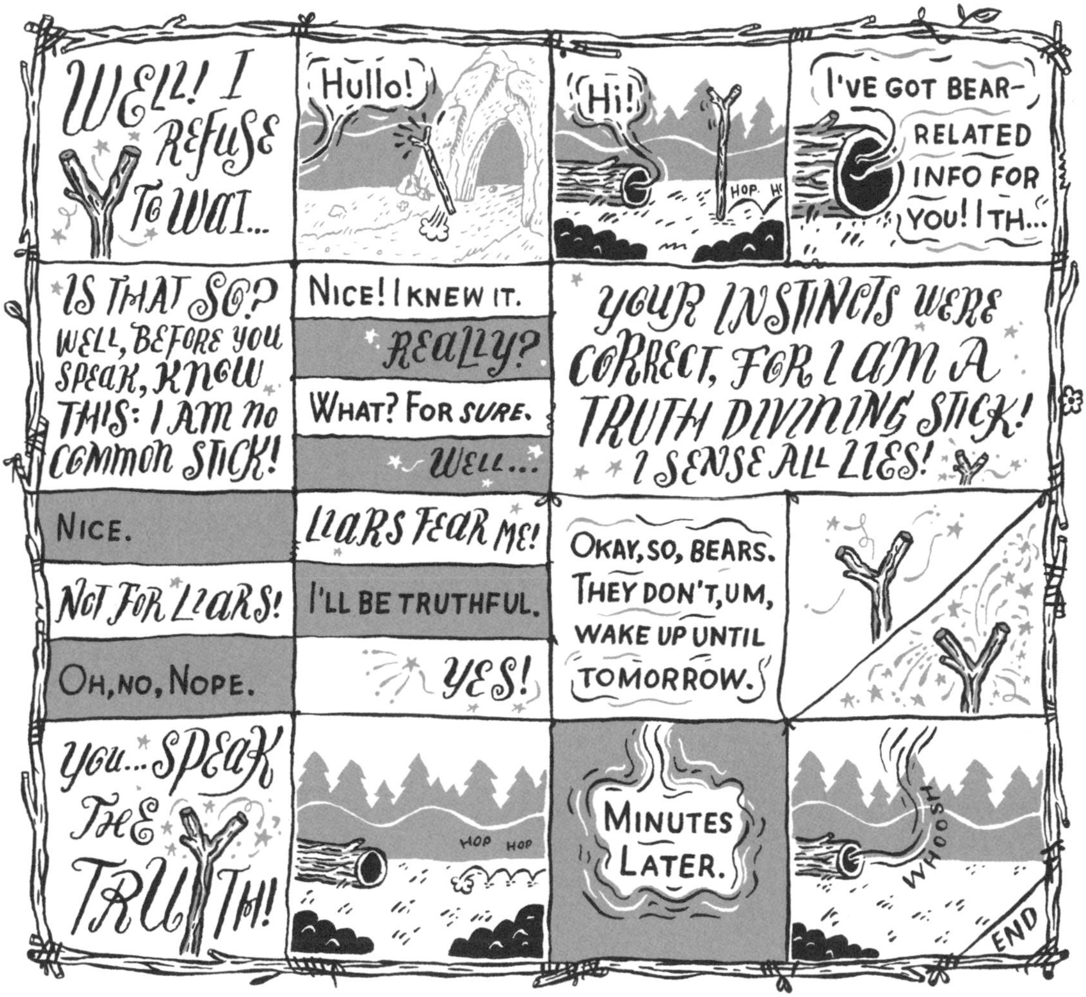
WELL! I REFUSE TO WAIT...
Hullo!
Hi!
HOP.
I'VE GOT BEAR-RELATED INFO FOR YOU! I TH...
IS THAT SO? WELL, BEFORE YOU SPEAK, KNOW THIS: I AM NO COMMON STICK!
NICE! I KNEW IT.
REALLY?
WHAT? FOR SURE.
WELL...
YOUR INSTINCTS WERE CORRECT, FOR I AM A TRUTH DIVINING STICK! I SENSE ALL LIES!
NICE.
NOT FOR LIARS!
OH, NO, NOPE.
LIARS FEAR ME!
I'LL BE TRUTHFUL.
YES!
OKAY, SO, BEARS. THEY DON'T, UM, WAKE UP UNTIL TOMORROW.
YOU... SPEAK THE TRUTH!
HOP HOP
MINUTES LATER.
WHOOSH
END

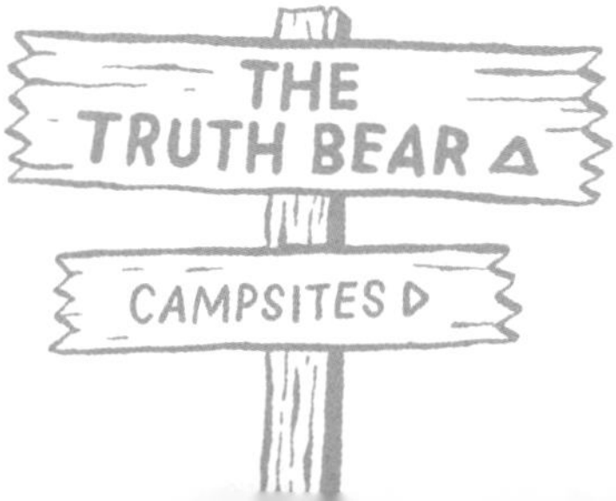
THE TRUTH BEAR
CAMPSITES

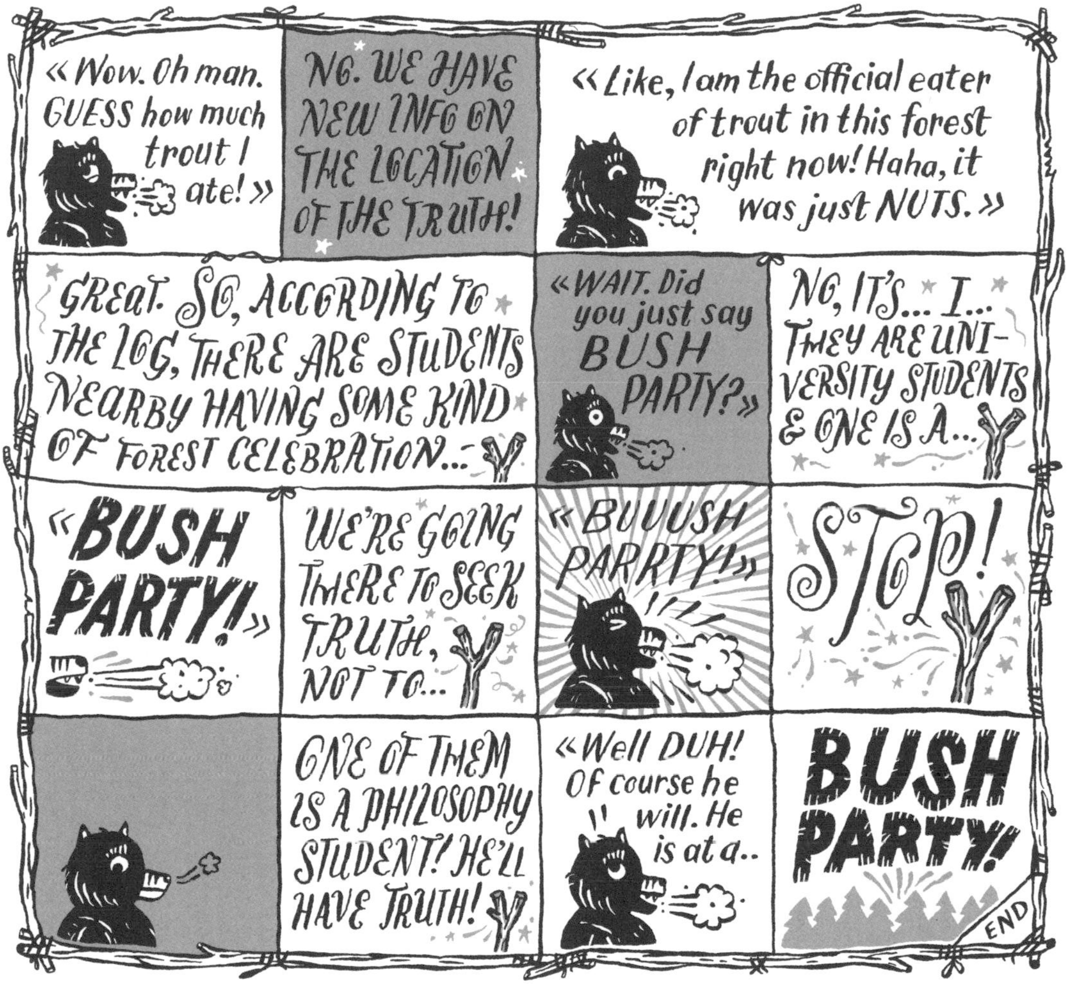
« Wow. Oh man. GUESS how much trout I ate! »
NO. WE HAVE NEW INFO ON THE LOCATION OF THE TRUTH!
« Like, I am the official eater of trout in this forest right now! Haha, it was just NUTS. »
GREAT. SO, ACCORDING TO THE LOG, THERE ARE STUDENTS NEARBY HAVING SOME KIND OF FOREST CELEBRATION...
« WAIT. Did you just say BUSH PARTY? »
NO, IT'S... I... THEY ARE UNIVERSITY STUDENTS & ONE IS A...
« BUSH PARTY! »
WE'RE GOING THERE TO SEEK TRUTH, NOT TO...
« BUUUSH PARRTY! »
STOP!
ONE OF THEM IS A PHILOSOPHY STUDENT! HE'LL HAVE TRUTH!
« Well DUH! Of course he will. He is at a..
BUSH PARTY!
END

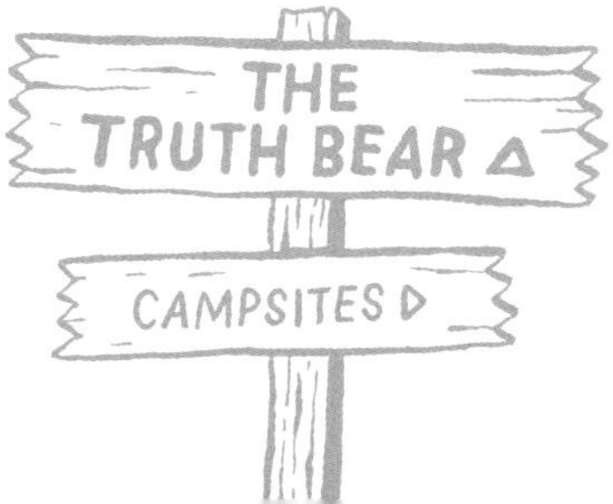
THE TRUTH BEAR
CAMPSITES

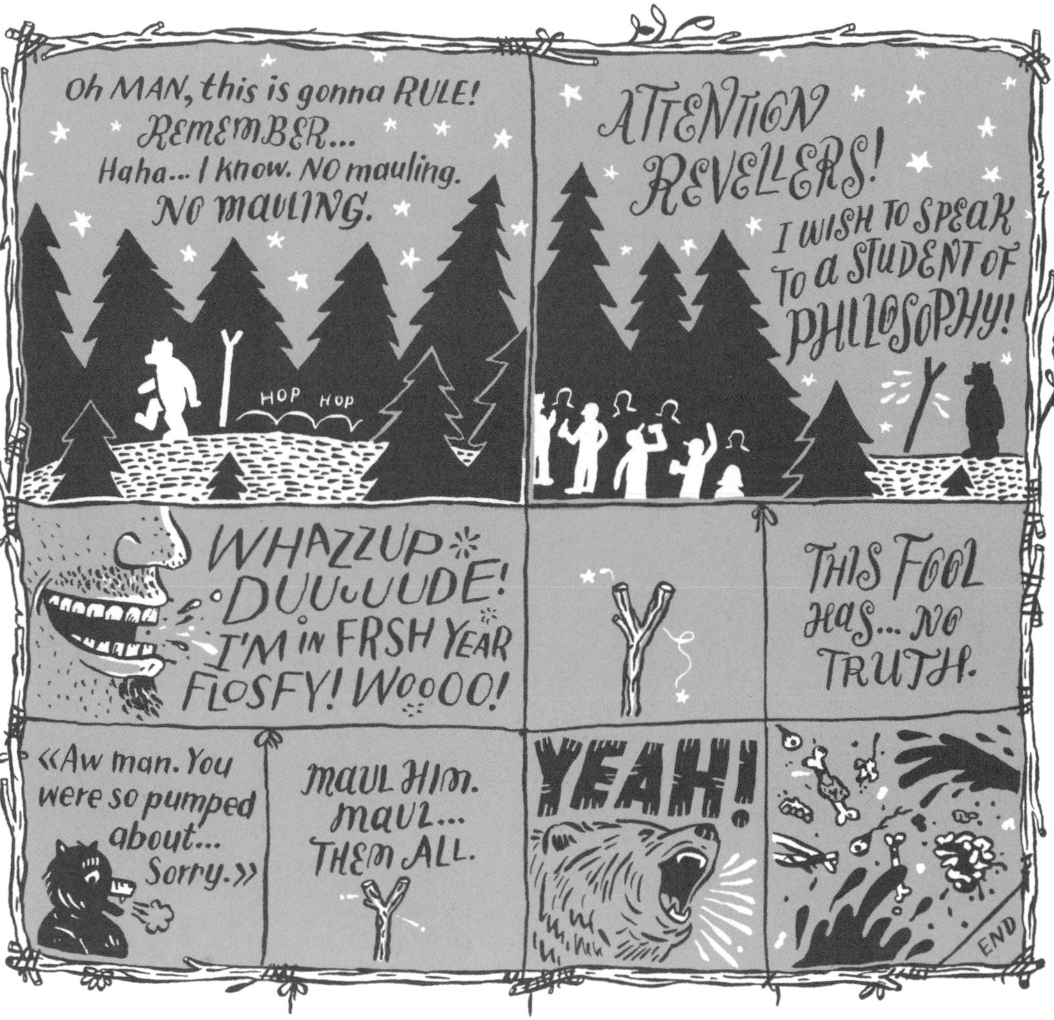
Oh MAN, this is gonna RULE!
REMEMBER...
Haha... I know. NO mauling.
NO MAULING.
HOP HOP
ATTENTION REVELLERS!
I WISH TO SPEAK TO A STUDENT OF PHILOSOPHY!
WHAZZUP DUUuUUDE! I'M IN FRSH YEAR FLOSFY! WOoOOO!
THIS FOOL HAS... NO TRUTH.
«Aw man. You were so pumped about... Sorry.»
MAUL HIM. MAUL... THEM ALL.
YEAH!
END

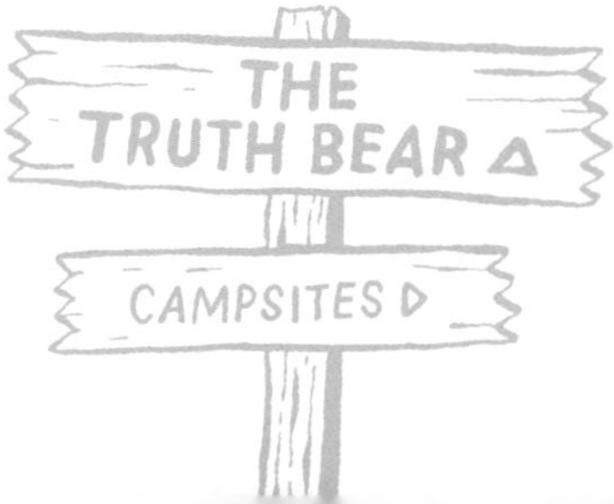
THE TRUTH BEAR
CAMPSITES

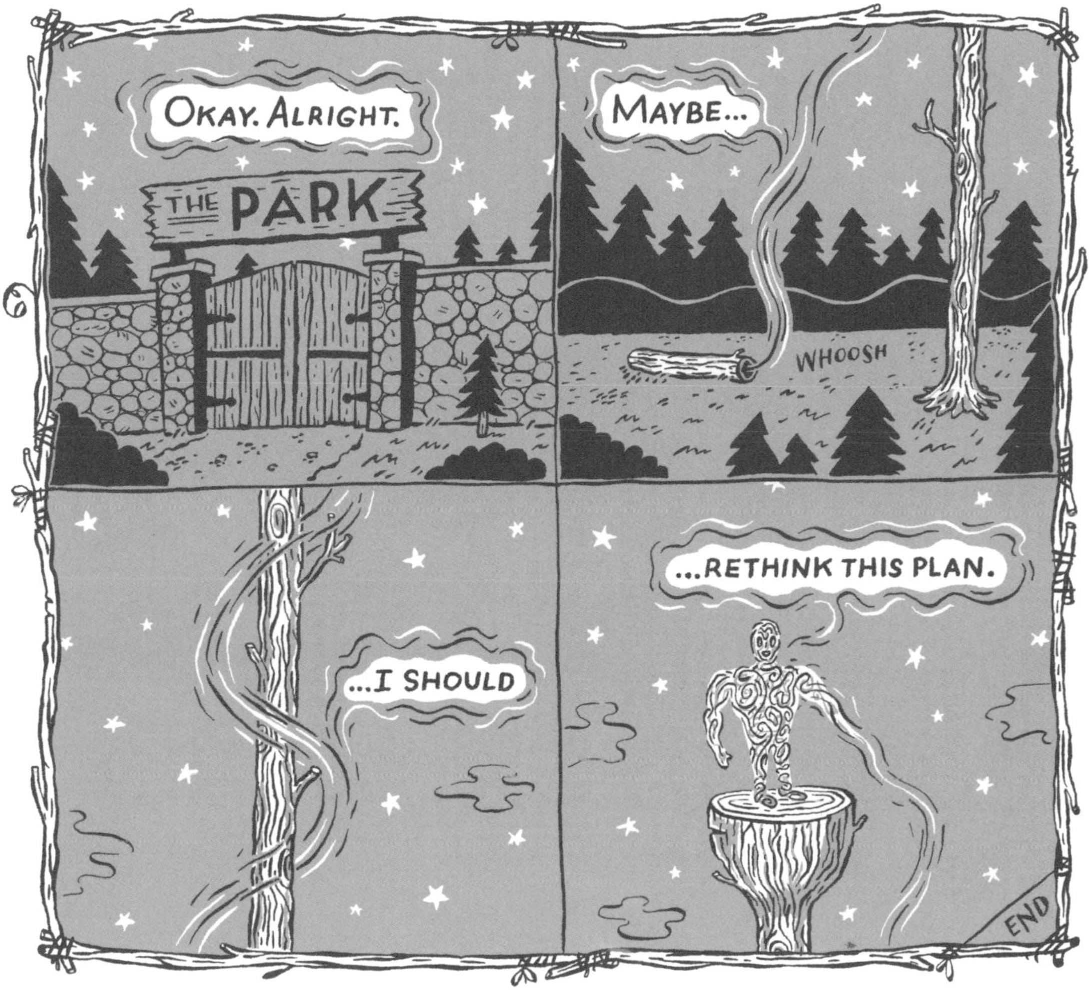
OKAY. ALRIGHT.
THE PARK
MAYBE...
WHOOSH
...I SHOULD
...RETHINK THIS PLAN.
END

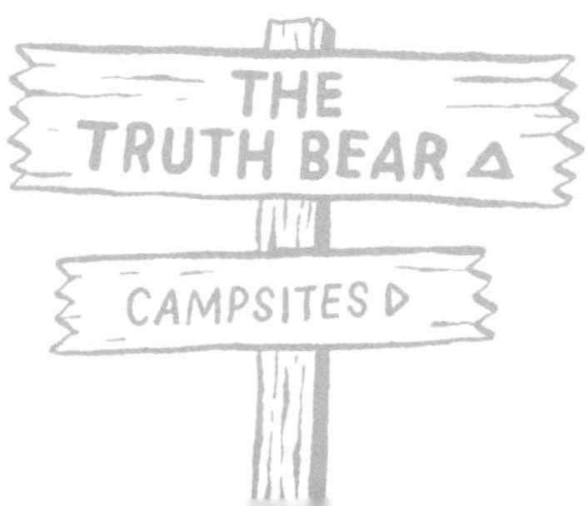
THE TRUTH BEAR
CAMPSITES

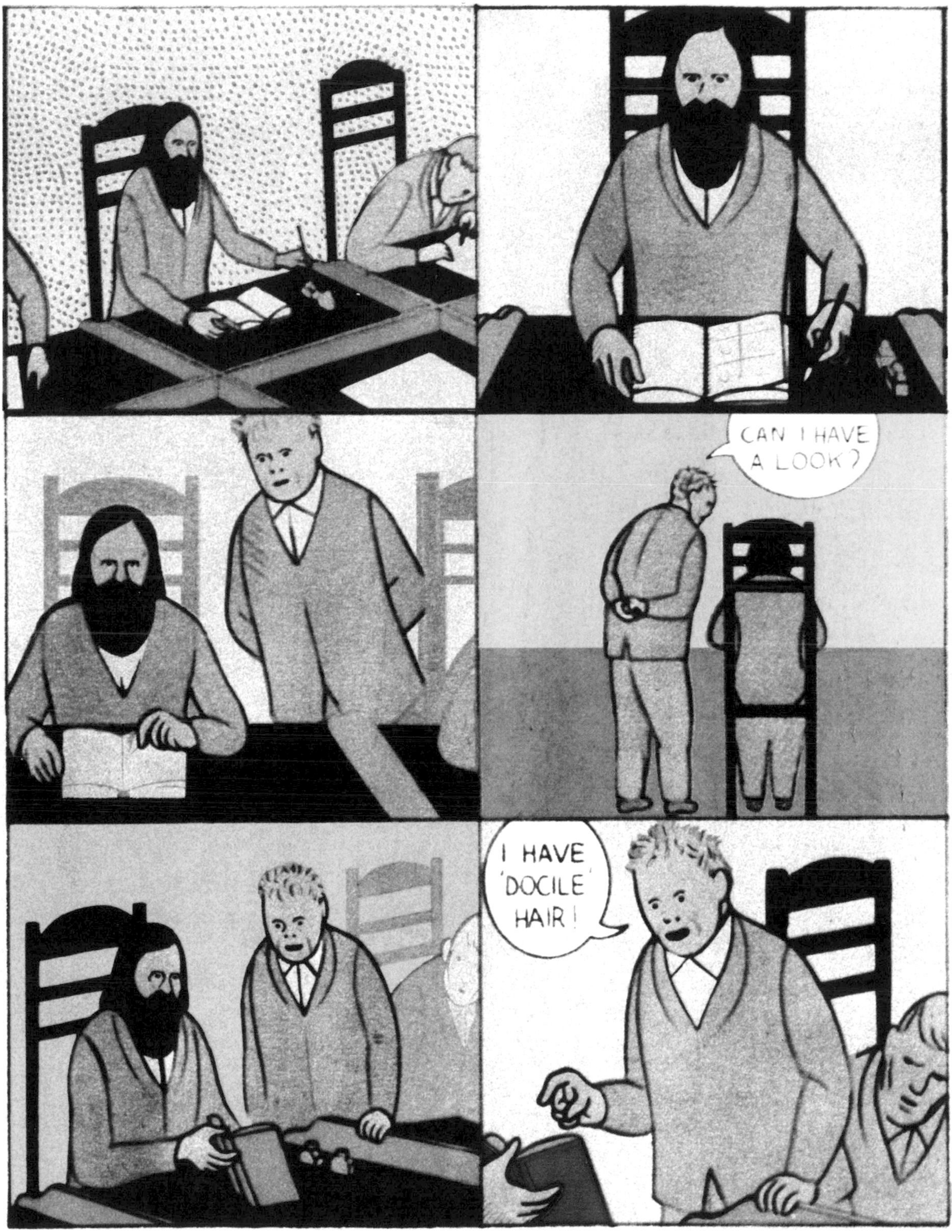
CAN I HAVE A LOOK?
I HAVE 'DOCILE' HAIR!

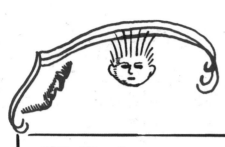

HAIR
TYPES

FIG. A

DOCILE

FIG. B

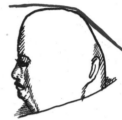

RIGID

FIG. C

FRIVOLOUS

FIG. D

INTRUSIVE

FIG. E

WILD

FIG. F

CRAZY

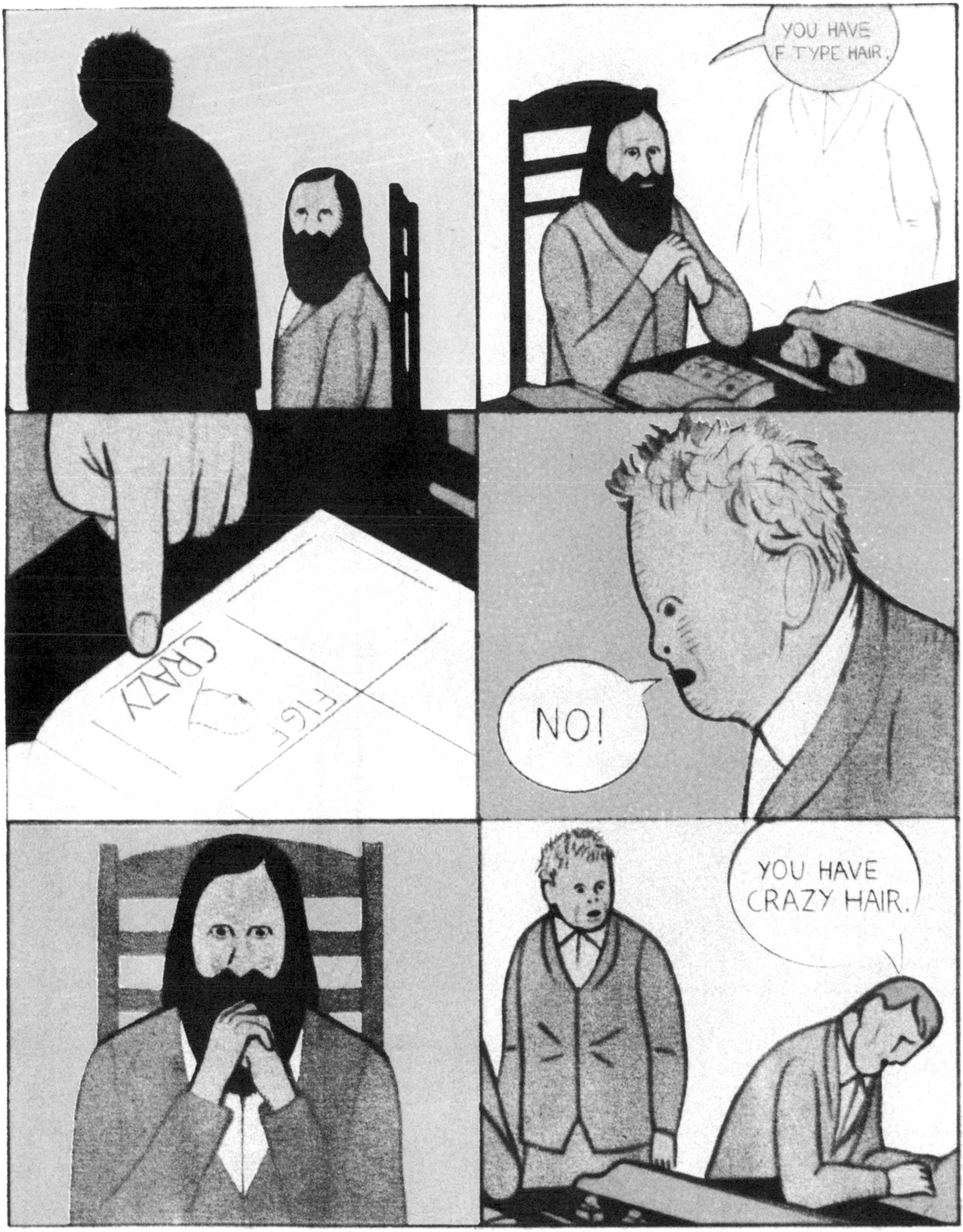
YOU HAVE F TYPE HAIR.
FIG F
CRAZY
NO!
YOU HAVE CRAZY HAIR.

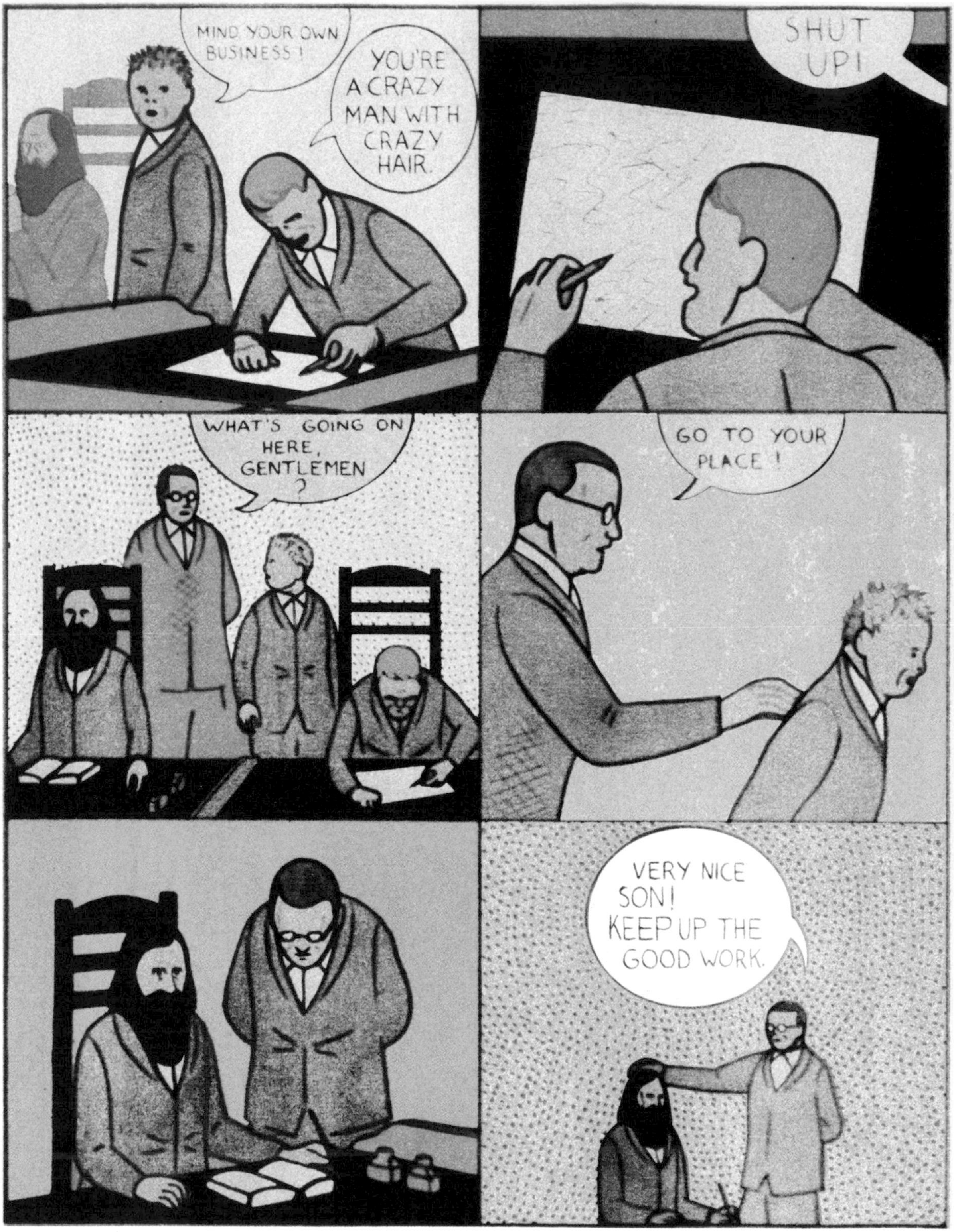
MIND YOUR OWN BUSINESS!
YOU'RE A CRAZY MAN WITH CRAZY HAIR.
SHUT UP!
WHAT'S GOING ON HERE, GENTLEMEN ?
GO TO YOUR PLACE!
VERY NICE SON! KEEP UP THE GOOD WORK.

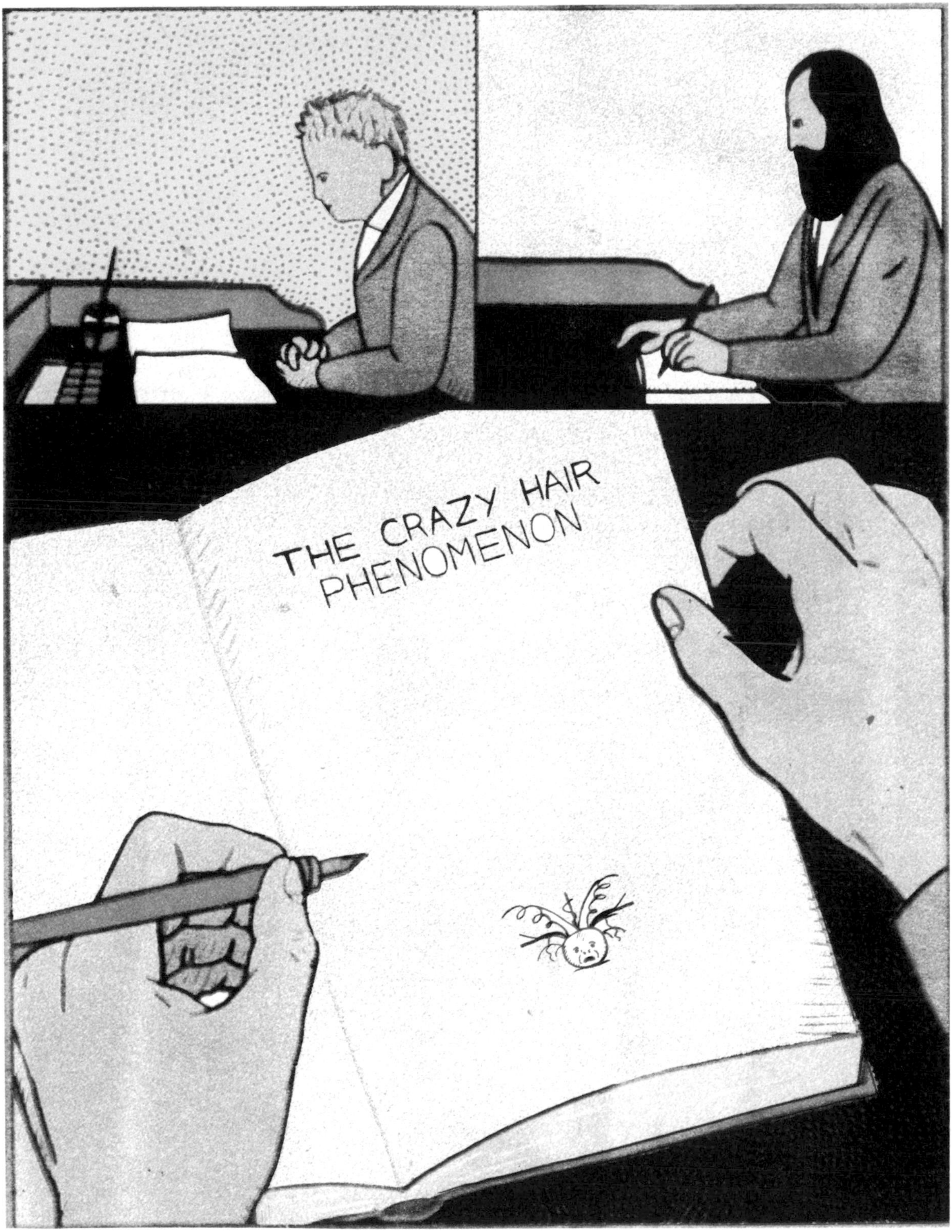
THE CRAZY HAIR
PHENOMENON

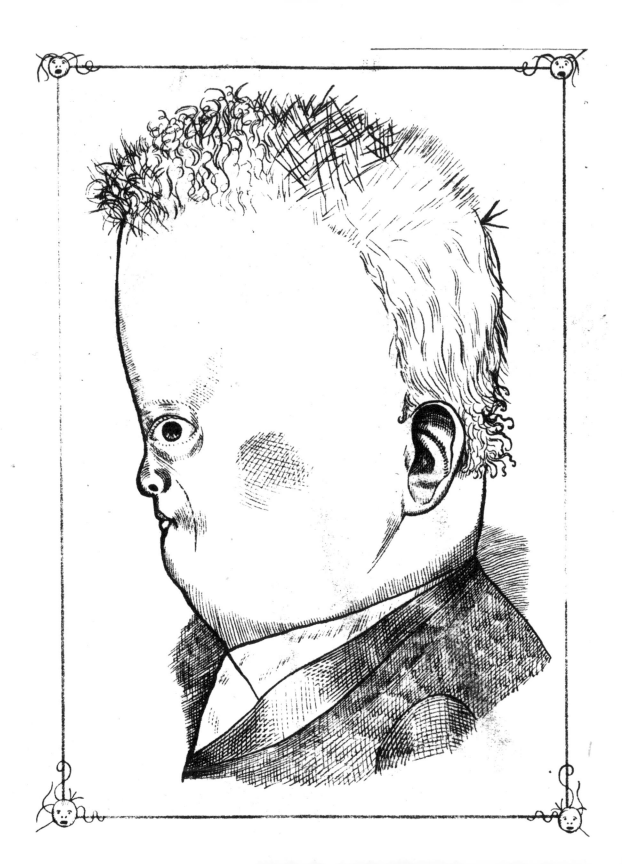

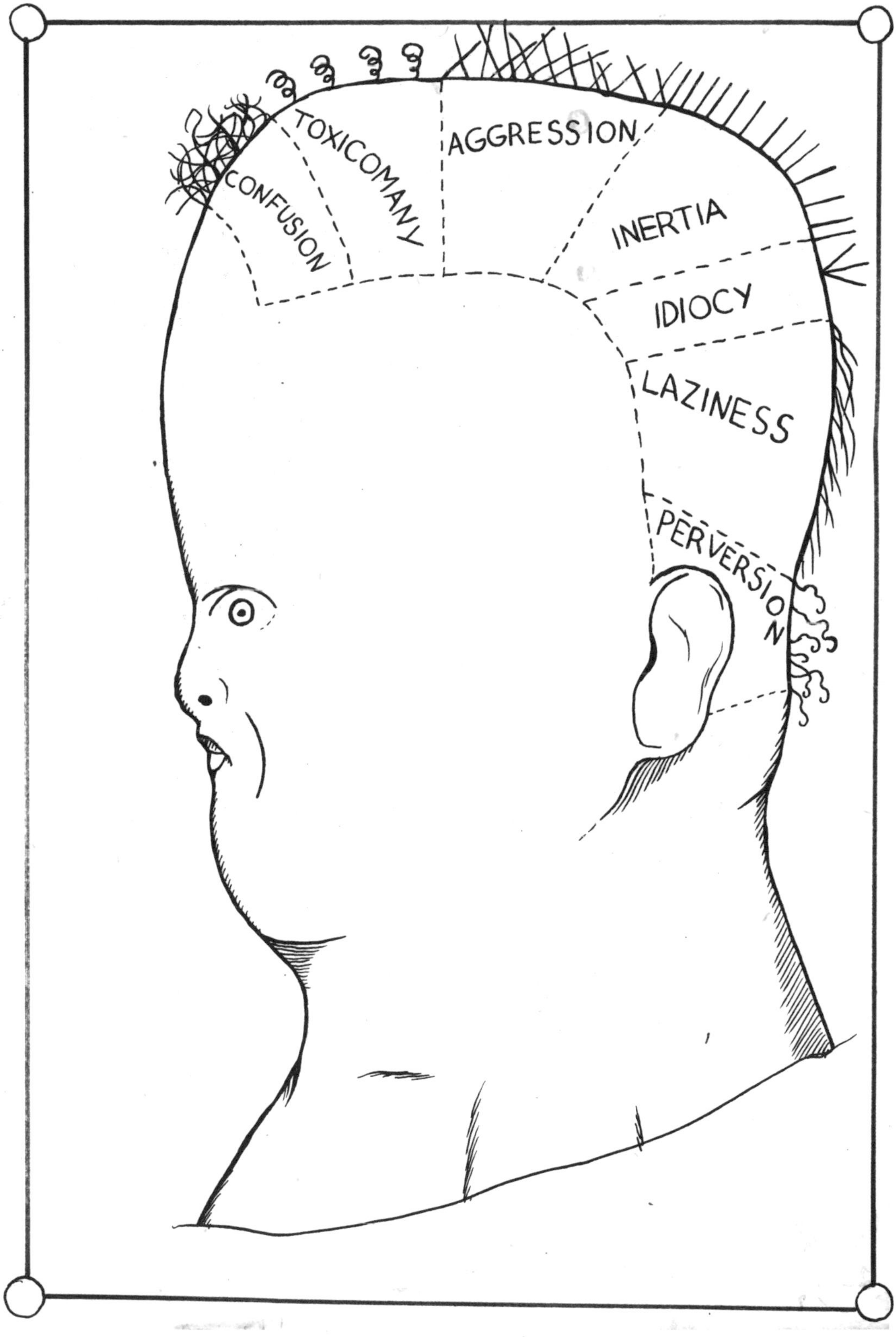
CONFUSION
TOXICOMANY
AGGRESSION
INERTIA
IDIOCY
LAZINESS
PERVERSION

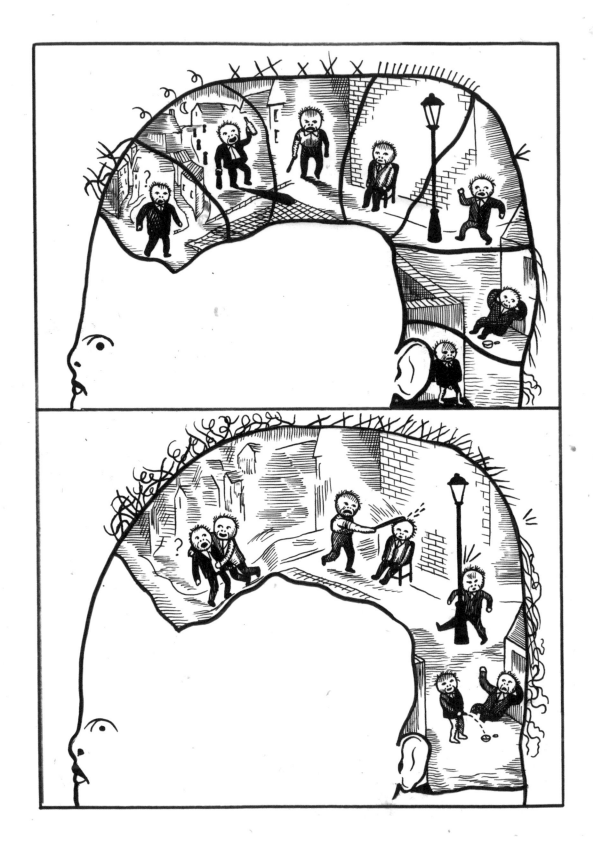

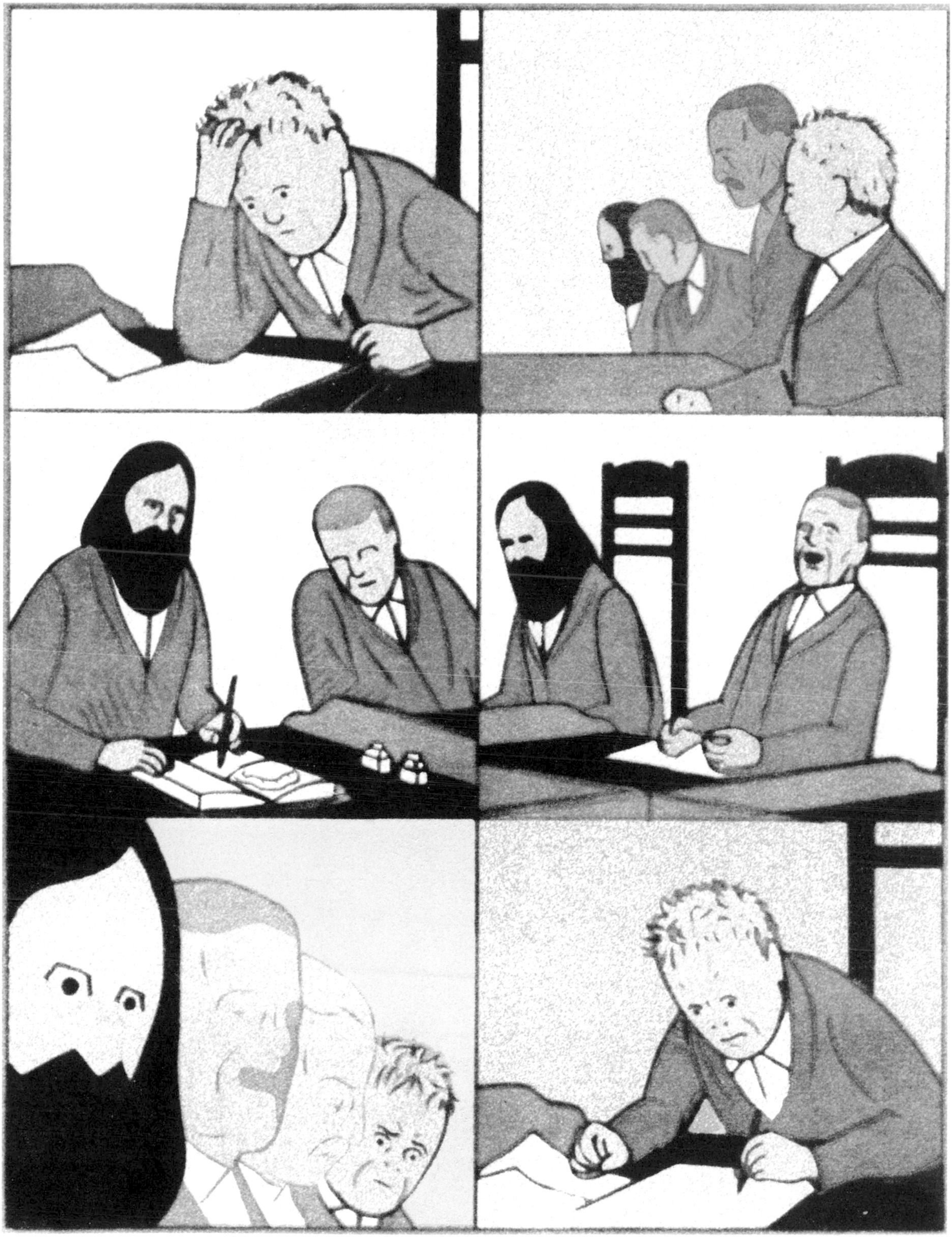

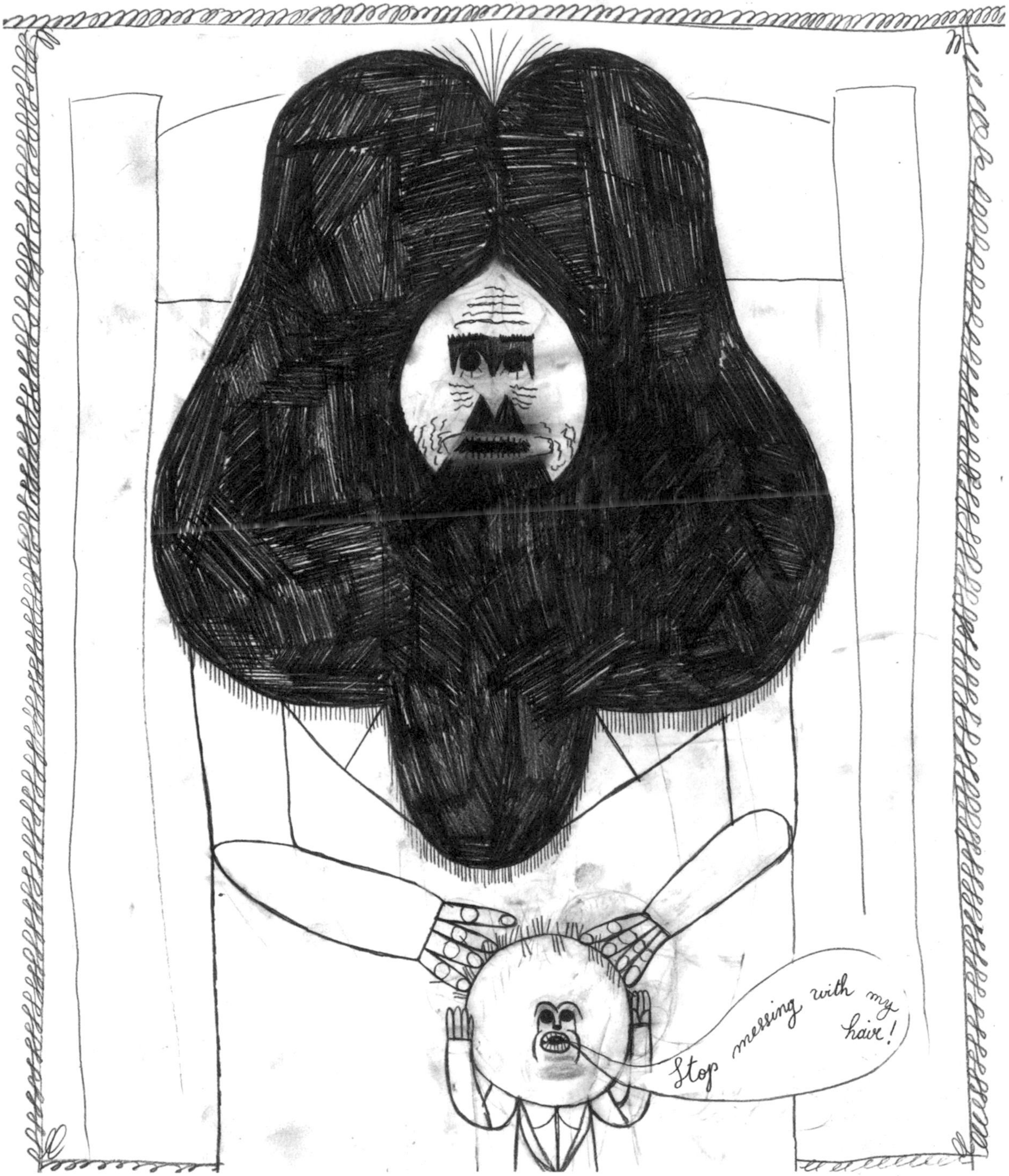
Stop messing with my hair!

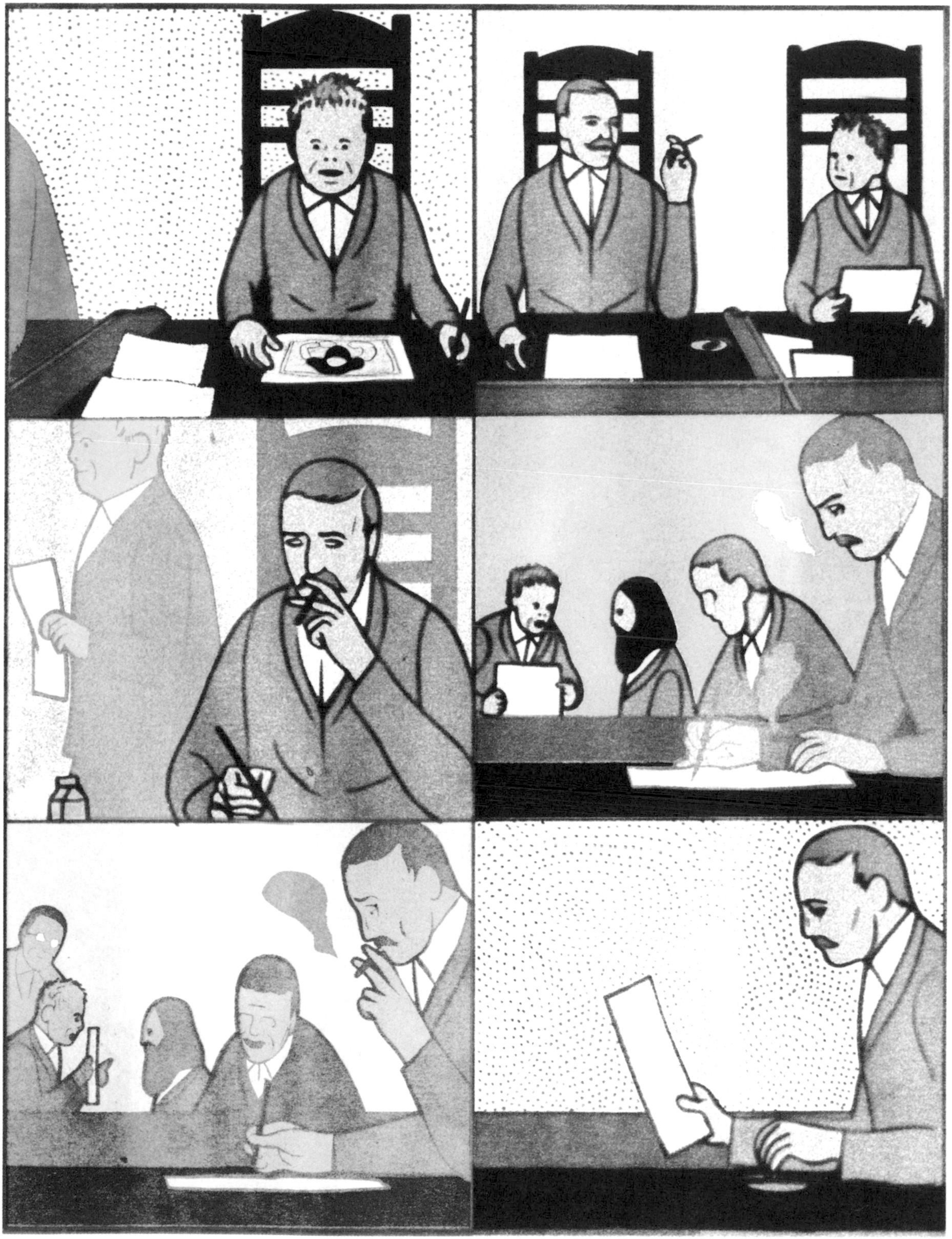

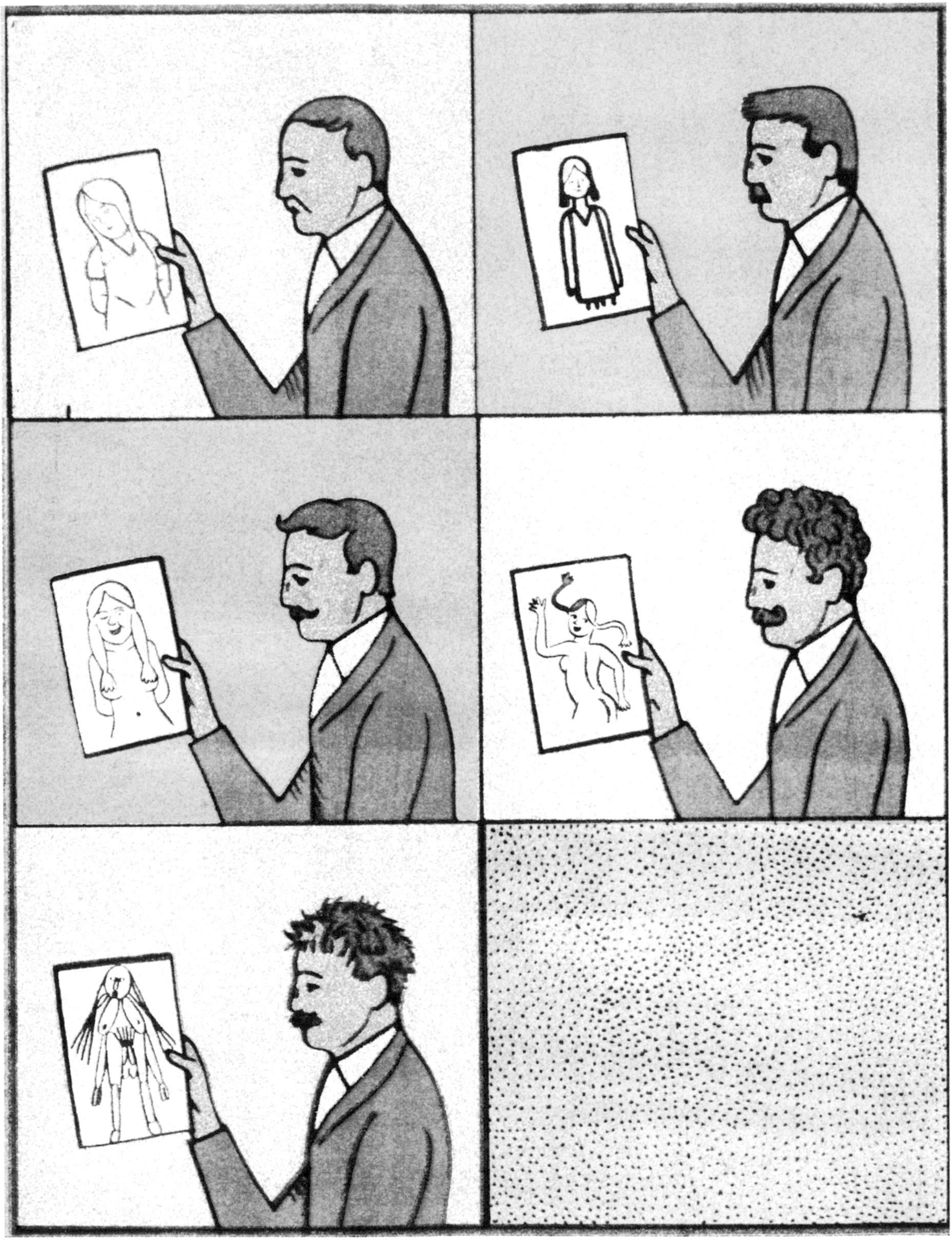

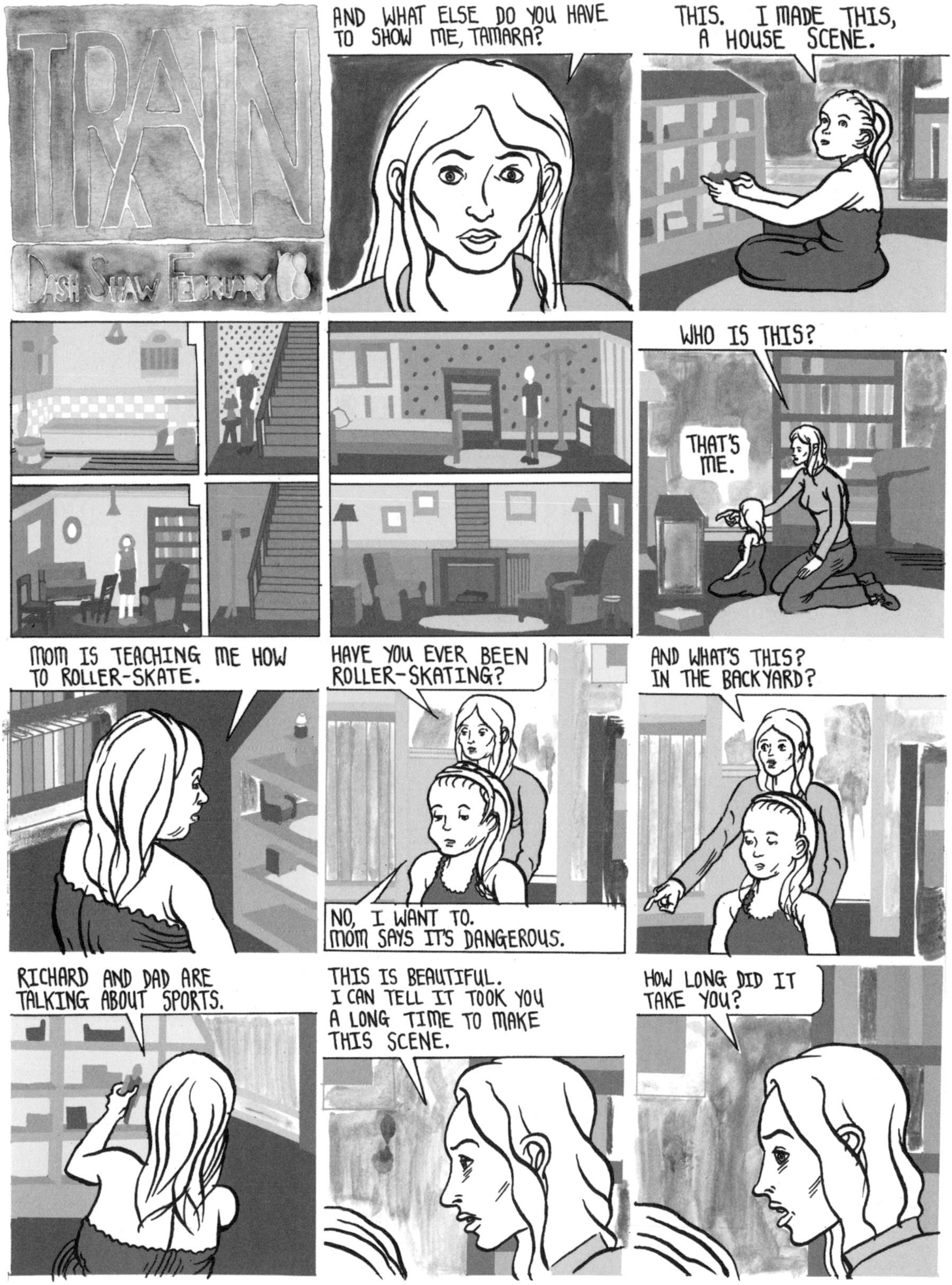

TRAIN
DASH SHAW FEBRUARY 08
AND WHAT ELSE DO YOU HAVE TO SHOW ME, TAMARA?
THIS. I MADE THIS, A HOUSE SCENE.
WHO IS THIS?
THAT'S ME.
MOM IS TEACHING ME HOW TO ROLLER-SKATE.
HAVE YOU EVER BEEN ROLLER-SKATING?
NO, I WANT TO. MOM SAYS IT'S DANGEROUS.
AND WHAT'S THIS? IN THE BACKYARD?
RICHARD AND DAD ARE TALKING ABOUT SPORTS.
THIS IS BEAUTIFUL. I CAN TELL IT TOOK YOU A LONG TIME TO MAKE THIS SCENE.
HOW LONG DID IT TAKE YOU?

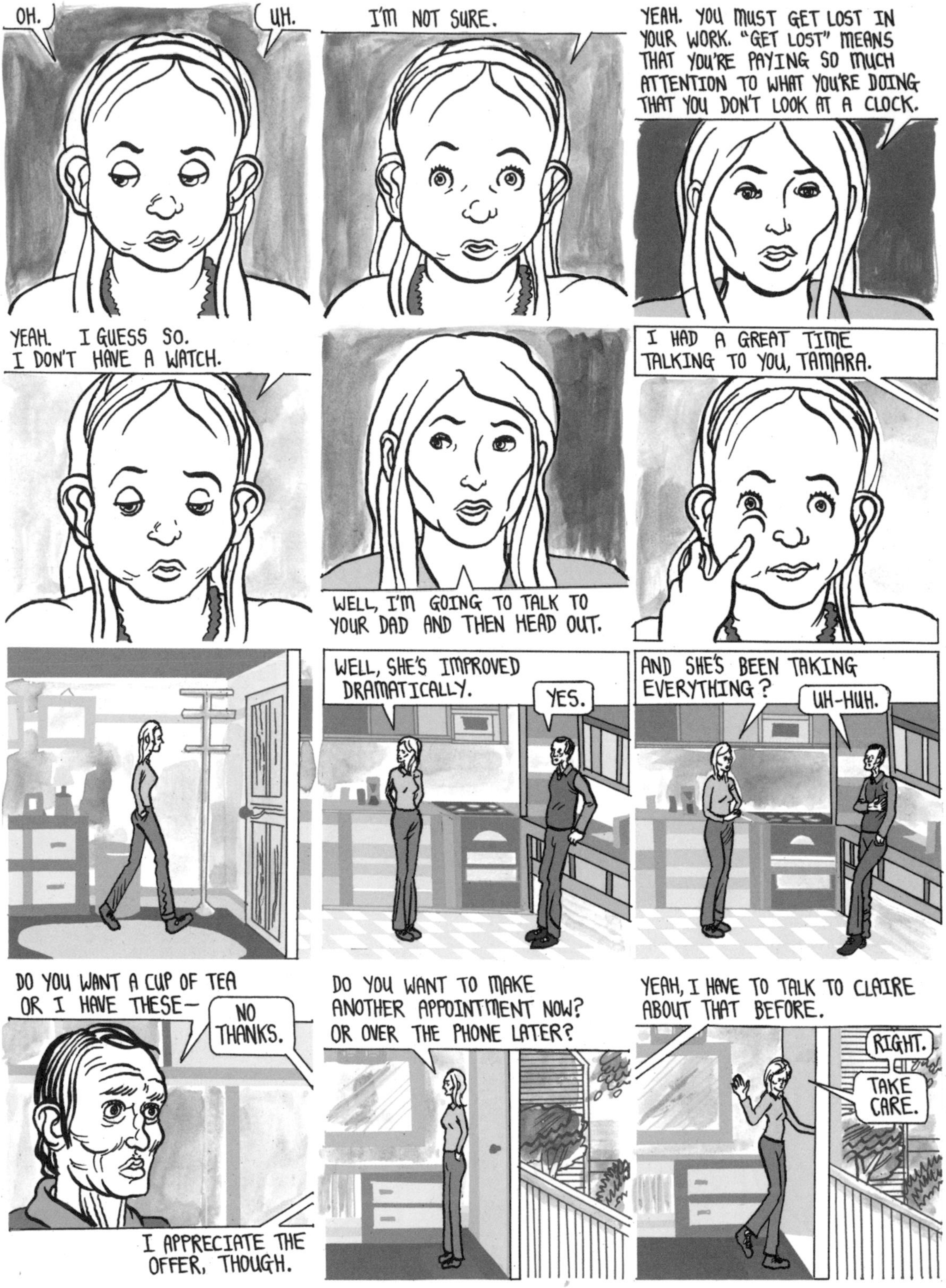
OH.
UH.
I'M NOT SURE.
YEAH. YOU MUST GET LOST IN YOUR WORK. "GET LOST" MEANS THAT YOU'RE PAYING SO MUCH ATTENTION TO WHAT YOU'RE DOING THAT YOU DON'T LOOK AT A CLOCK.
YEAH. I GUESS SO. I DON'T HAVE A WATCH.
WELL, I'M GOING TO TALK TO YOUR DAD AND THEN HEAD OUT.
I HAD A GREAT TIME TALKING TO YOU, TAMARA.
WELL, SHE'S IMPROVED DRAMATICALLY.
YES.
AND SHE'S BEEN TAKING EVERYTHING?
UH-HUH.
DO YOU WANT A CUP OF TEA OR I HAVE THESE—
NO THANKS.
I APPRECIATE THE OFFER, THOUGH.
DO YOU WANT TO MAKE ANOTHER APPOINTMENT NOW? OR OVER THE PHONE LATER?
YEAH, I HAVE TO TALK TO CLAIRE ABOUT THAT BEFORE.
RIGHT.
TAKE CARE.

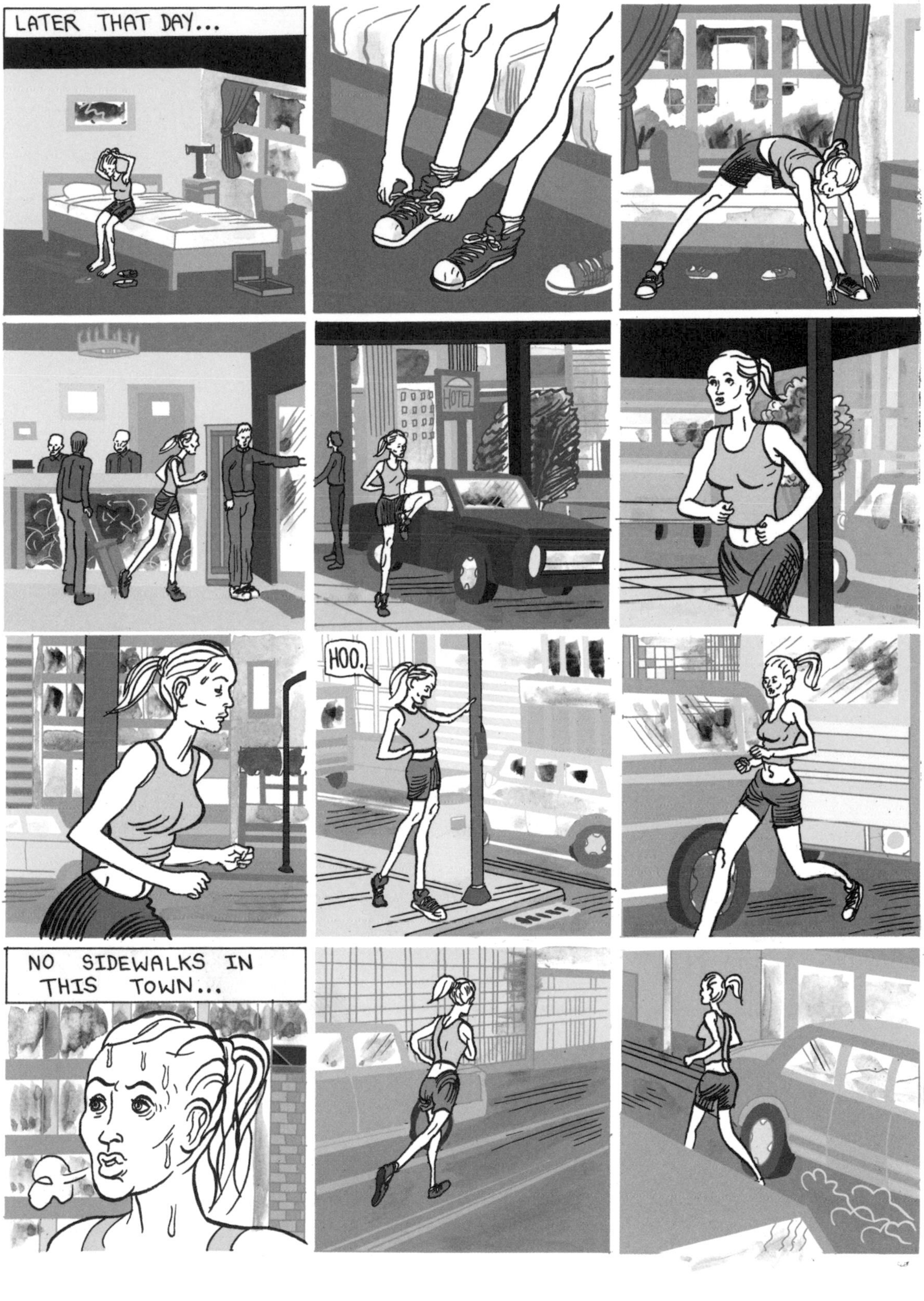
LATER THAT DAY...
HOTEL
HOO.
NO SIDEWALKS IN THIS TOWN...

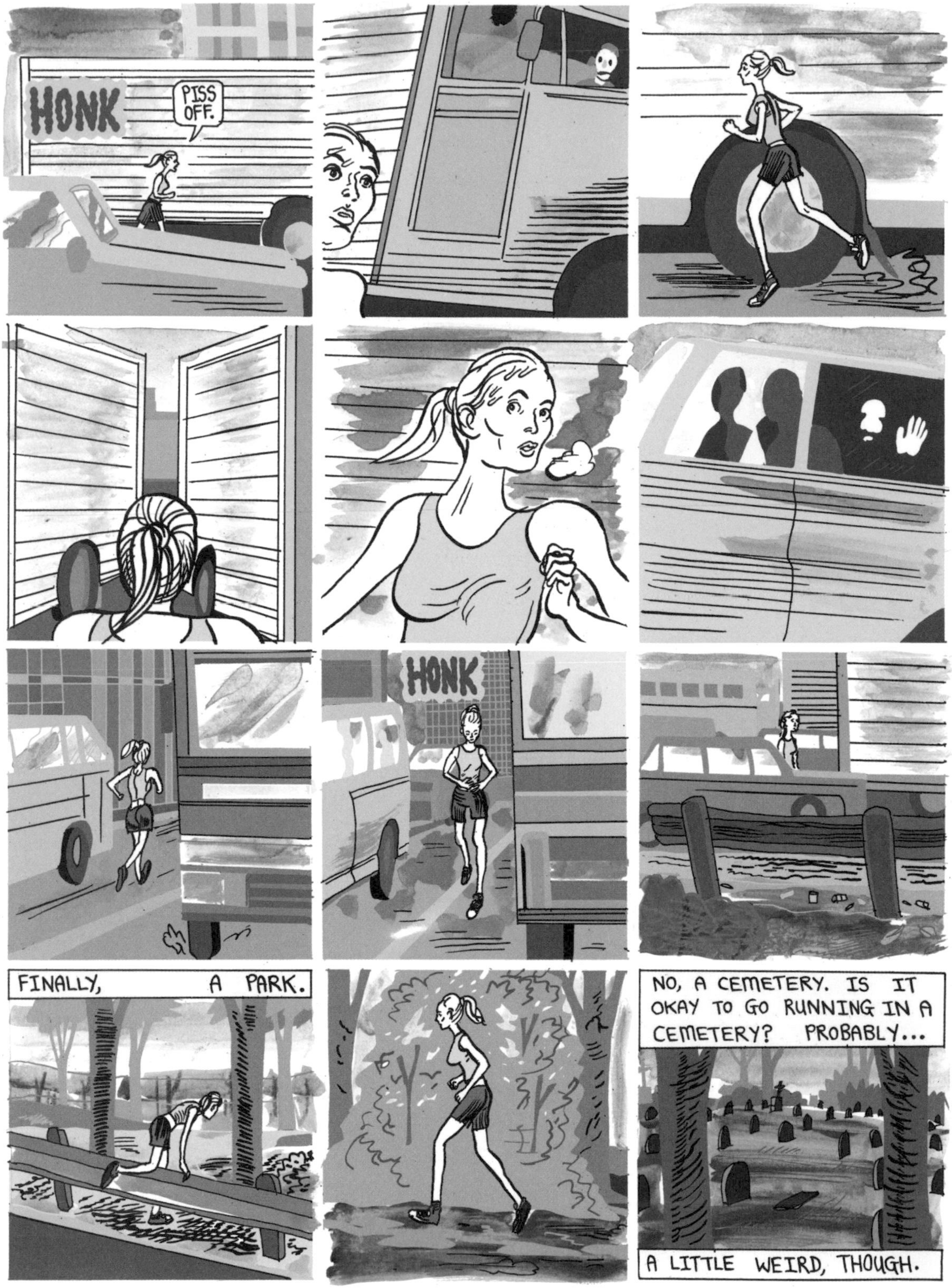
HONK
PISS OFF.
HONK
FINALLY, A PARK.
NO, A CEMETERY. IS IT OKAY TO GO RUNNING IN A CEMETERY? PROBABLY...
A LITTLE WEIRD, THOUGH.

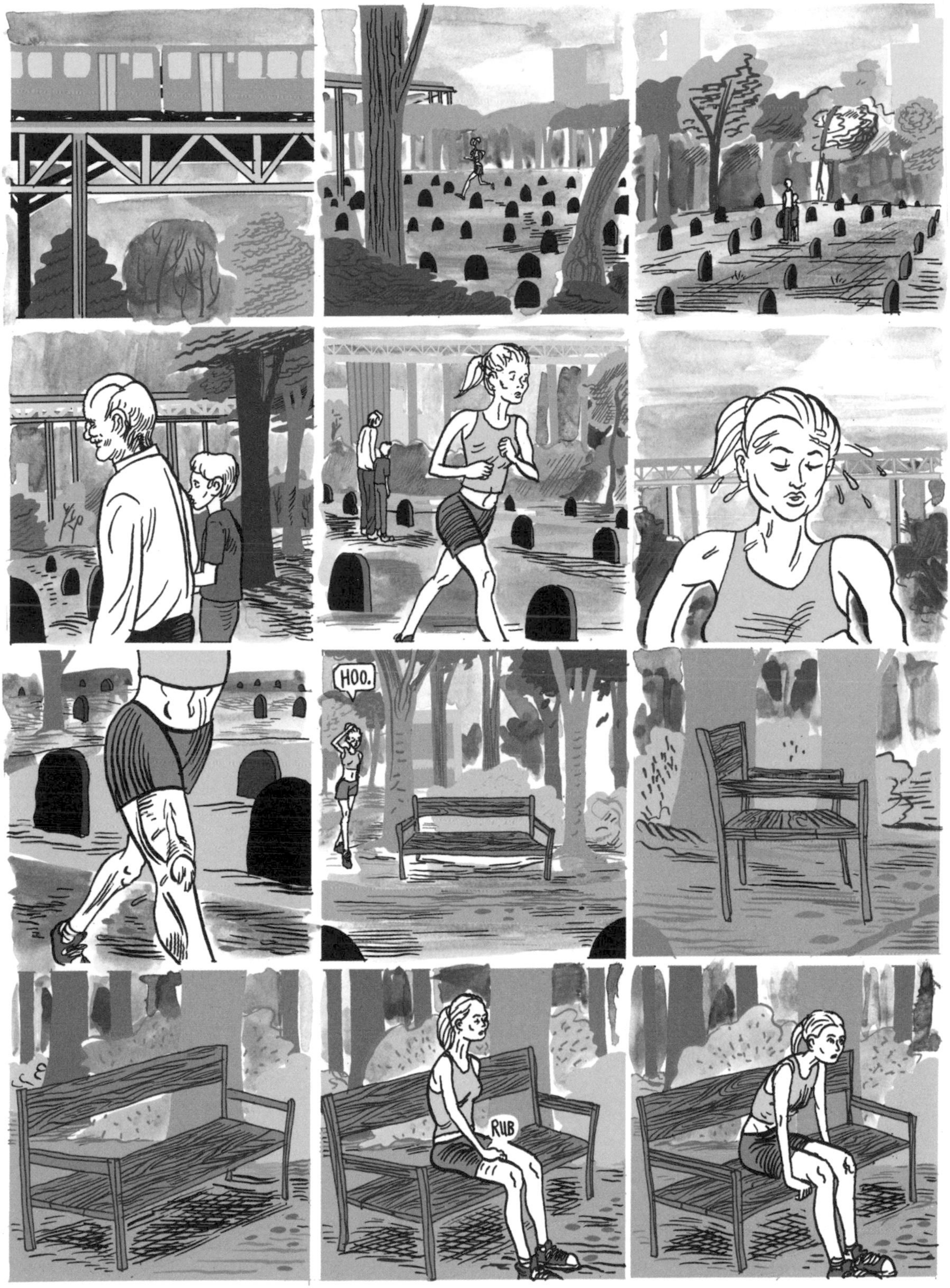
HOO.
RUB

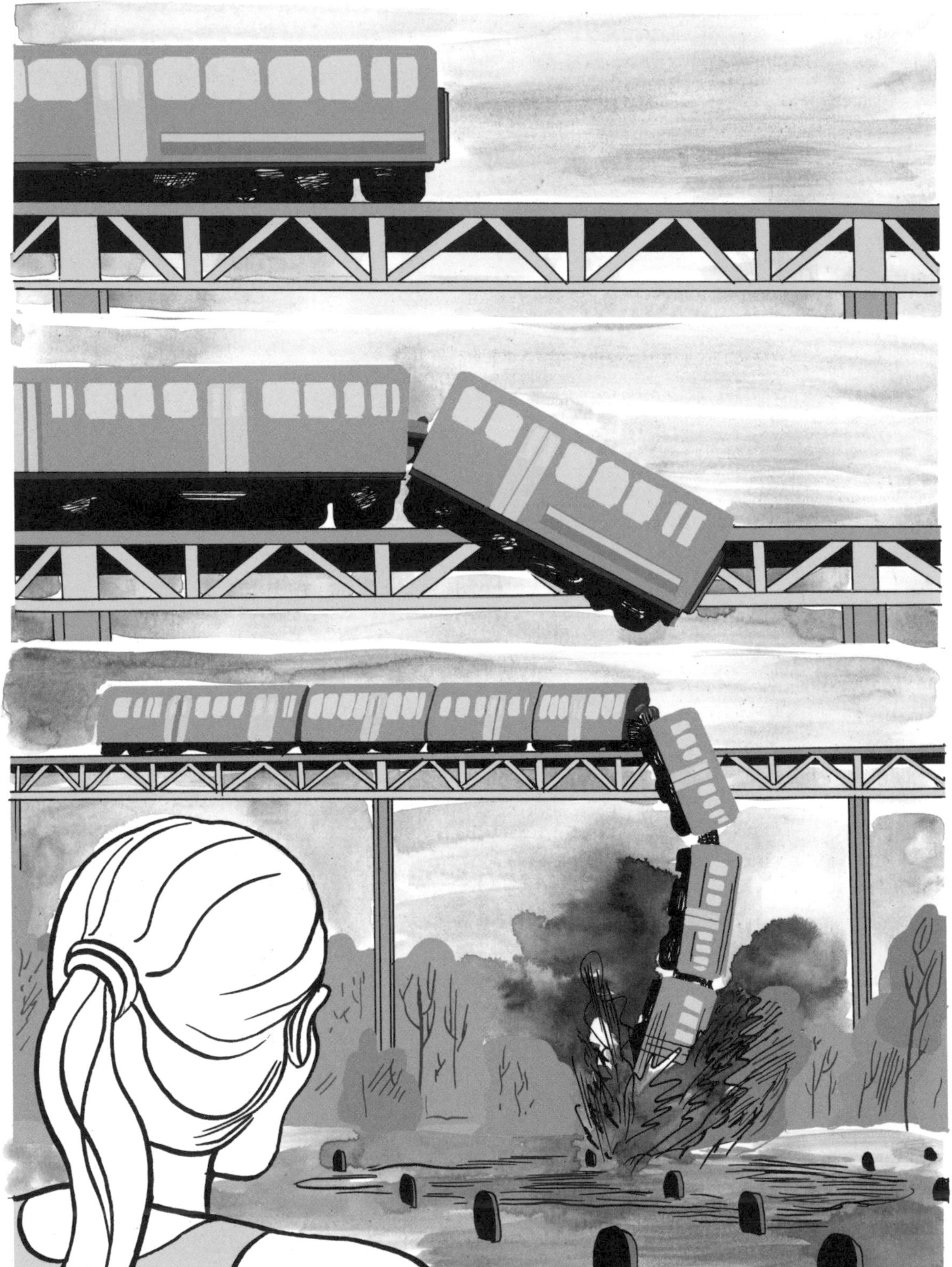

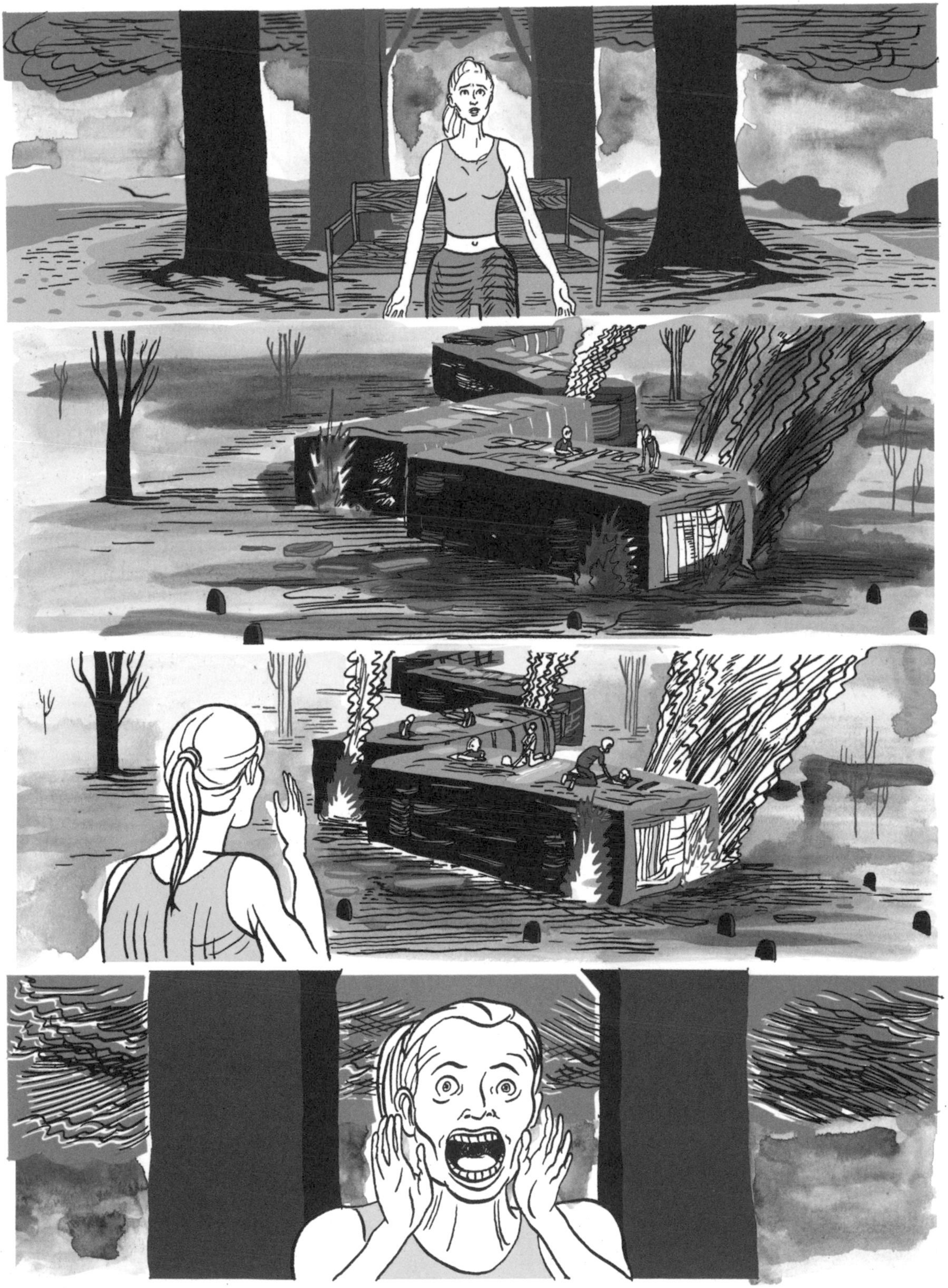

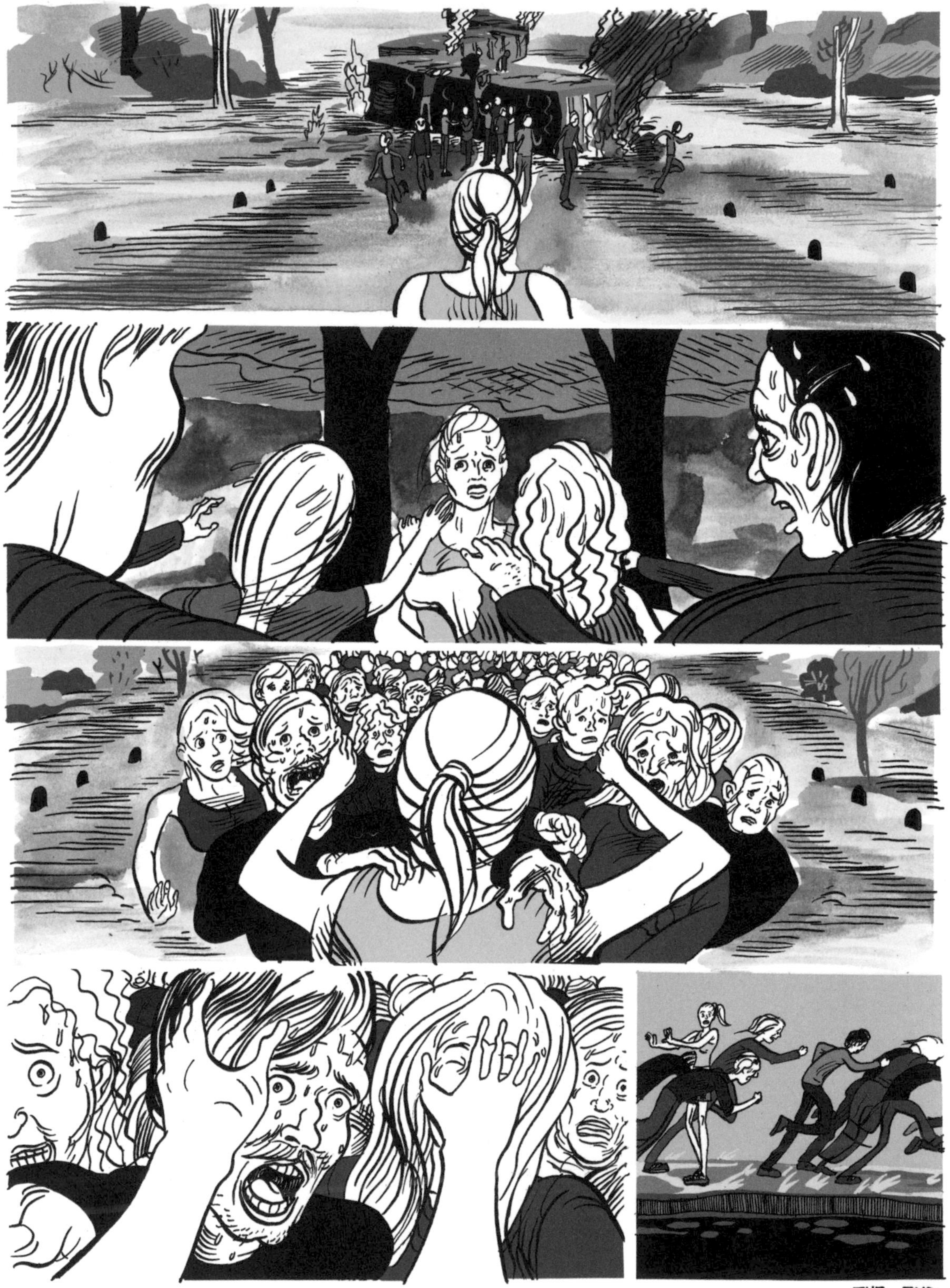

THE END.

NOISE a history

BIG BANG. 14 BILLION BC. ?DB

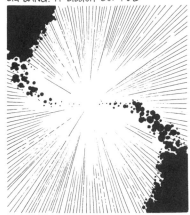

WATERFALL. 80,000 BC. 60 DB

SANTORINI ERUPTION. 1650 BC. 200 DB

THE TURKISH BOMBARD AT THE SIEGE OF CONSTANTINOPLE. 1453 AD. 120 DB

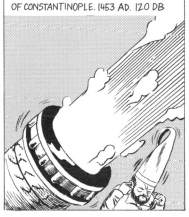

TWENTIETH CENTURY LIMITED. NORTH AMERICA. 1905 AD. 95 DB

RUSTLING OF LEAVES. CENTRAL PARK. 1885 AD. 10 DB

SYMPHONY OF THE CITY. 1914 AD. 95 DB

NUCLEAR EXPLOSION. NAGASAKI. 1945 AD. 248 DB

PERSONAL AUDIO DEVICE. NOW. 90 DB

T.KACZYNSKI

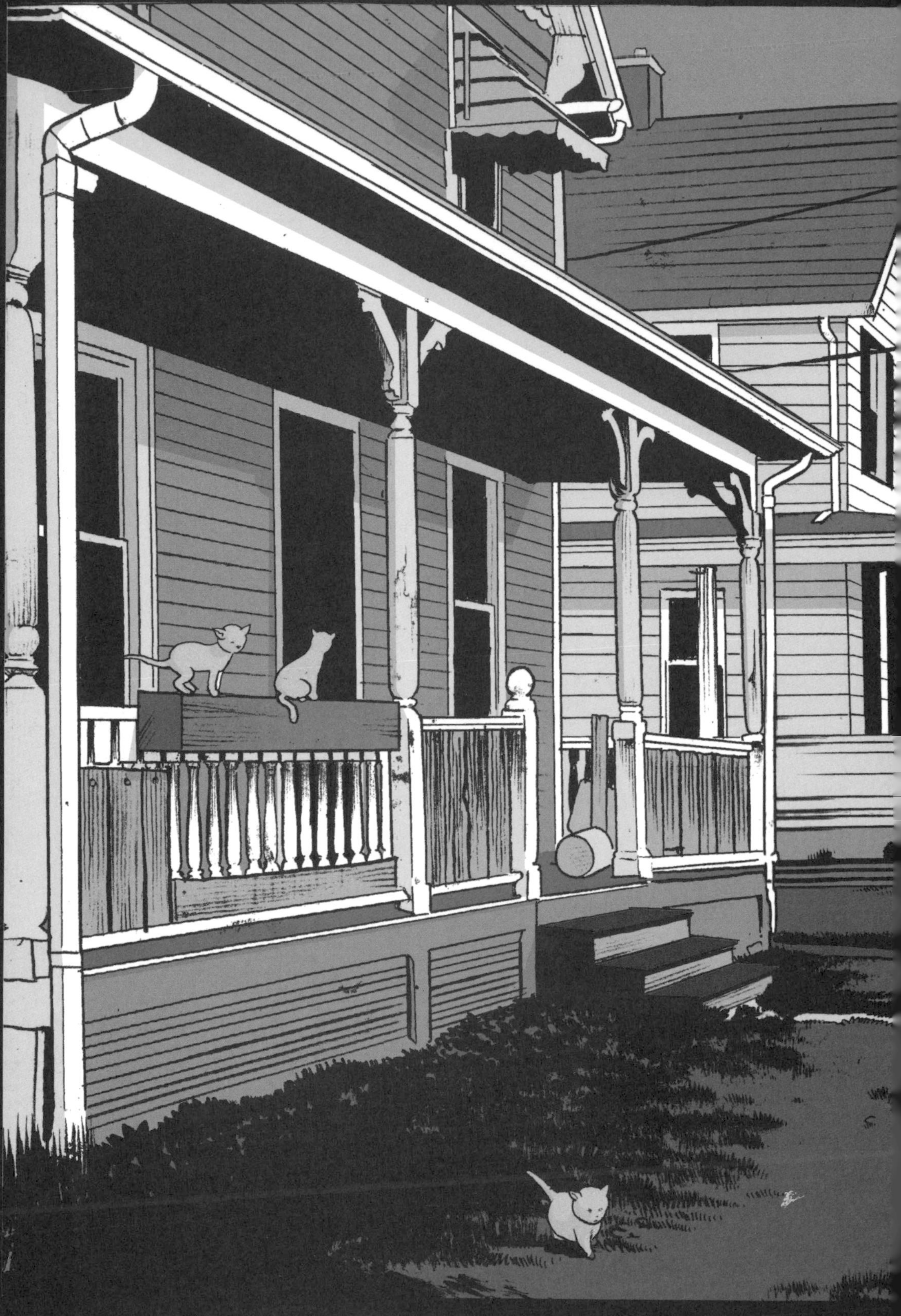

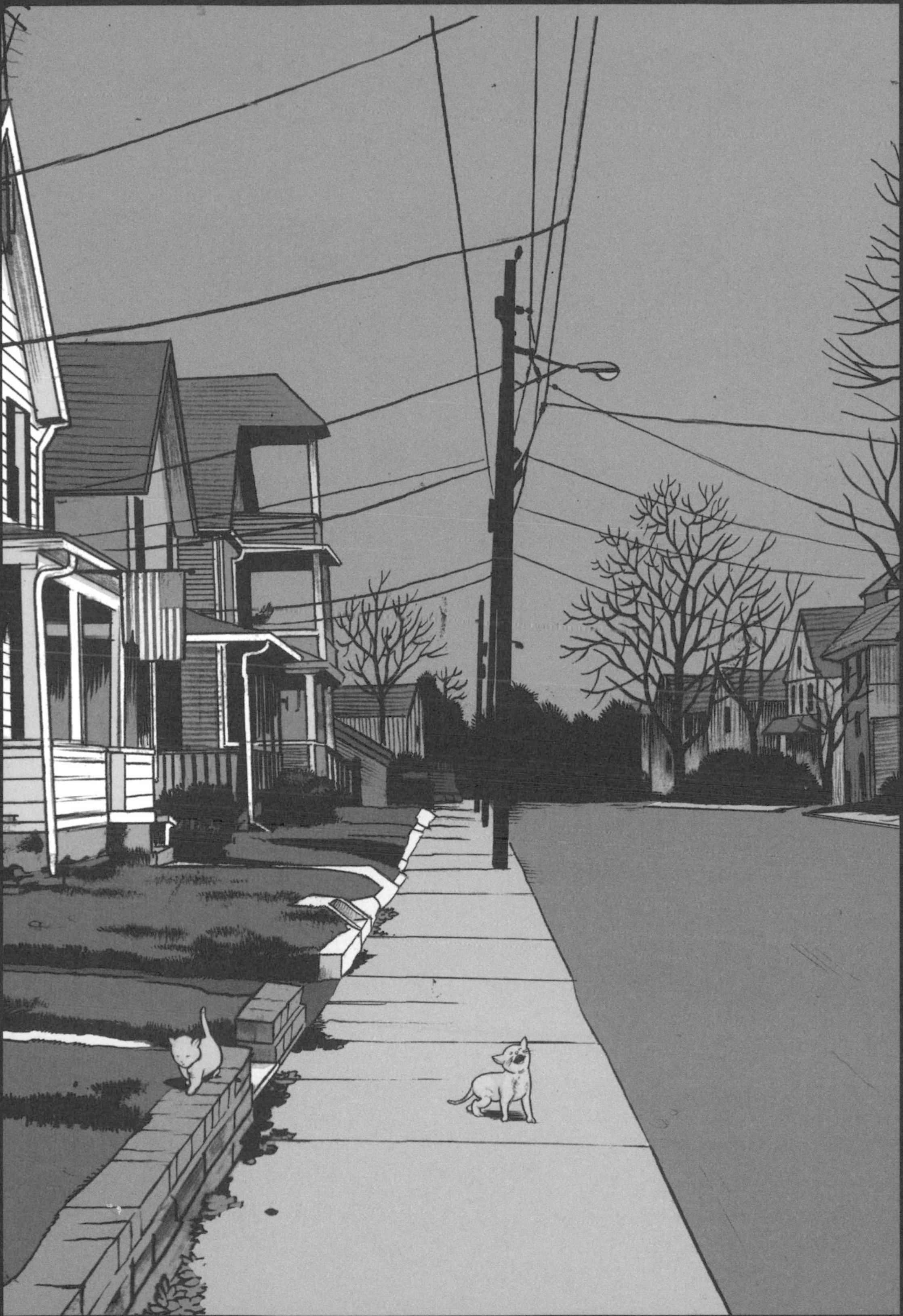

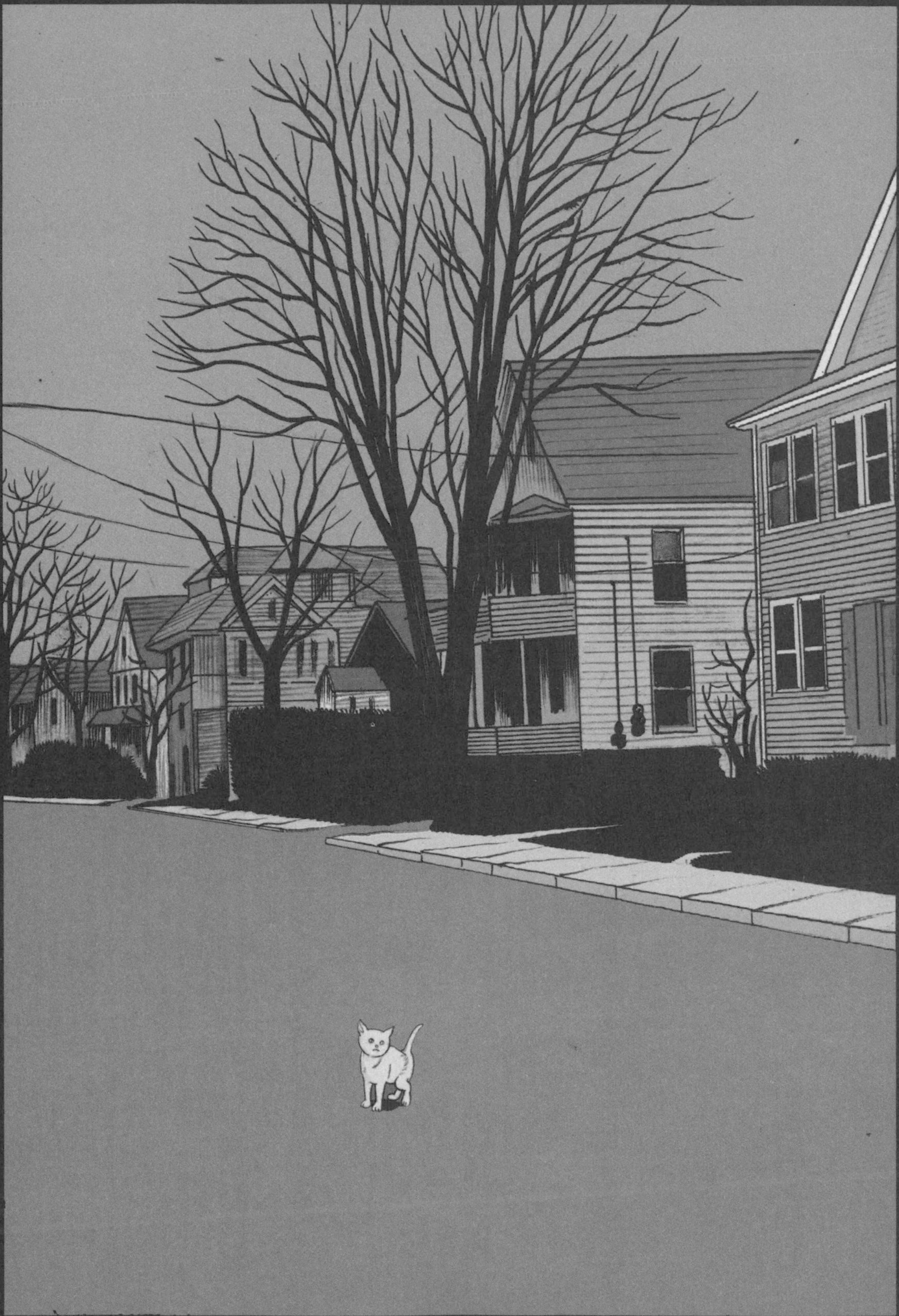

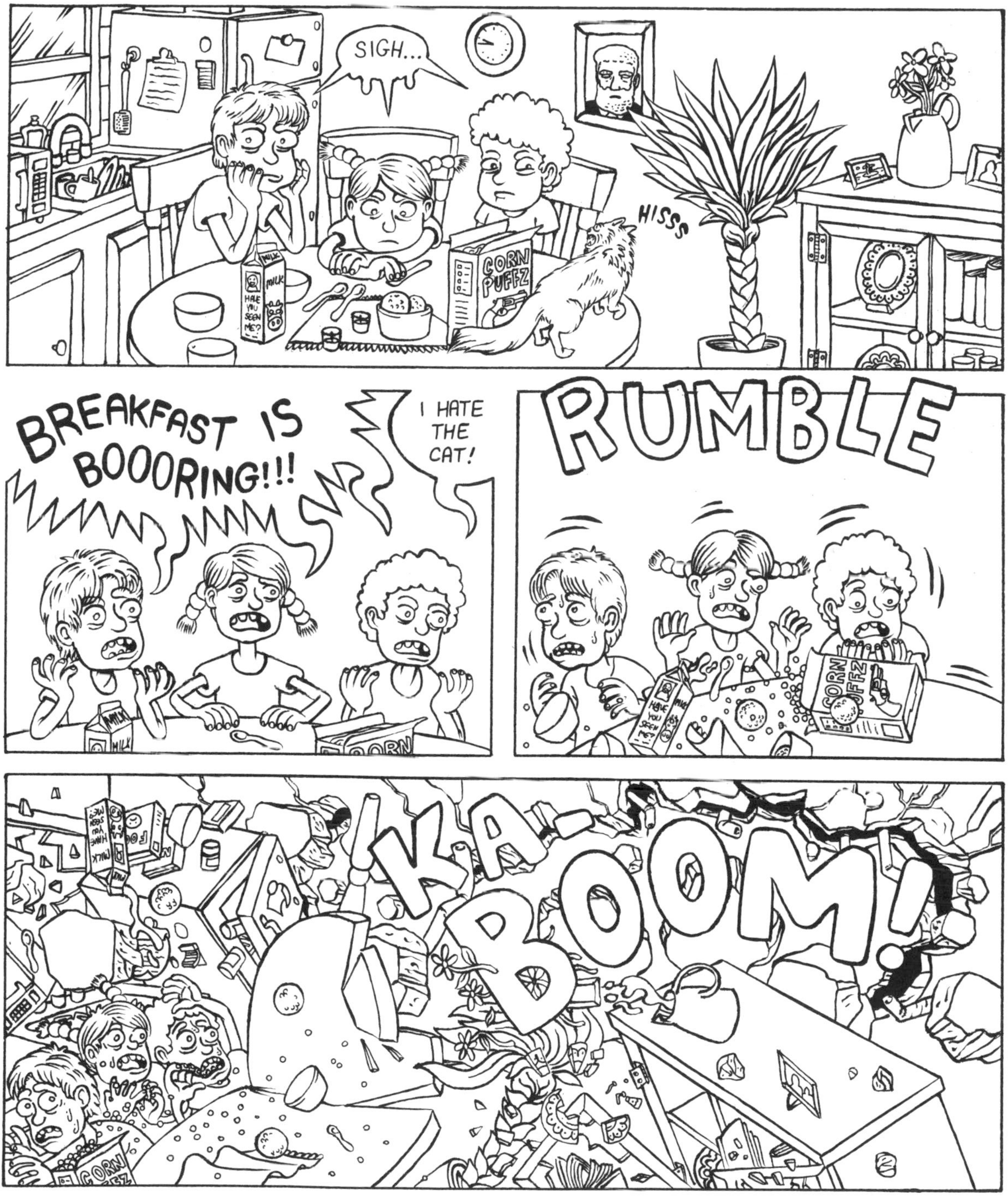
SIGH...
HISSS
CORN PUFFZ
MILK
HAVE YOU SEEN ME?
BREAKFAST IS BOOORING!!!
I HATE THE CAT!
RUMBLE
KA-BOOM!

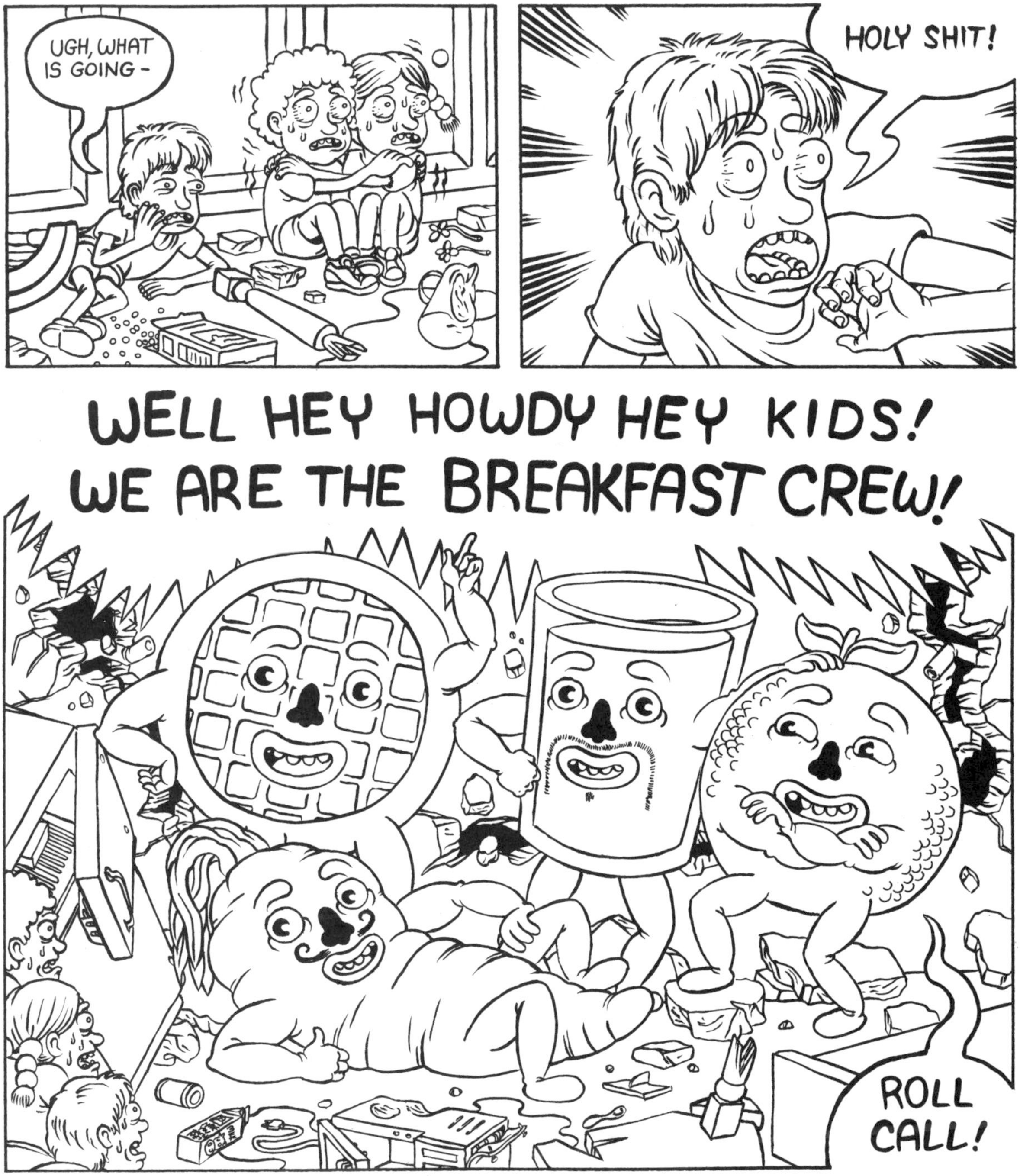
UGH, WHAT IS GOING -
HOLY SHIT!
WELL HEY HOWDY HEY KIDS!
WE ARE THE BREAKFAST CREW!
ROLL CALL!

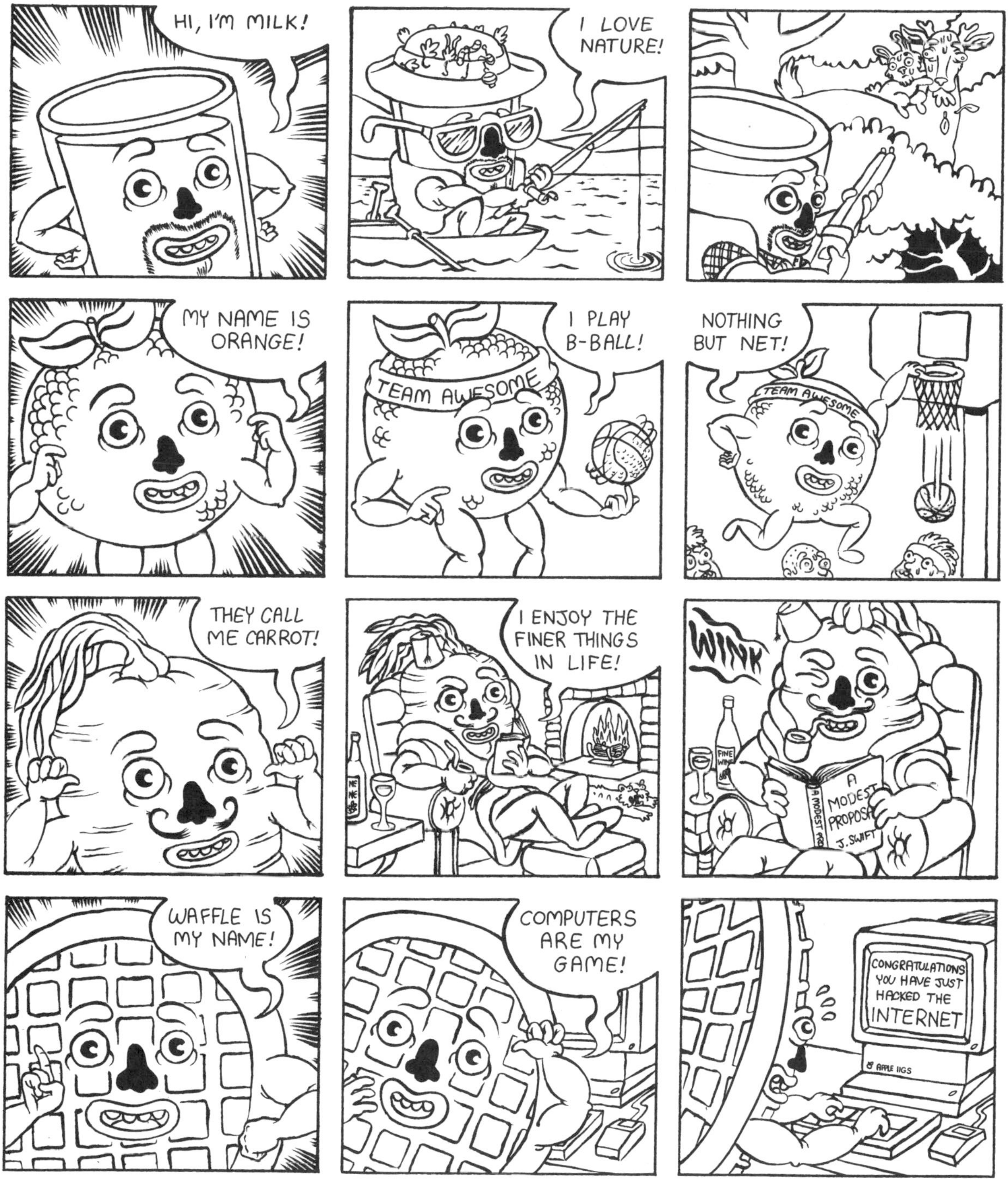
HI, I'M MILK!
I LOVE NATURE!
MY NAME IS ORANGE!
I PLAY B-BALL!
TEAM AWESOME
NOTHING BUT NET!
TEAM AWESOME
THEY CALL ME CARROT!
I ENJOY THE FINER THINGS IN LIFE!
WINK
FINE WINE
A MODEST PROPOSAL
J. SWIFT
WAFFLE IS MY NAME!
COMPUTERS ARE MY GAME!
CONGRATULATIONS YOU HAVE JUST HACKED THE INTERNET
APPLE IIGS

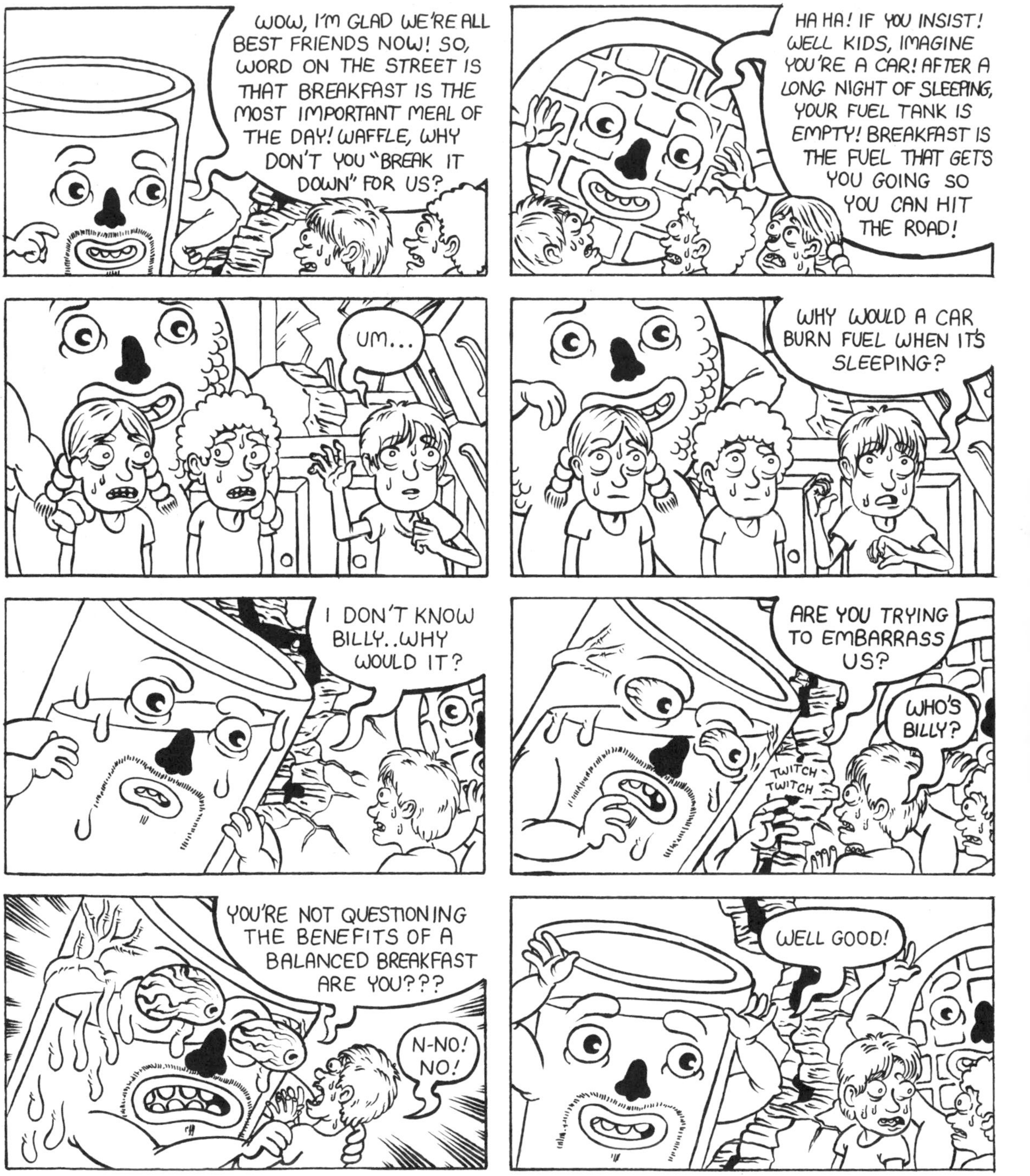
WOW, I'M GLAD WE'RE ALL BEST FRIENDS NOW! SO, WORD ON THE STREET IS THAT BREAKFAST IS THE MOST IMPORTANT MEAL OF THE DAY! WAFFLE, WHY DON'T YOU "BREAK IT DOWN" FOR US?
HA HA! IF YOU INSIST! WELL KIDS, IMAGINE YOU'RE A CAR! AFTER A LONG NIGHT OF SLEEPING, YOUR FUEL TANK IS EMPTY! BREAKFAST IS THE FUEL THAT GETS YOU GOING SO YOU CAN HIT THE ROAD!
UM...
WHY WOULD A CAR BURN FUEL WHEN IT'S SLEEPING?
I DON'T KNOW BILLY..WHY WOULD IT?
ARE YOU TRYING TO EMBARRASS US?
TWITCH TWITCH
WHO'S BILLY?
YOU'RE NOT QUESTIONING THE BENEFITS OF A BALANCED BREAKFAST ARE YOU???
N-NO! NO!
WELL GOOD!

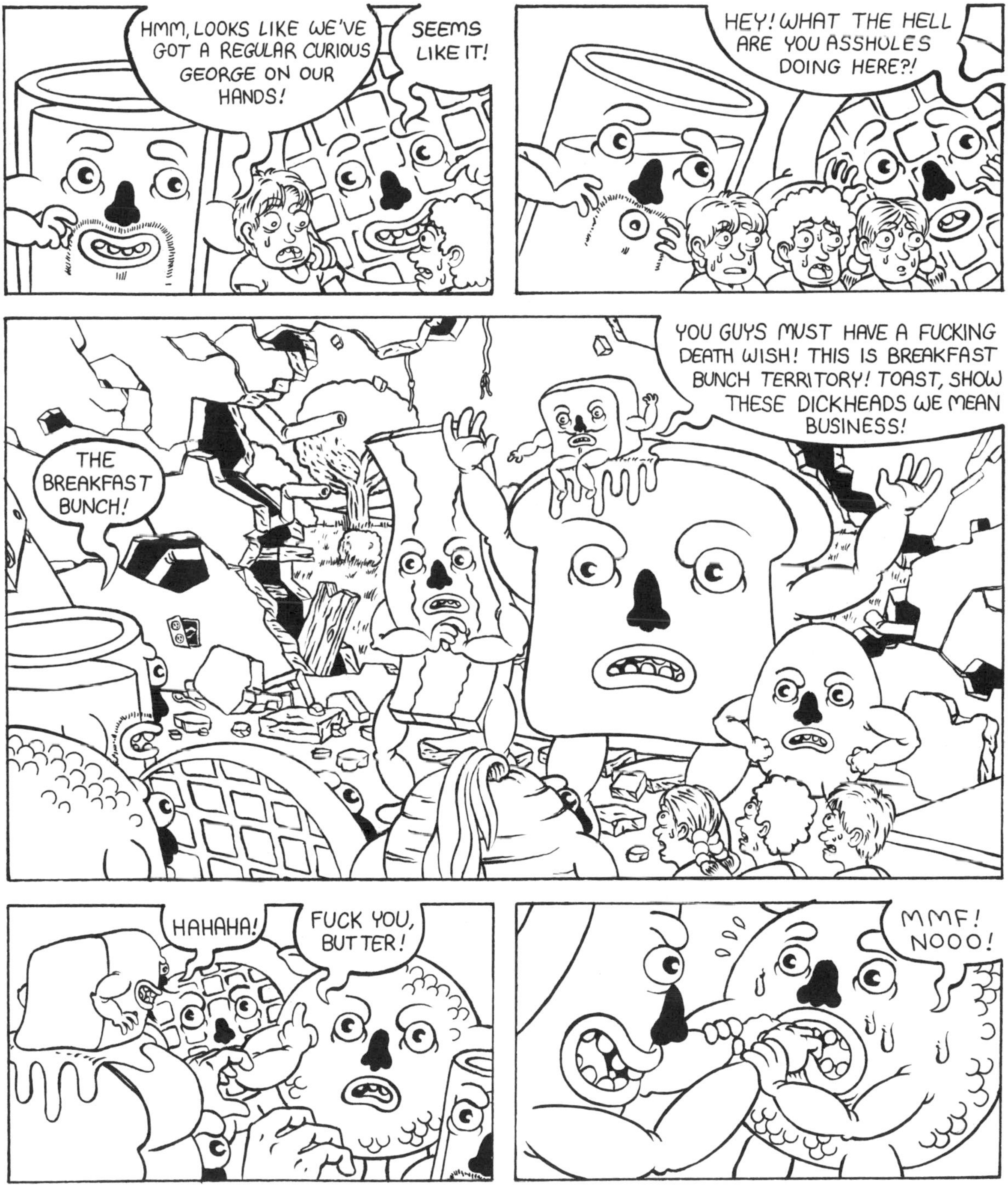
HMM, LOOKS LIKE WE'VE GOT A REGULAR CURIOUS GEORGE ON OUR HANDS!
SEEMS LIKE IT!
HEY! WHAT THE HELL ARE YOU ASSHOLES DOING HERE?!
YOU GUYS MUST HAVE A FUCKING DEATH WISH! THIS IS BREAKFAST BUNCH TERRITORY! TOAST, SHOW THESE DICKHEADS WE MEAN BUSINESS!
THE BREAKFAST BUNCH!
HAHAHA!
FUCK YOU, BUTTER!
MMF! NOOO!

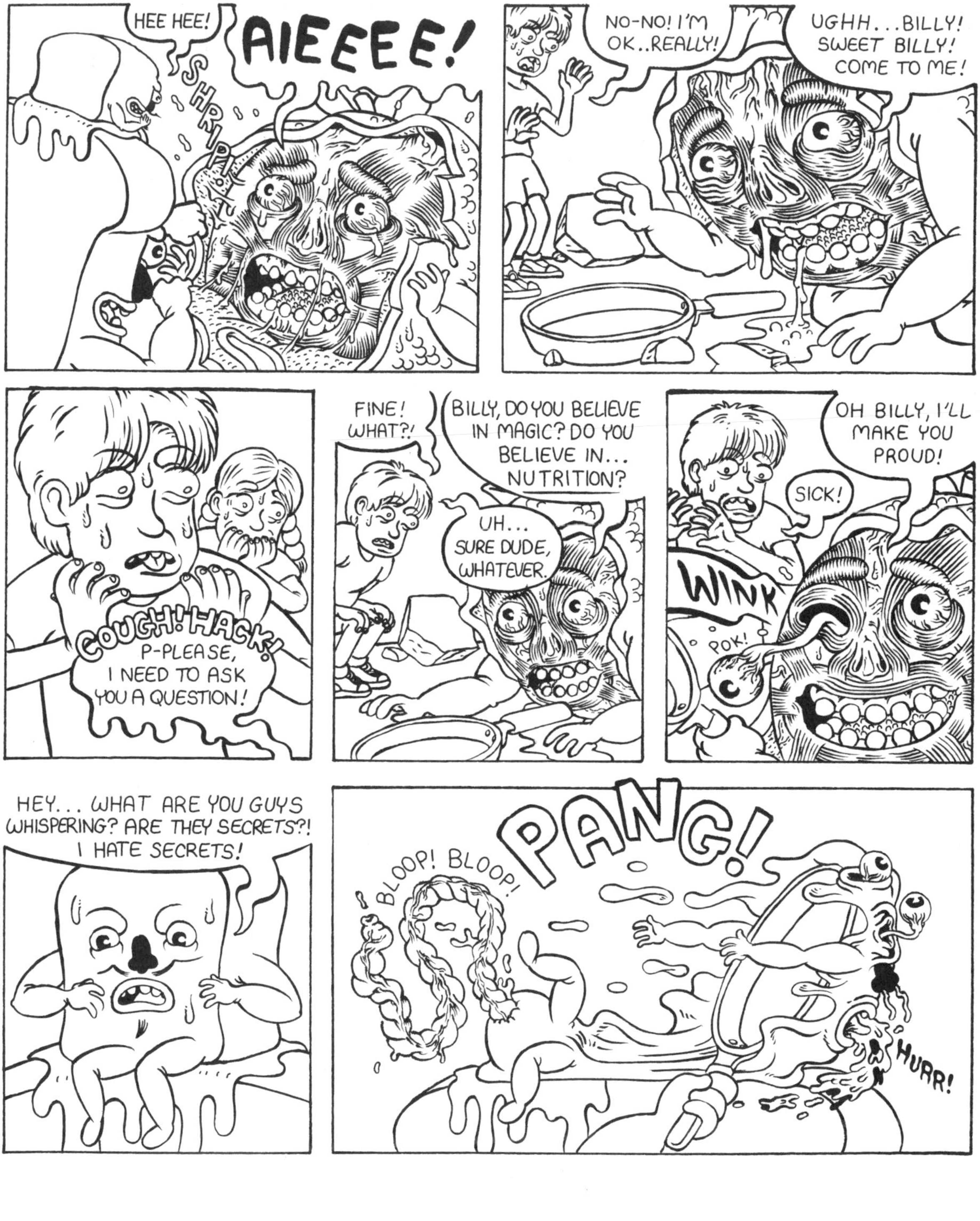
HEE HEE!
AIEEEE!
SHRIP!
NO-NO! I'M OK..REALLY!
UGHH...BILLY! SWEET BILLY! COME TO ME!
COUGH! HACK!
P-PLEASE, I NEED TO ASK YOU A QUESTION!
FINE! WHAT?!
BILLY, DO YOU BELIEVE IN MAGIC? DO YOU BELIEVE IN... NUTRITION?
UH... SURE DUDE, WHATEVER.
OH BILLY, I'LL MAKE YOU PROUD!
SICK!
WINK
POK!
HEY... WHAT ARE YOU GUYS WHISPERING? ARE THEY SECRETS?! I HATE SECRETS!
PANG!
BLOOP! BLOOP!
HURR!

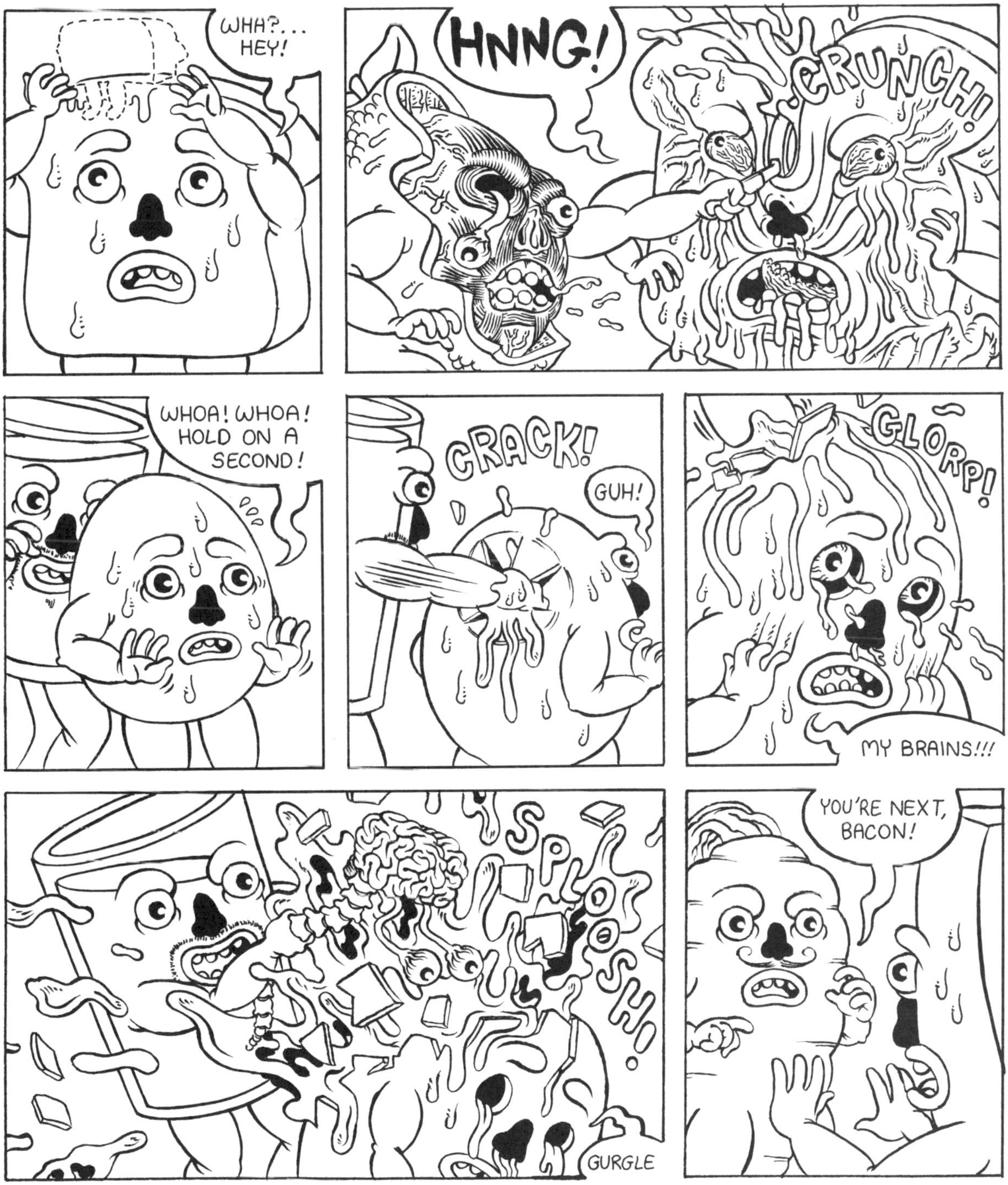

WHA?... HEY!
HNNG!
CRUNCH!
WHOA! WHOA! HOLD ON A SECOND!
CRACK!
GUH!
GLORP!
MY BRAINS!!!
SPLOOSH!
GURGLE
YOU'RE NEXT, BACON!

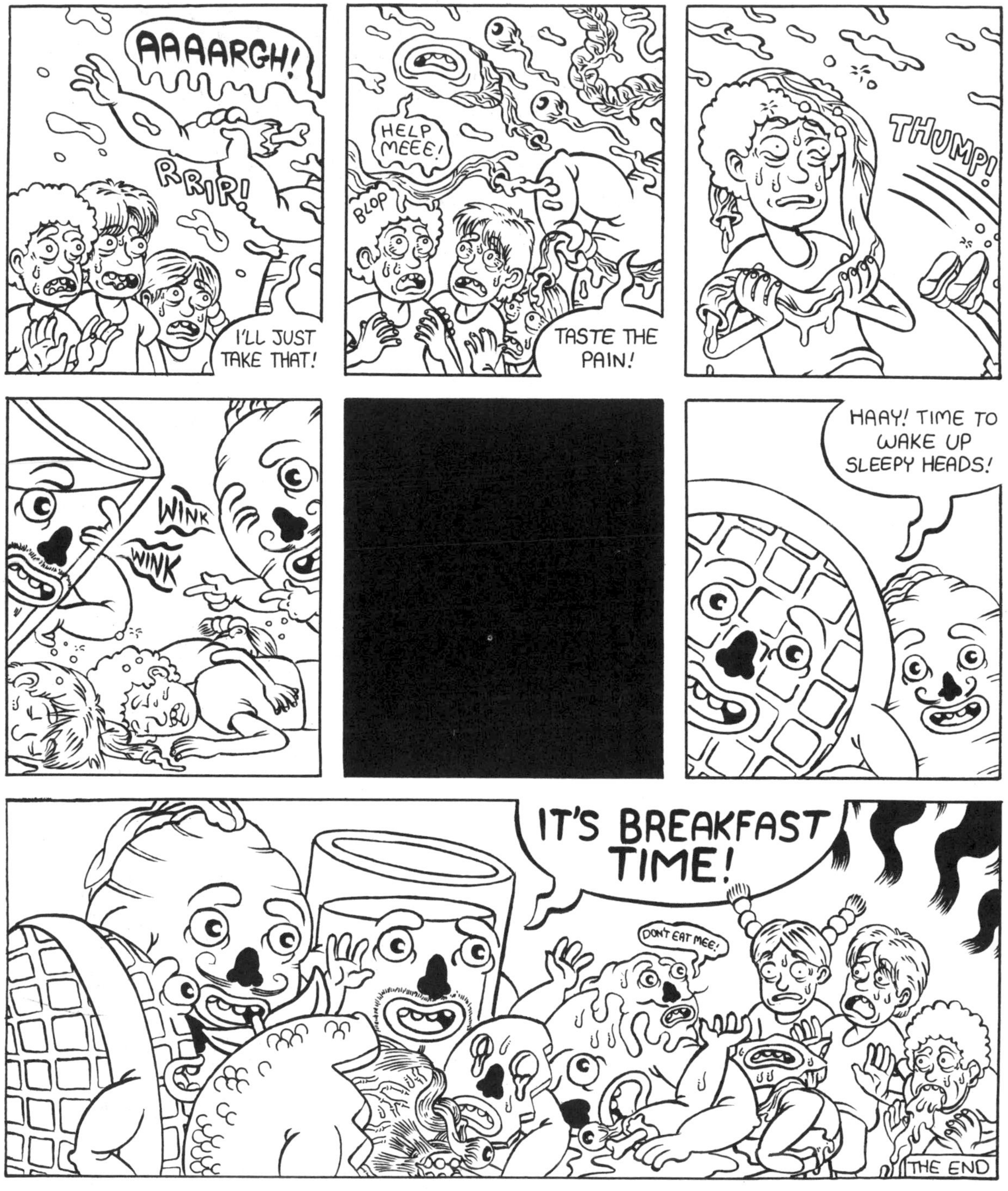
AAAARGH!
RRIP!
I'LL JUST TAKE THAT!
HELP MEEE!
BLOP
TASTE THE PAIN!
THUMP!
WINK
WINK
HAAY! TIME TO WAKE UP SLEEPY HEADS!
IT'S BREAKFAST TIME!
DON'T EAT MEE!
THE END

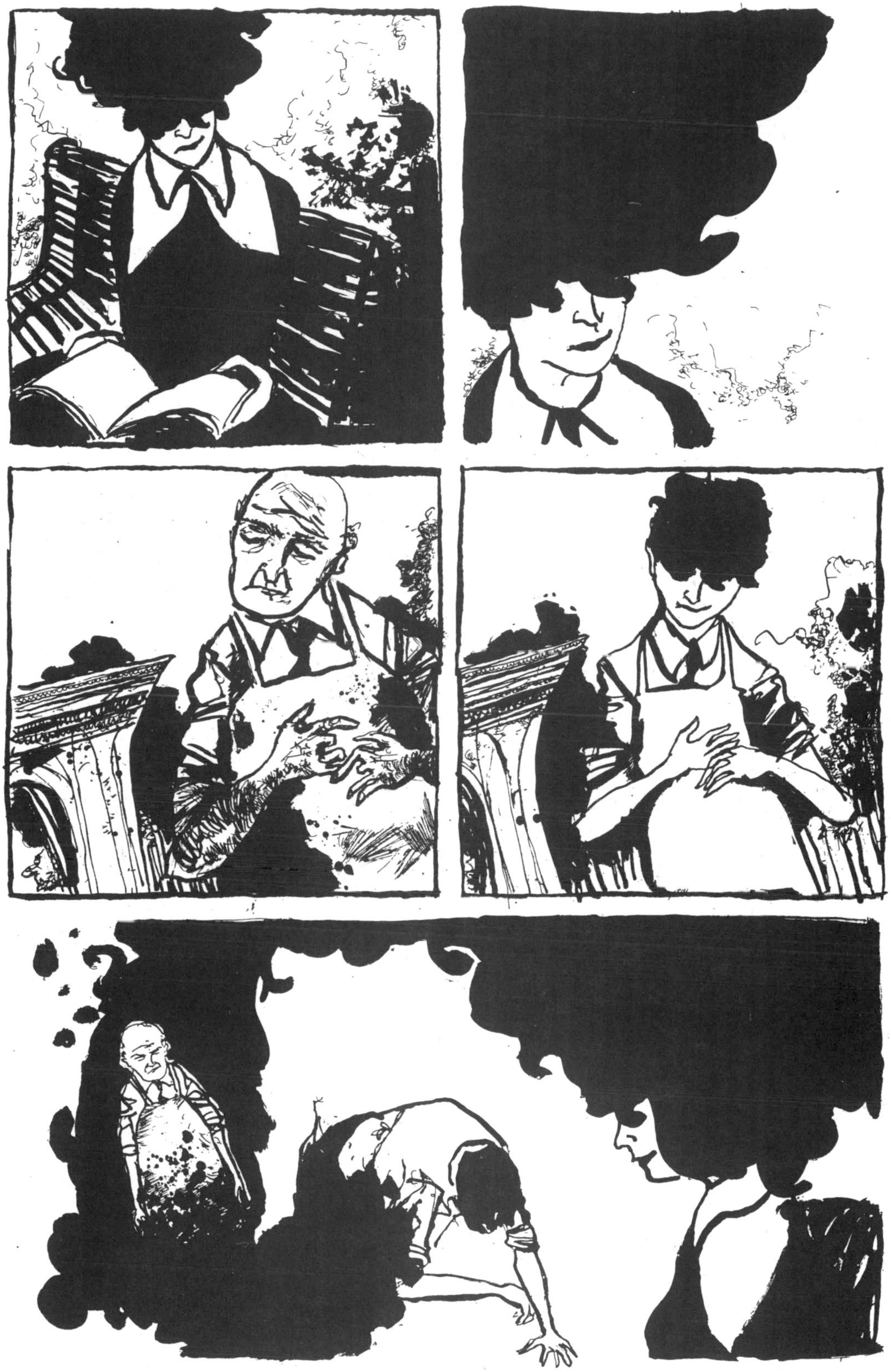

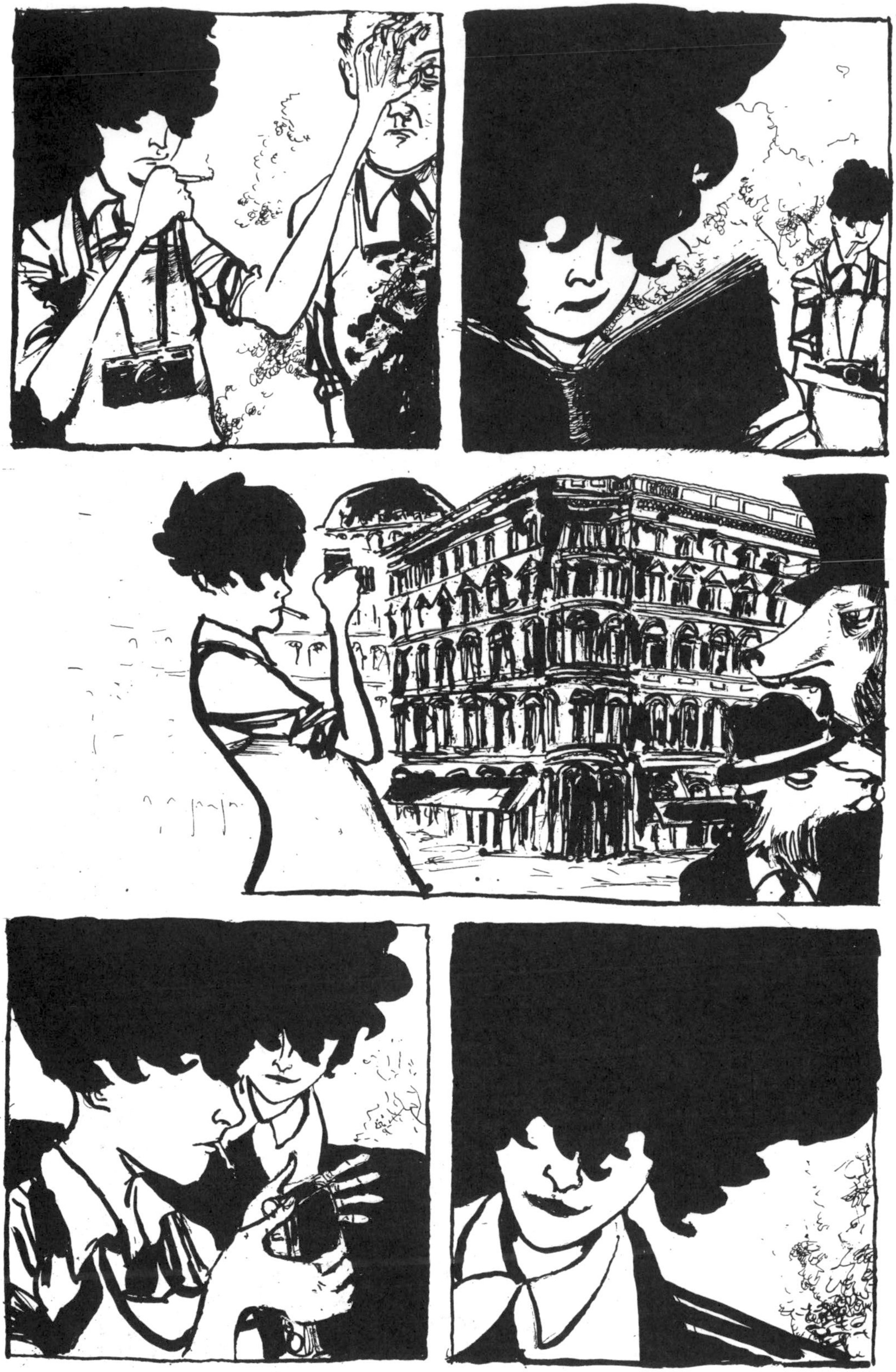

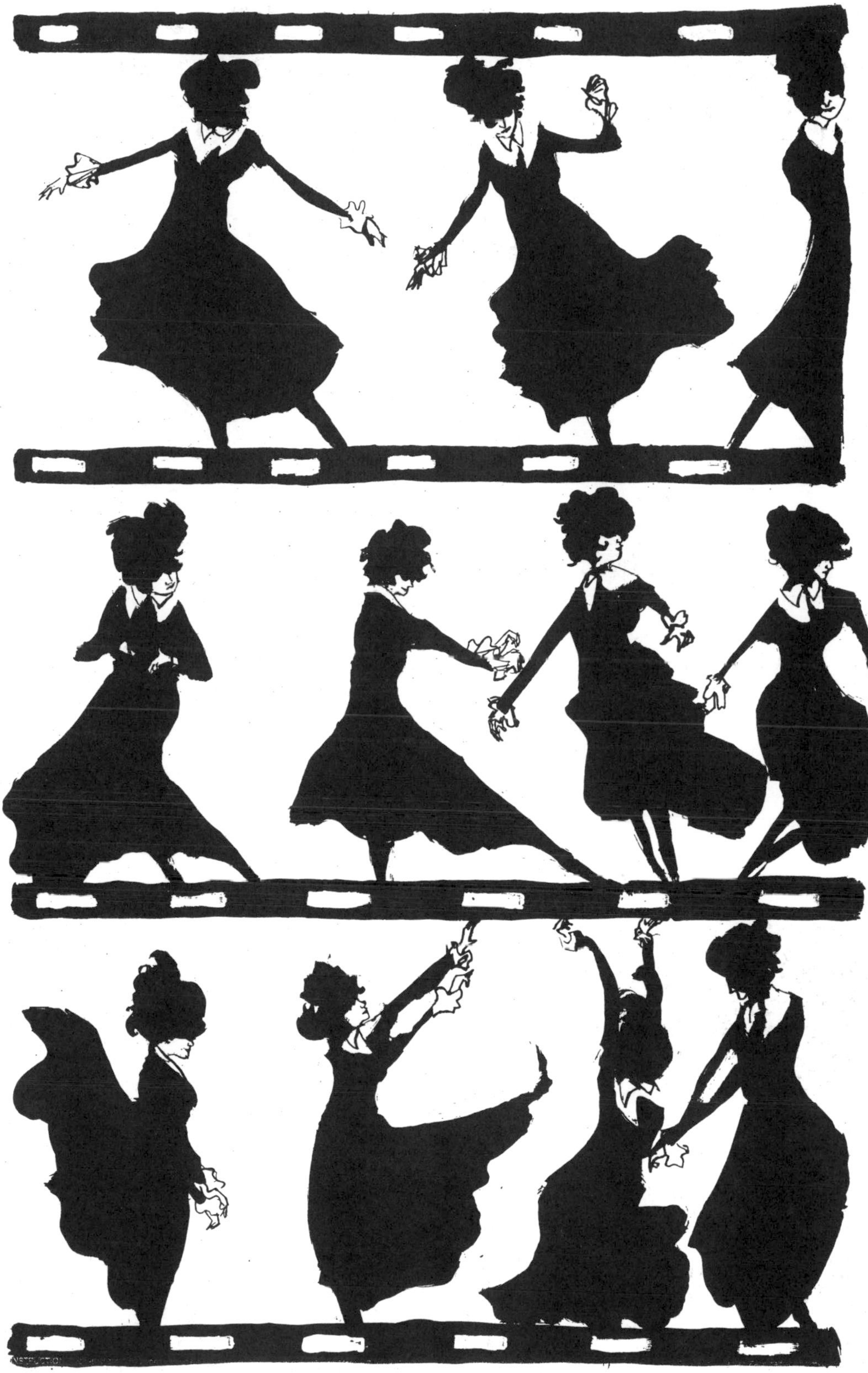

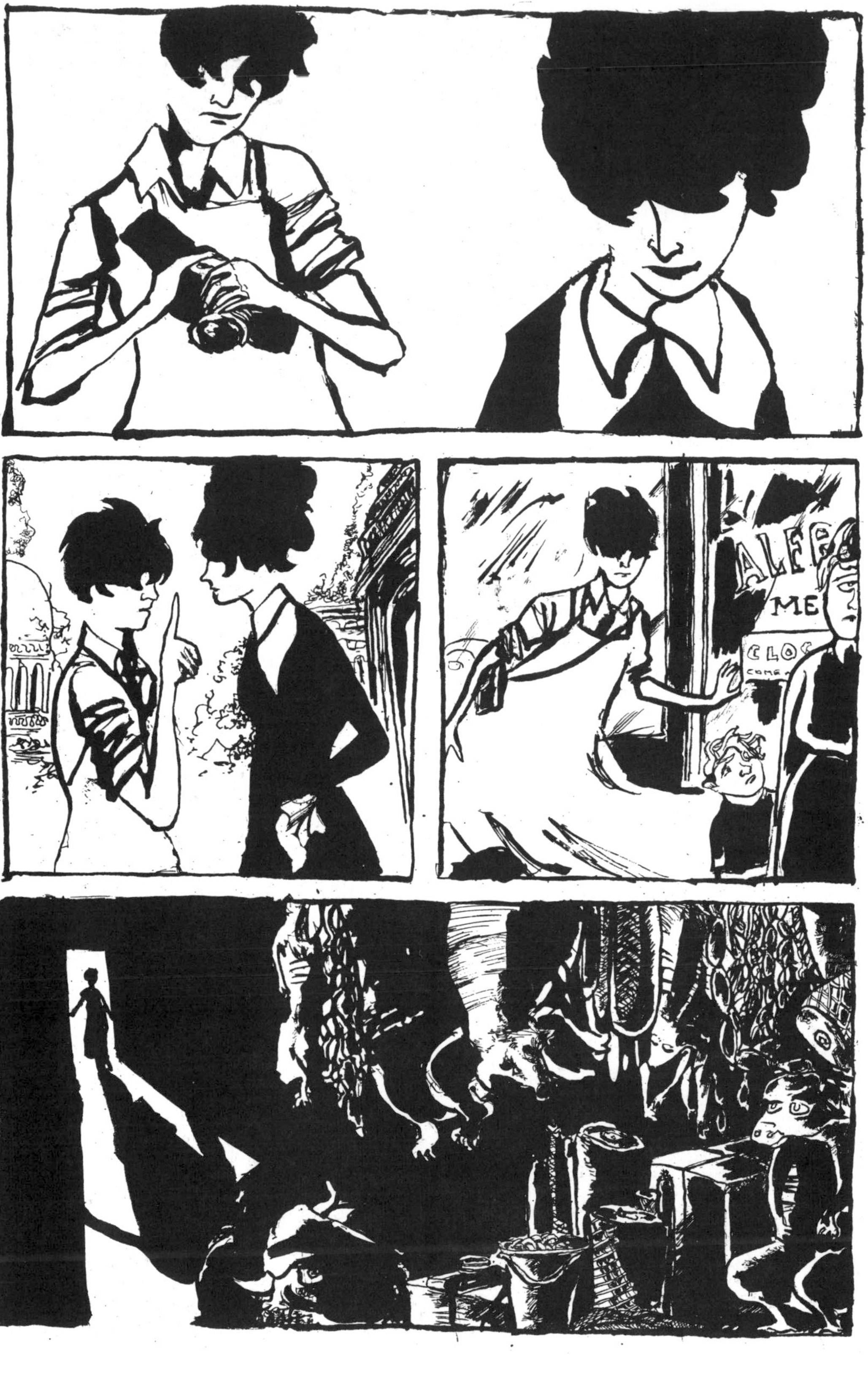

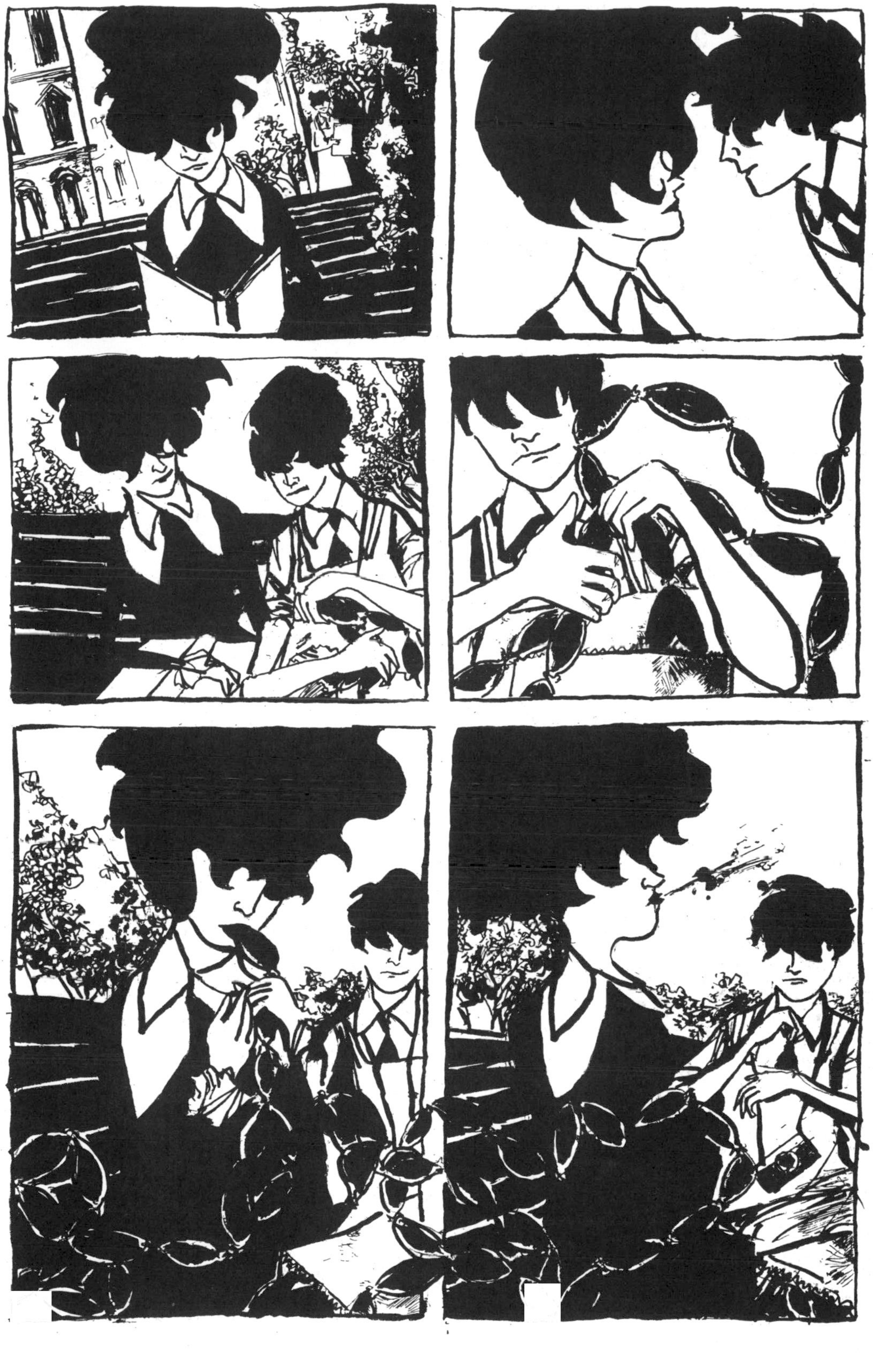

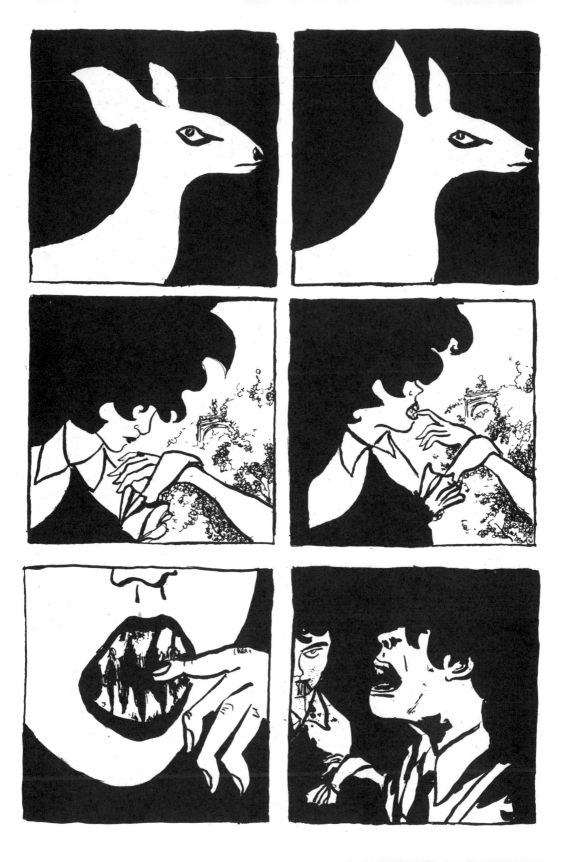

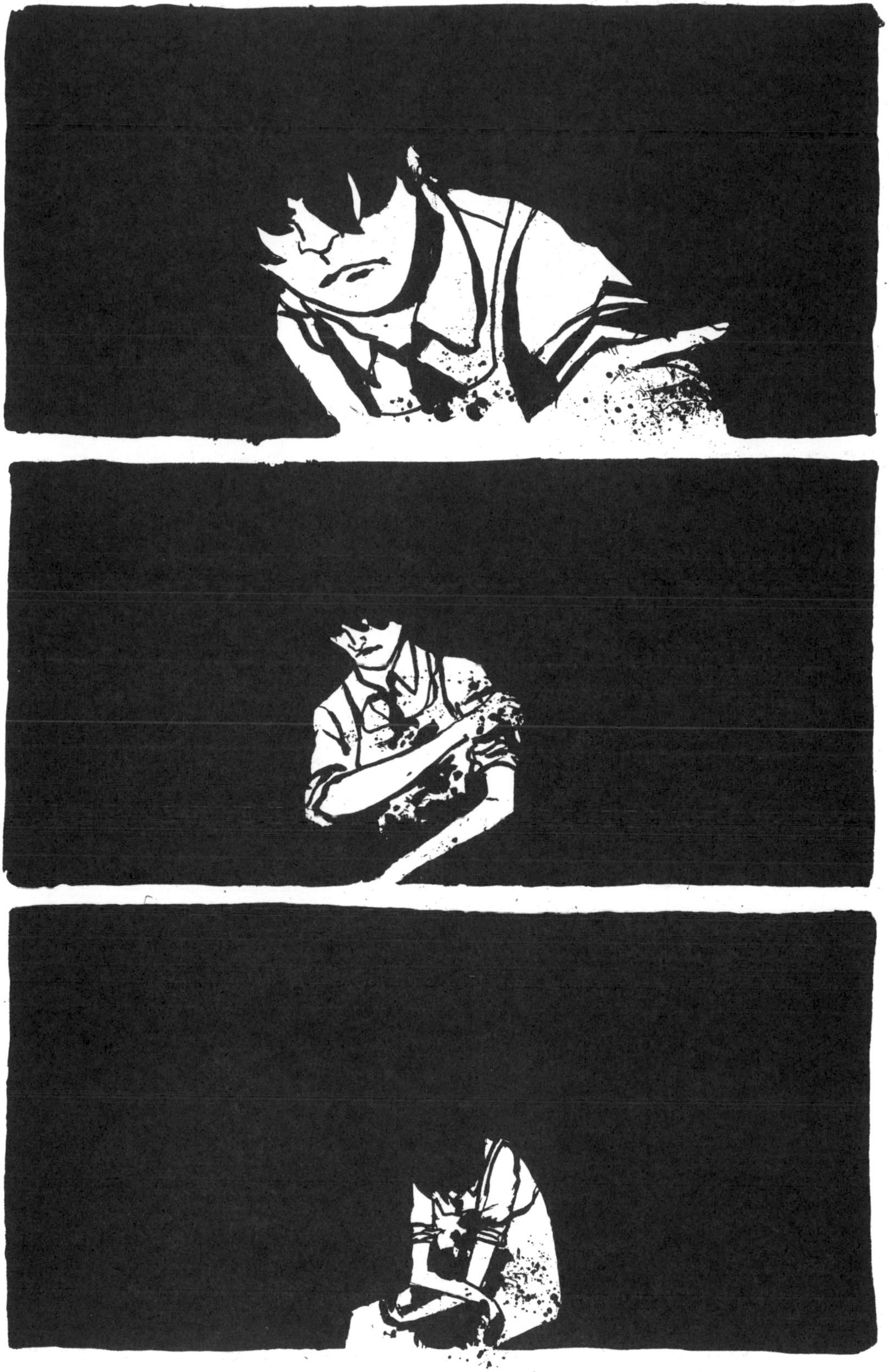

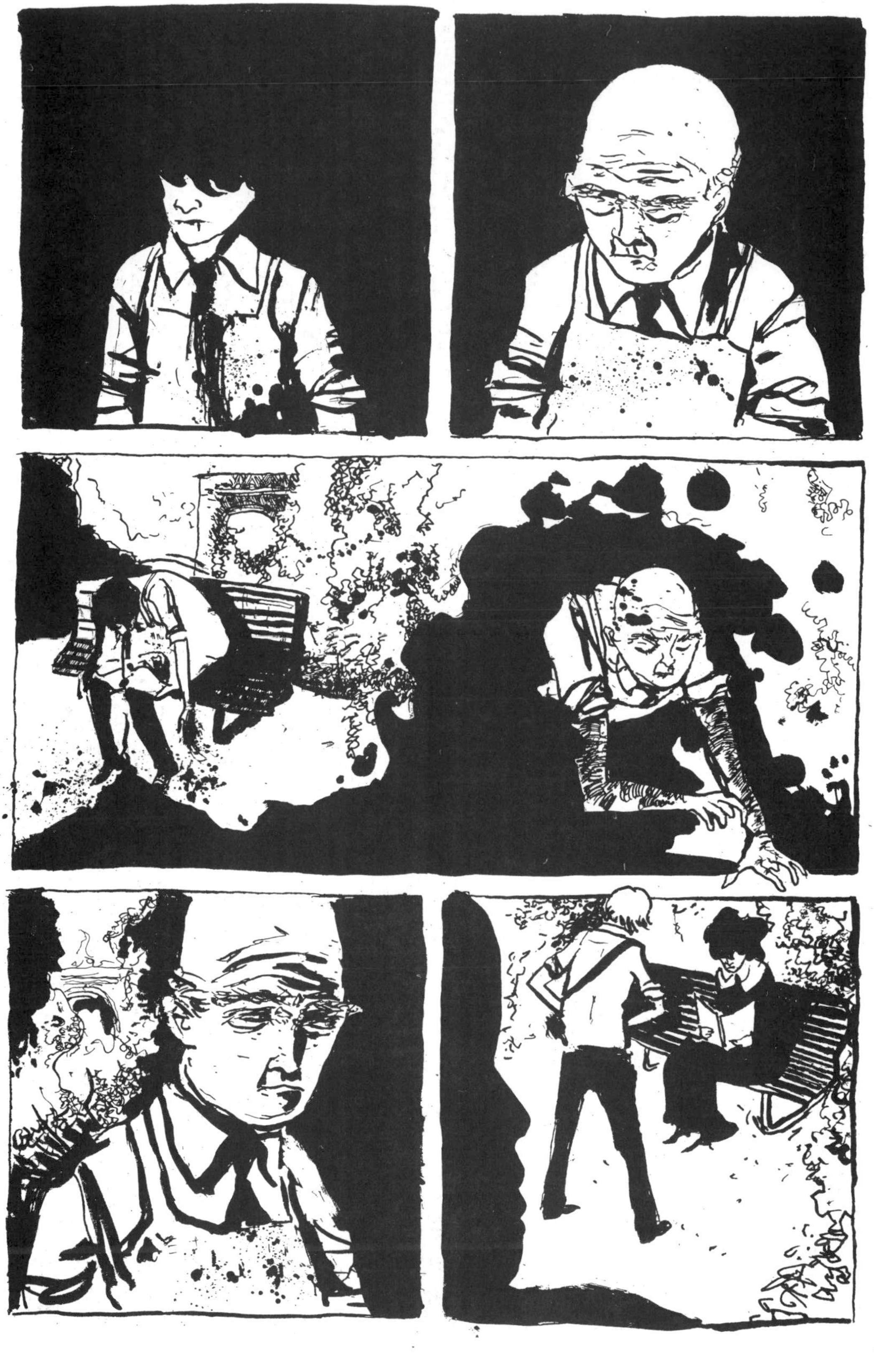

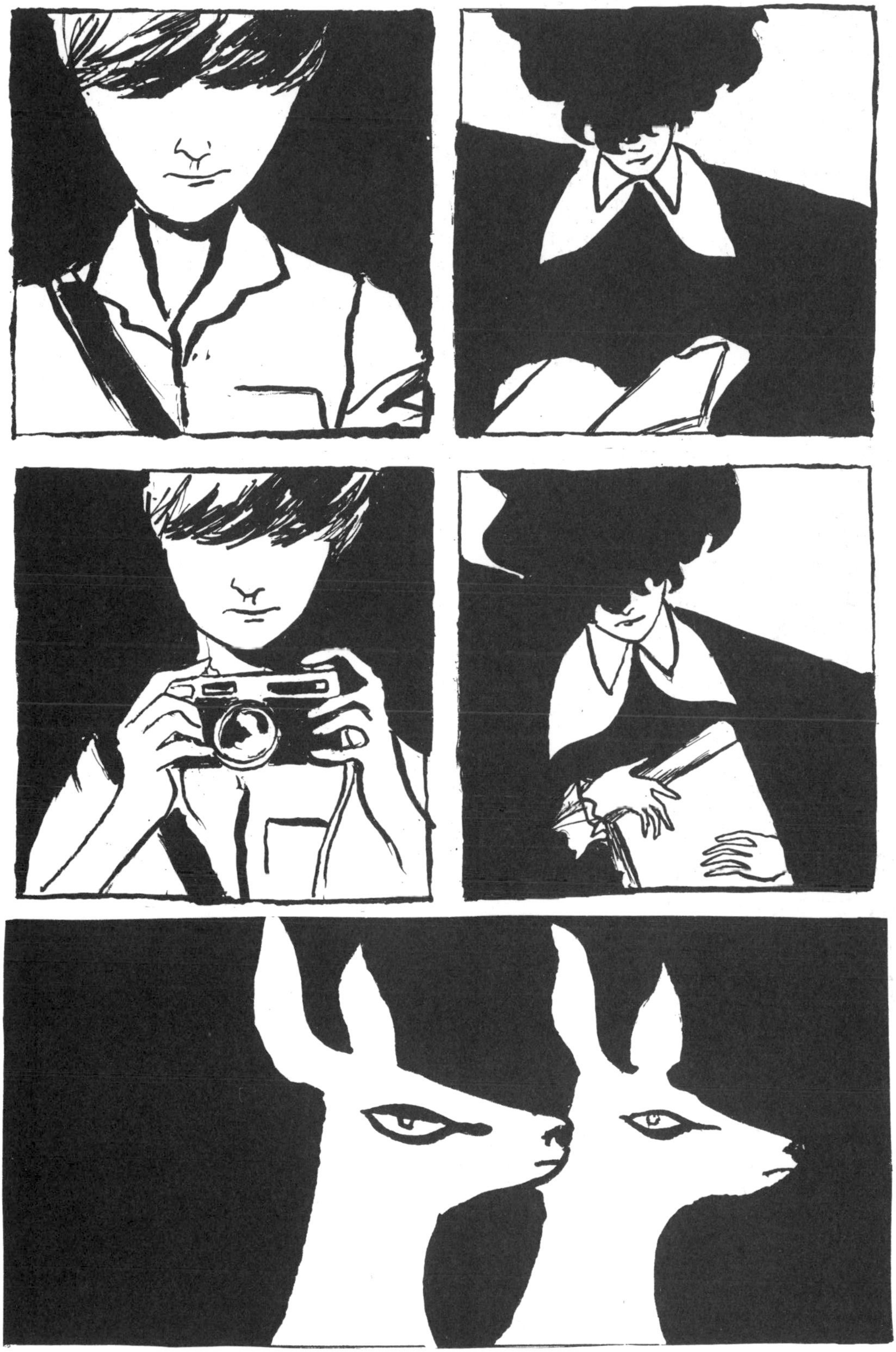

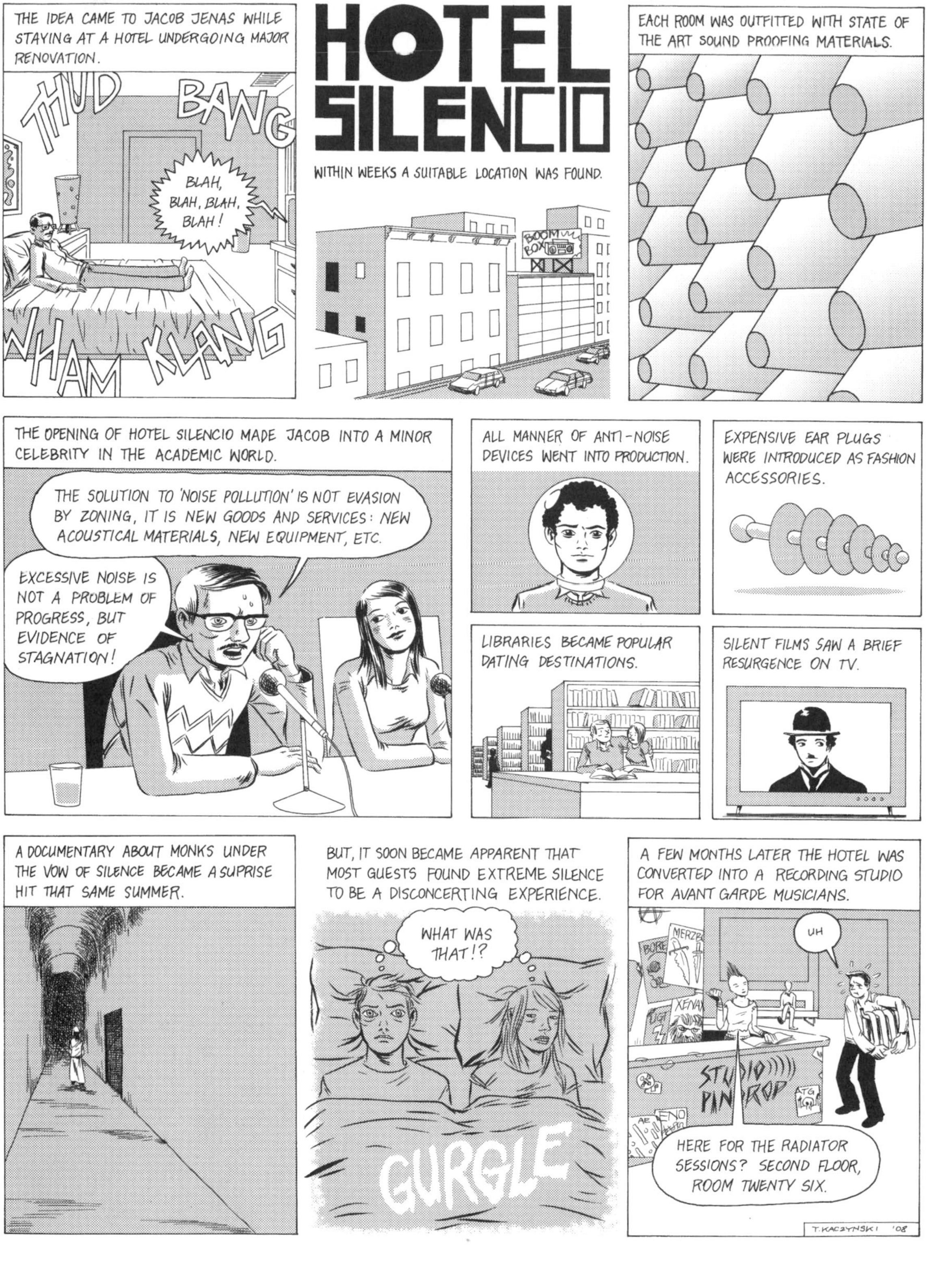
HOTEL SILENCIO
THE IDEA CAME TO JACOB JENAS WHILE STAYING AT A HOTEL UNDERGOING MAJOR RENOVATION.
THUD
BANG
BLAH, BLAH, BLAH, BLAH!
WHAM
KLANG
WITHIN WEEKS A SUITABLE LOCATION WAS FOUND.
BOOM BOX
EACH ROOM WAS OUTFITTED WITH STATE OF THE ART SOUND PROOFING MATERIALS.
THE OPENING OF HOTEL SILENCIO MADE JACOB INTO A MINOR CELEBRITY IN THE ACADEMIC WORLD.
THE SOLUTION TO 'NOISE POLLUTION' IS NOT EVASION BY ZONING, IT IS NEW GOODS AND SERVICES: NEW ACOUSTICAL MATERIALS, NEW EQUIPMENT, ETC.
EXCESSIVE NOISE IS NOT A PROBLEM OF PROGRESS, BUT EVIDENCE OF STAGNATION!
ALL MANNER OF ANTI-NOISE DEVICES WENT INTO PRODUCTION.
EXPENSIVE EAR PLUGS WERE INTRODUCED AS FASHION ACCESSORIES.
LIBRARIES BECAME POPULAR DATING DESTINATIONS.
SILENT FILMS SAW A BRIEF RESURGENCE ON TV.
A DOCUMENTARY ABOUT MONKS UNDER THE VOW OF SILENCE BECAME A SUPRISE HIT THAT SAME SUMMER.
BUT, IT SOON BECAME APPARENT THAT MOST GUESTS FOUND EXTREME SILENCE TO BE A DISCONCERTING EXPERIENCE.
WHAT WAS THAT!?
GURGLE
A FEW MONTHS LATER THE HOTEL WAS CONVERTED INTO A RECORDING STUDIO FOR AVANT GARDE MUSICIANS.
UH
HERE FOR THE RADIATOR SESSIONS? SECOND FLOOR, ROOM TWENTY SIX.
T. KACZYNSKI '08

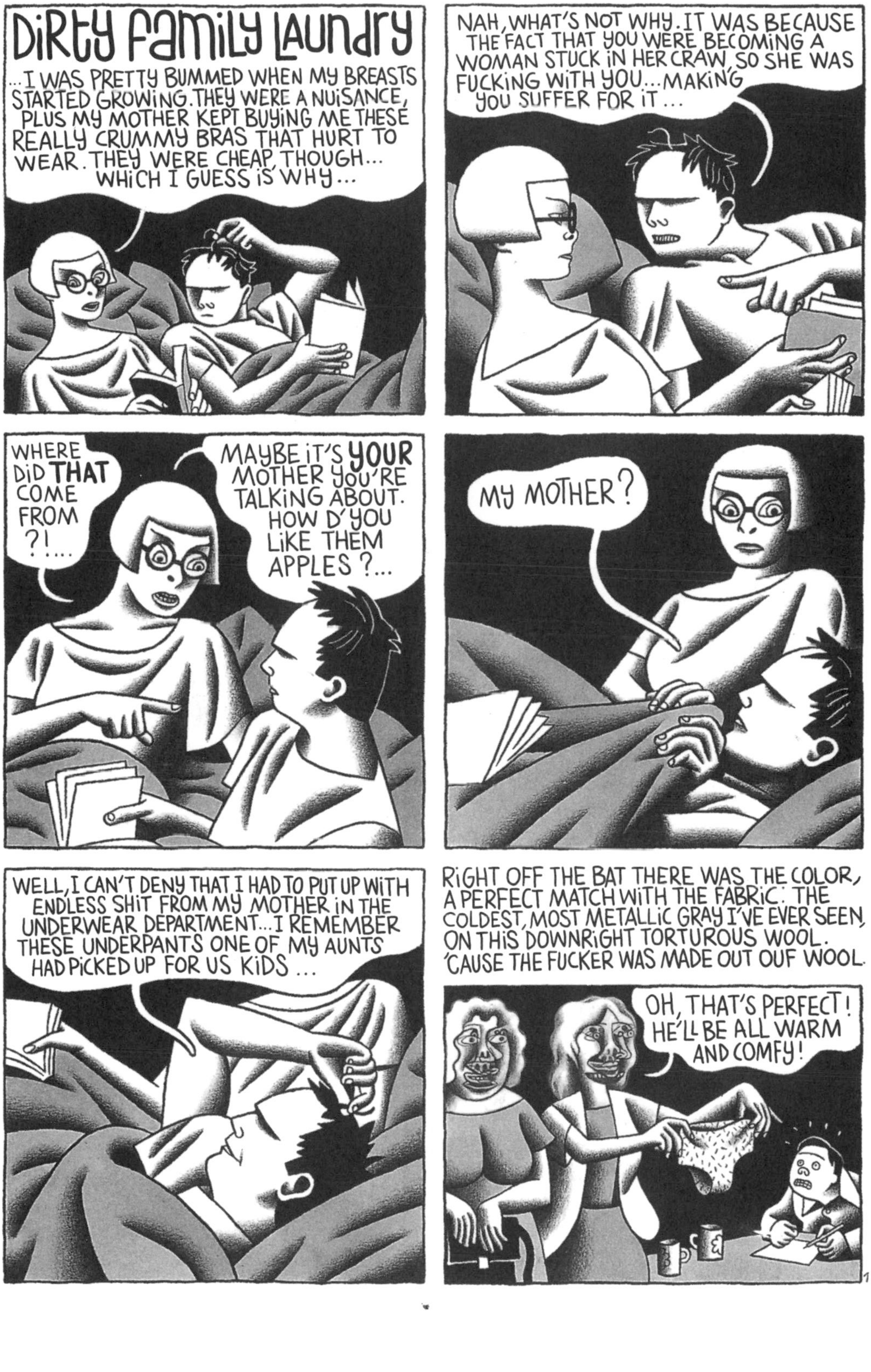

Dirty Family Laundry
...I WAS PRETTY BUMMED WHEN MY BREASTS STARTED GROWING. THEY WERE A NUISANCE, PLUS MY MOTHER KEPT BUYING ME THESE REALLY CRUMMY BRAS THAT HURT TO WEAR. THEY WERE CHEAP, THOUGH... WHICH I GUESS IS WHY...
NAH, WHAT'S NOT WHY. IT WAS BECAUSE THE FACT THAT YOU WERE BECOMING A WOMAN STUCK IN HER CRAW, SO SHE WAS FUCKING WITH YOU... MAKING YOU SUFFER FOR IT...
WHERE DID THAT COME FROM ?!...
MAYBE IT'S YOUR MOTHER YOU'RE TALKING ABOUT. HOW D'YOU LIKE THEM APPLES ?...
MY MOTHER?
WELL, I CAN'T DENY THAT I HAD TO PUT UP WITH ENDLESS SHIT FROM MY MOTHER IN THE UNDERWEAR DEPARTMENT... I REMEMBER THESE UNDERPANTS ONE OF MY AUNTS HAD PICKED UP FOR US KIDS...
RIGHT OFF THE BAT THERE WAS THE COLOR, A PERFECT MATCH WITH THE FABRIC: THE COLDEST, MOST METALLIC GRAY I'VE EVER SEEN, ON THIS DOWNRIGHT TORTUROUS WOOL. 'CAUSE THE FUCKER WAS MADE OUT OUF WOOL.
OH, THAT'S PERFECT! HE'LL BE ALL WARM AND COMFY!

EVERY TIME I TRIED TO IMAGINE FROM WHAT HIDEOUS MONSTER THIS FABRIC MIGHT HAVE BEEN HARVESTED I WOULD BE THROWN INTO AN ABYSS OF PUZZLEMENT.

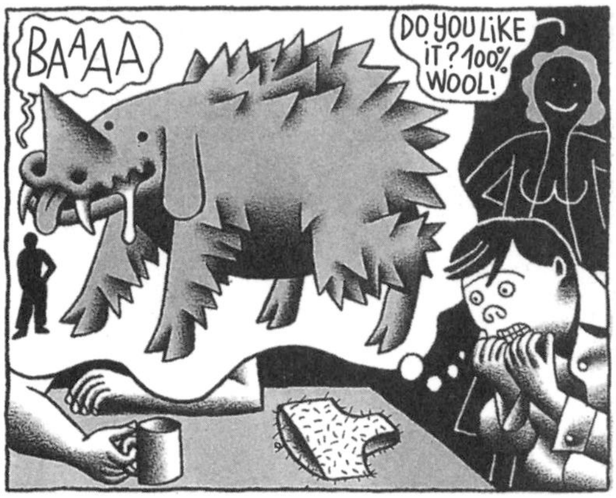
BAAAA
DO YOU LIKE IT? 100% WOOL!

YEAH, WELL, FROM WHERE I WAS STANDING IT MIGHT AS WELL'VE BEEN **STEEL** WOOL.

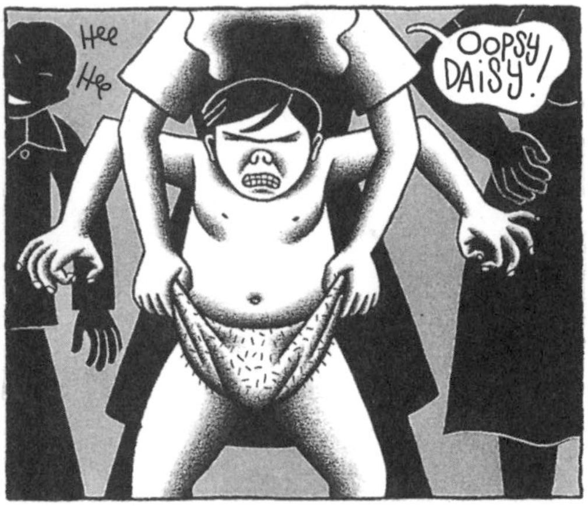
Hee Hee
OOPSY DAISY!

ADDING INSULT TO INJURY, IT WAS BULKY AS FUCK. I'M SURE IT CREATED ALL MANNER OF UNSIGHTLY BULGES IN MY FASHIONABLY TIGHT BELLBOTTOMS.

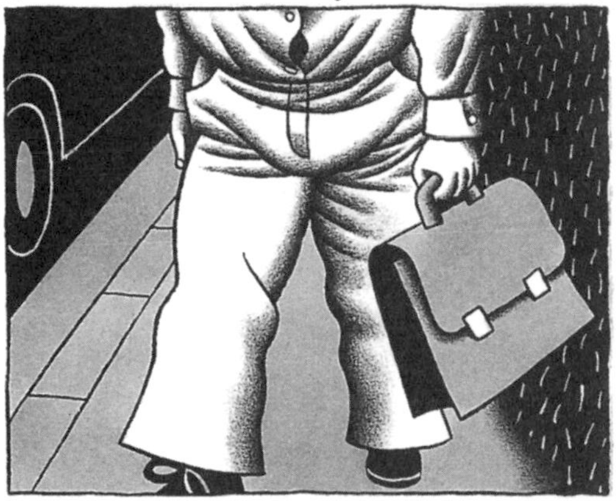

ESPECIALLY SINCE THEY WERE USUALLY TOO SMALL FOR ME FROM DAY ONE. I WAS INHERITING HAND-ME-DOWNS FROM MY BIG BROTHER, BUT LET'S FACE IT, AT THAT TIME IN MY LIFE I WAS A BIT OF A PORKER. I REMEMBER SUFFERING THROUGH A SCHOOLDAY WITH ONE PANTS LEG TOTALLY RIPPED TO SHIT BECAUSE THE SEAM HAD SPLIT EARLIER THAT MORNING.

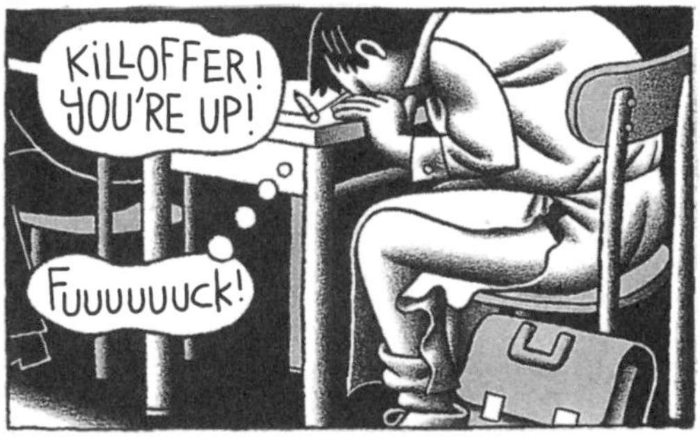
KILLOFFER! YOU'RE UP!
FUUUUUUCK!

IN OUR HOUSE, WE WORE CLOTHES ALL THE WAY TO THE BITTER END. IT'S NOT LIKE MONEY GREW ON TREES. RIGHT? ALTHOUGH THAT ALSO MEANT THAT WHEN THE WEATHER GOT HOT, I WAS SENT OFF TO SCHOOL IN TRUNKS... **SWIM** TRUNKS, THAT IS.

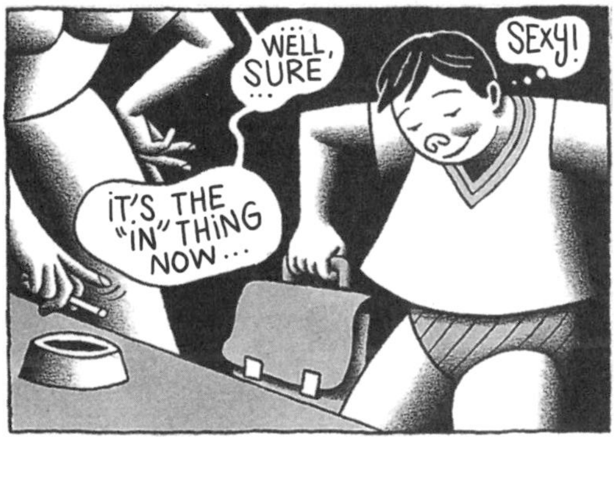
WELL, SURE...
SEXY!
IT'S THE "IN" THING NOW...

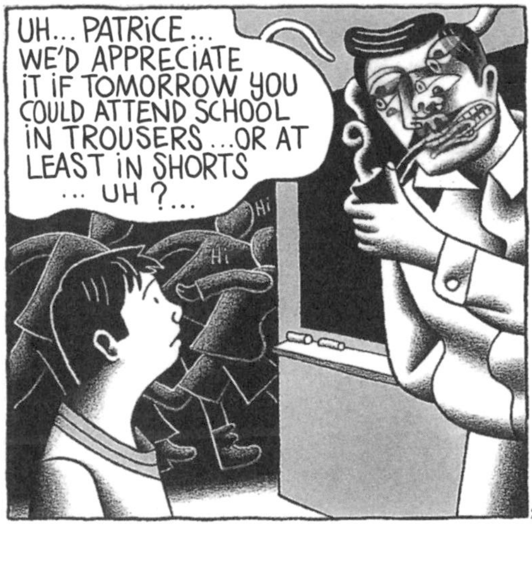
UH... PATRICE... WE'D APPRECIATE IT IF TOMORROW YOU COULD ATTEND SCHOOL IN TROUSERS... OR AT LEAST IN SHORTS ... UH?...
Hi
Hi

ANYWAY, MY PROBLEMS WOULD VAULT TO A WHOLE NEW LEVEL WHEN I WAS WEARING **THE** UNDERPANTS. ESTHETICS BECOME AN ISSUE ONLY ONCE THE ITCHING STOPS, YA KNOW? I RECKON PERSPIRATION MUST DISSOLVE STYLISHNESS OR SOMETHING. ANYWAY IN TERMS OF KEEPING WARM, HEY, NO PROBLEM THERE, I WAS DEFINITELY OFF THE HIGH-RISK LIST FOR CATCHING PNEUMONIA OF THE BALLS, OR A DICK COLD.

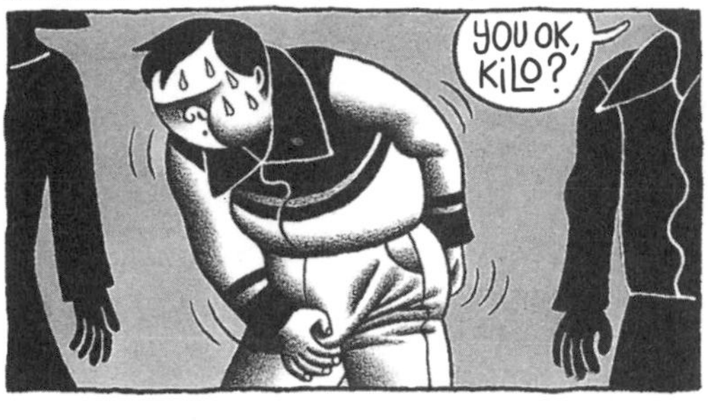
YOU OK, KILO?

THANKS TO MOMMY, AND THANKS TO AUNTIE, I WAS NEVER COLD, NO SIRREE. BUT I WAS WEARING THIS CROWN OF THORNS ON MY ASS. NOT QUITE AS OBVIOUS AS THE TOP-OF-THE-HEAD MODEL, BUT STILL ALL TOO CLEARLY AN INSTRUMENT OF TORTURE. OKAY, SO MY MOM'S NAME IS MARIA, THAT DON'T NECESSARILY MAKE ME BABY JESUS.

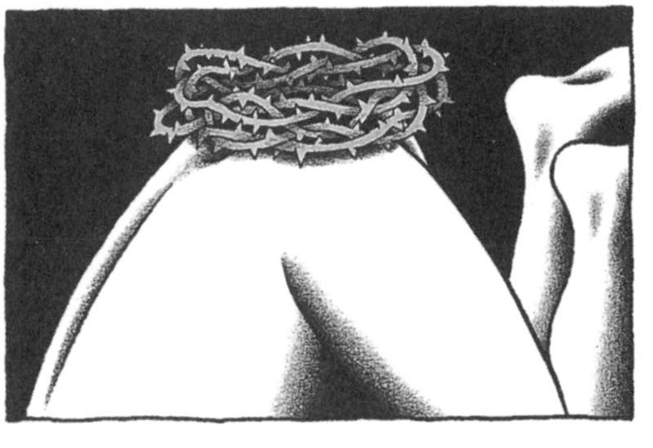

FORTUNATELY, SHE DIDN'T MAKE ME WEAR IT ALL THAT OFTEN, EVEN THOUGH I ENJOYED THE REPUTATION OF HAVING THE HIDE OF A RHINOCEROS. WHICH WAS ACTUALLY KIND OF COOL, 'CAUSE I DUG RHINOS.

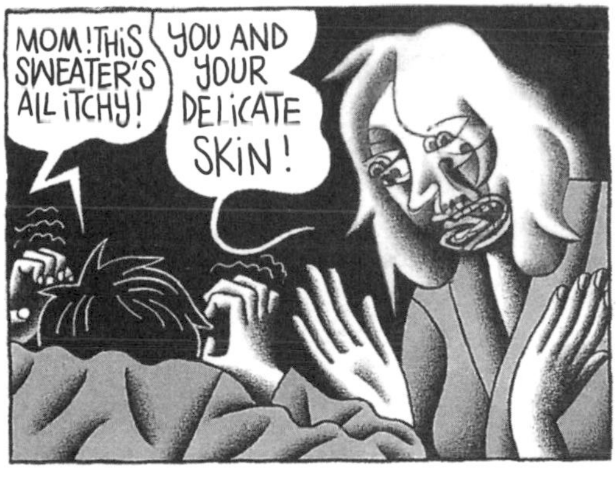
MOM! THIS SWEATER'S ALL ITCHY!
YOU AND YOUR DELICATE SKIN!

OKAY, EVEN THOUGH I WAS TOTALLY INTO KNIGHTS FROM MEDIEVAL TIMES, I DON'T THINK THAT WAS A GOOD REASON TO SWADDLE ME IN ARMOR DISGUISED AS UNDERPANTS. AND I'LL BET THOSE GUYS WEREN'T PARTICULARLY ENAMORED OF HAVING BRILLO PADS GROUND INTO THEIR ASSES EITHER...

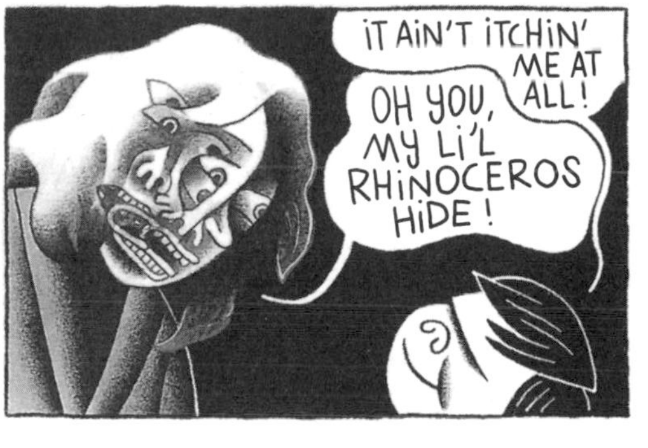
IT AIN'T ITCHIN' ME AT ALL!
OH YOU, MY LI'L RHINOCEROS HIDE!

THAT PAIR OF UNDIES STAYED IN THE CLOSET FOR AGES. SOMETIMES I'D JUST STAND AROUND EYEBALLIN' 'EM FOR A WHILE, THAT'S HOW STOKED I WAS NOT TO HAVE THEM ON MY BODY.

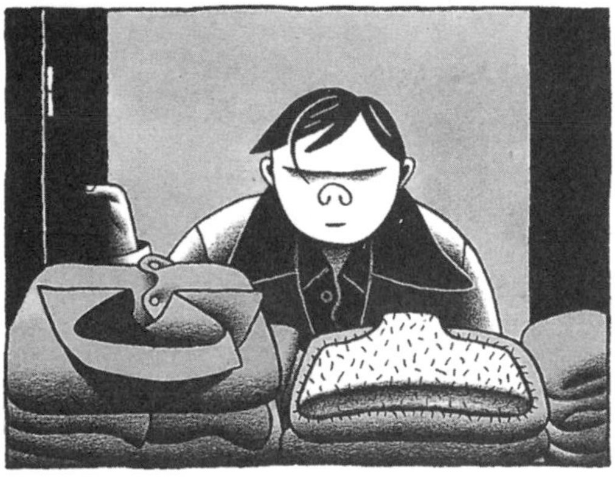

THEN THERE WAS THE "BIG-BOY UNDERWEAR", AS MY MOTHER CALLED IT, WHICH SHE USED TO TAUNT ME WITH. IT WAS A PAIR OF CLASSIC TIGHTY-WHITIES. I HAVE NO IDEA WHERE THIS WAS ALL COMING FROM, BUT SHE'D BUILT THEM UP INTO THIS HUGE RITE OF PASSAGE.

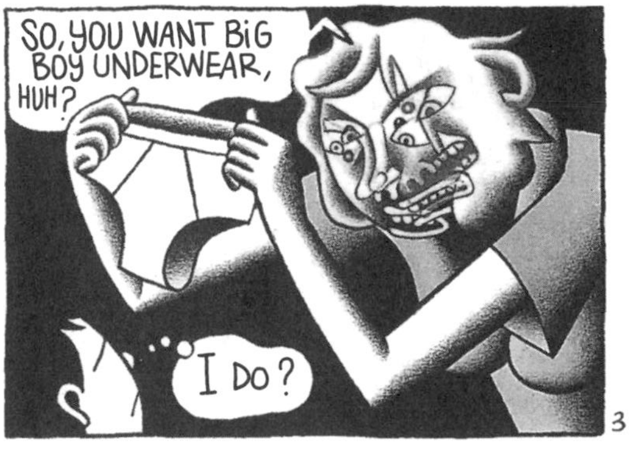
SO, YOU WANT BIG BOY UNDERWEAR, HUH?
I DO?

I WASN'T REALLY SHITTING IN MY PANTS–THAT WASN'T WHAT WAS HAPPENING. THE PROBLEM WAS THAT I JUST DIDN'T WANT TO SHIT AT ALL. WHEN THE URGE WOULD HIT ME, I'D FIND HEADING OFF TO THE JOHN AN INSURMOUNTABLE EFFORT AND ANYWAY, I WAS BUSY. I DIDN'T WANT TO, OR WAS UNABLE TO, ADMIT THAT I WAS BEING CONTROLLED BY THIS BODILY FUNCTION!

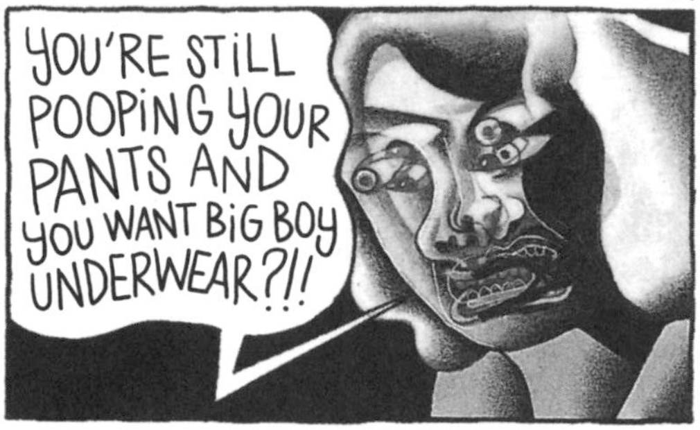
YOU'RE STILL POOPING YOUR PANTS AND YOU WANT BIG BOY UNDERWEAR?!!

EVENTUALLY I WOULD MAKE MY WAY TO THE CRAPPER, ALWAYS AT THE VERY LAST MOMENT. BUT NOT UNTIL I'D HELD OFF AS LONG AS HUMANLY POSSIBLE, AND OFTEN, NEEDLESS TO SAY, I'D END UP WITH SKID MARKS, TIRE TRACKS... AND FOR THAT MATTER ONCE IN A WHILE THE SHORTS WOULD END UP TOTALED.

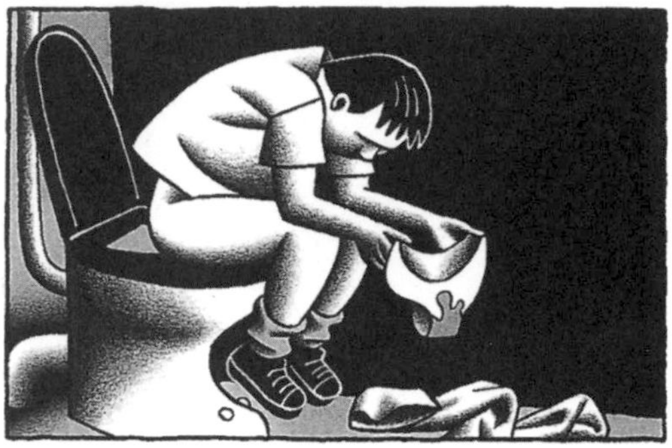

THIS DESPITE MY HAVING DEVELOPED A RATHER SOPHISTICATED TECHNIQUE. SQUATTING, I WOULD JAM MY HEEL UP MY ANUS AND WAIT FOR THE NEED TO PASS, FOR EVERYTHING TO CLIMB BACK UP AGAIN. BUT THERE'S A LIMIT TO HOW LONG ONE CAN THWART THE FORCES OF GRAVITY. BESIDES, "IT'S STRONGER THAN LOVE", AS MY FOLKS USED TO SAY.

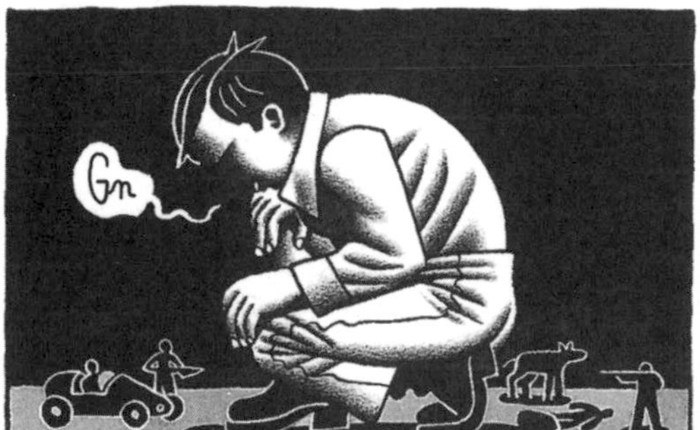
Gn

SO SHE WAS PRETTY FED WITH HAVING TO LAUNDER MY POOPY UNDIES, MY MOM WAS. NOW ADMITTELY AT THIS TIME, SHE WAS KIND OF FUCKED UP, SHE SUFFERED FROM CHRONIC PANIC ATTACKS, OR SOME SORT OF HYTERIA. HER NERVES WERE SHOT... ANYWAY, SOME SERIOUS SHIT.

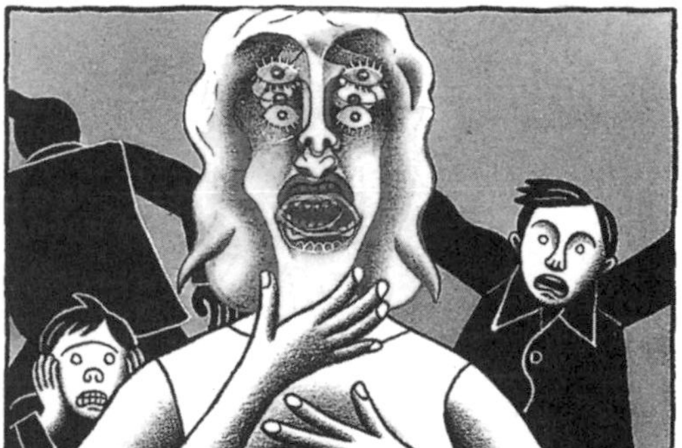

WE EVENTUALLY FIGURED OUT HOW TO DEAL WITH IT. ALL MY DAD HAD TO DO WAS PITCH A NICE BIG GLASS OF ICE COLD WATER STRAIGHT IN HER MUG, AND SHE'D START BREATHING AGAIN. THAT WAS HER PROBLEM, NOT BEING ABLE TO CATCH HER BREATH. THEN WE'D MAKE HER LIE DOWN FOR A WHILE. A COUPLE GOOD HARD SLAPS ACROSS HER FACE HAD PROVEN EFFECTIVE IN A PINCH AS WELL.

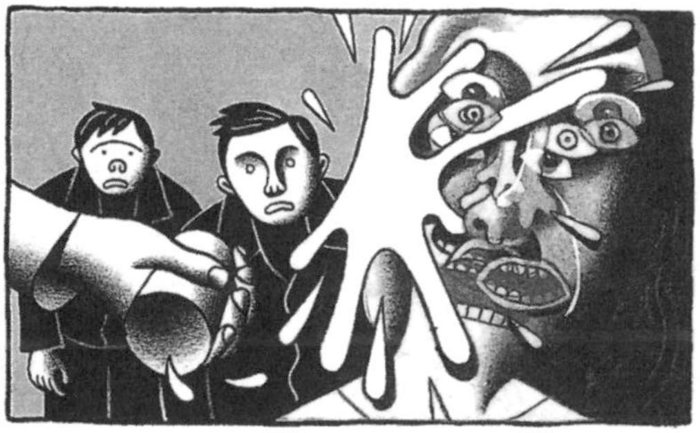

I DON'T KNOW IF THIS WAS A DREAM, BUT I SEEM TO REMEMBER, ONE NIGHT, THE THREE OF US HAVING TO CHASE HER ALL THE WAY DOWN THE STREET. SHE WAS RUNNING AWAY LIKE A LUNATIC, IN HER NIGHTGOWN.

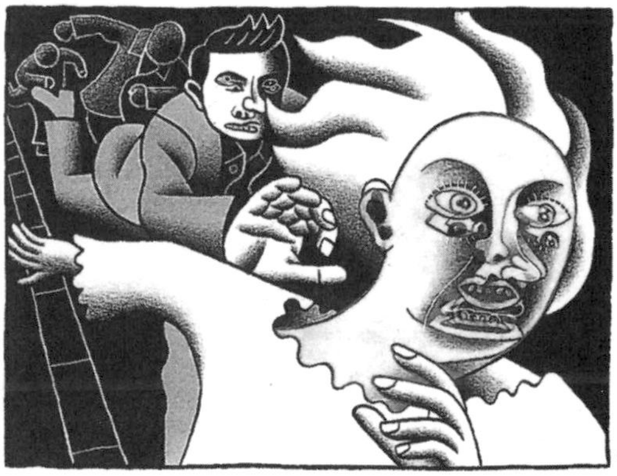

I MEAN THAT'S NOT TOO FAR FROM THE KIND OF DREAMS I WAS HAVING AT THAT TIME. THERE WAS ANOTHER ONE INVOLVING MY MOTHER, IN THE SAME BALLPARK. HER HEAD HAD SHRUNK DOWN TO THIS LITTLE STUB, ALL DESICCATED AND SHIT, IT LOOKED LIKE AN ALMOND. SHE WAS CALLING OUT FOR ME IN THIS TINY SQUEAKY VOICE, GROWING MORE AND MORE REMOTE. SHE WAS DYING. I DIDN'T REALLY KNOW WHAT TO DO.

MOmmy!

I SHOULD MENTION THAT SHE SUFFERED FROM THESE EPIC MIGRAINES LOUNGING AROUND FOR DAYS ON END IN HER BATHROBE, WITH A WET TOWEL DRAPED ACROSS HER FOREHEAD, AND LET'S NOT FORGET THE SERIAL DEPRESSIONS. BASICALLY, SHE WAS OFF HER ROCKER.

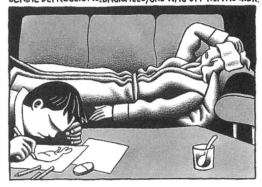

SHE'D TELL US ABOUT BEING SEIZED BY THESE URGES ON THE BRIDGE ABOVE THE TRAIN TRACKS, KIND OF LIKE A THREAT. THAT'S NOT THE ONE SHE ACTUALLY CARRIED OUT, THOUGH. NO, IT WAS A DIFFERENT ONCE.

I've Told you a MiLLiON Times!!!

YUP, IT HAD ALWAYS BEEN LOOMING RIGHT UNDER MY NOSE, BUT TODAY TURNED OUT TO BE D-DAY. SO IT WASN'T JUST BULLSHIT? IT WAS REALLY GONNA GO DOWN? RIGHT NOW? SHE WAS TOTALLY UNHINGED. THIS TIME I'D DROPPED A FULL LOAD ON HER.

NOW you're gonna Get iT!!!

IN MY MEMORY, SHE MADE ME CLIMB ONTO A CHAIR, AS IF FOR SOME SORT OF CEREMONY, TO GUARANTEE THAT I'D REMEMBER. NOT THAT THAT WOULD BE MUCH OF AN ISSUE.

C'MERE!

AND THEN SHE SHOVED THE UNDERWEAR HARD ONTO MY FACE, GIVING IT A LITTLE TWIST TO MAKE SURE SHE'D DRIVEN THE MESSAGE HOME?

I CAN STILL SEE MY MOTHER, TOTALLY OUT OF HER SKULL HOLLERING THE SAME BULLSHIT FIFTEEN TIMES IN A ROW, DRIVING INTO OUR HEADS THE DEPTH OF HER MISERY, ALL OF IT THROUGH THIS LAYER OF SHIT INTERMINGLED WITH MY TEARS.

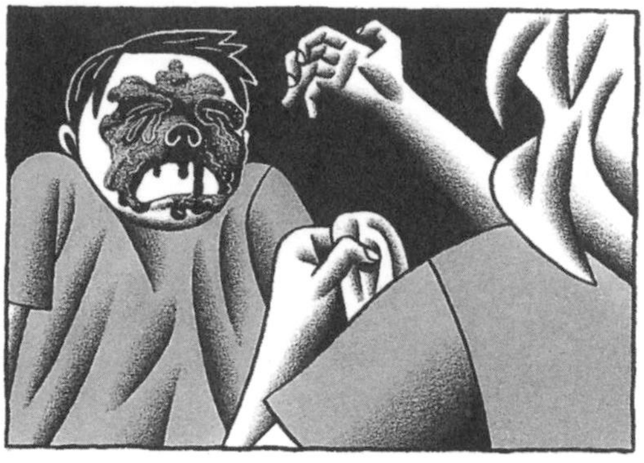

MY BROTHER MUST'VE BEEN LAUGHING HIS ASS OFF, SOMEWHERE OFF IN A CORNER. I DON'T REMEMBER ANY MORE IF MY FATHER WAS THERE...

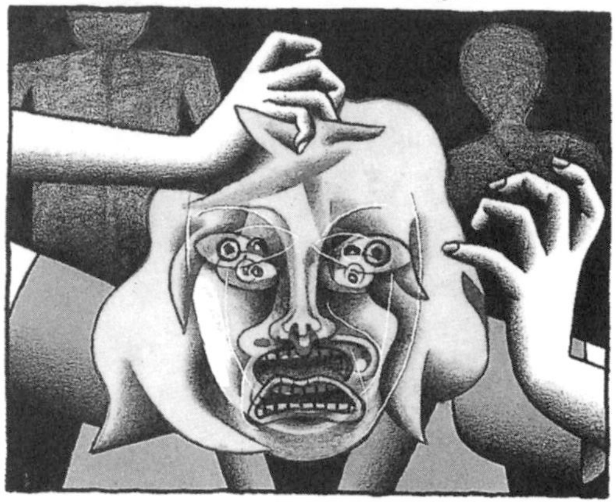

I WENT UP MY NOSE, IT SMEARED ALL OVER MY TEETH.

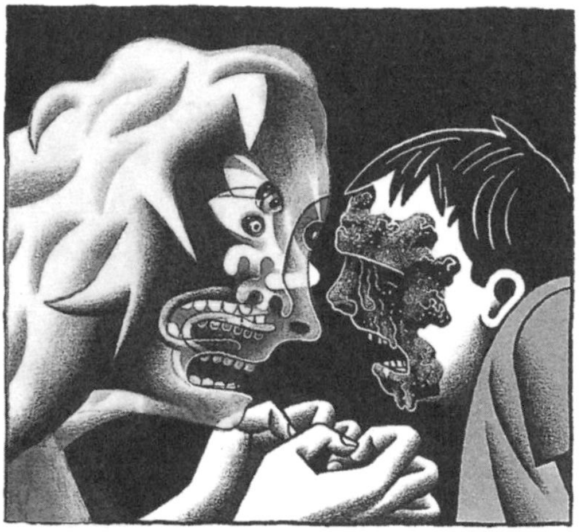

SO YOU SEE, I KNOW EXACTLY WHAT FLAVOR MY SHIT IS, BECAUSE I ACTUALLY GOT TO TASTE IT.

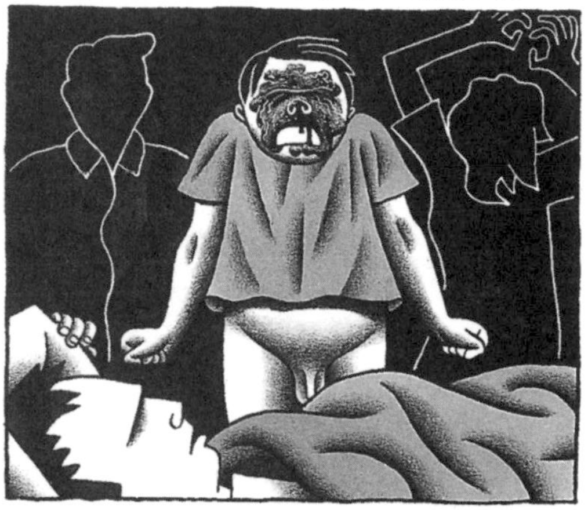

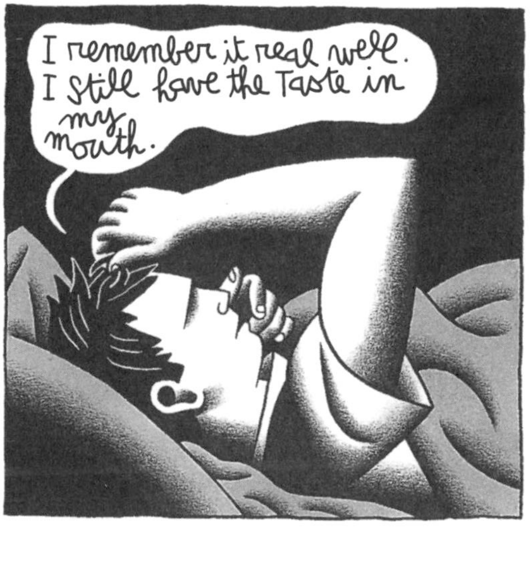
I remember it real well. I still have the taste in my mouth.

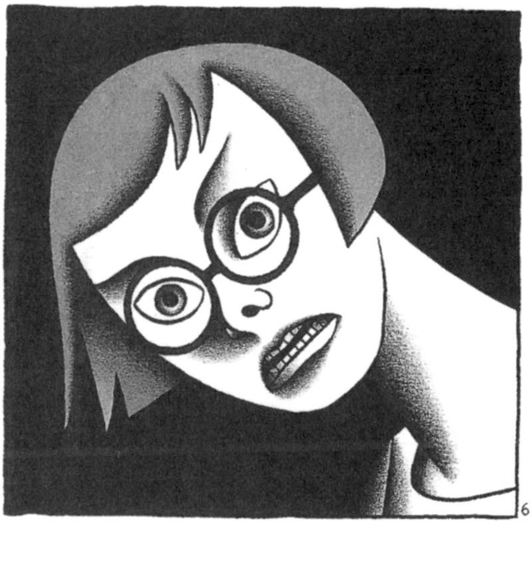

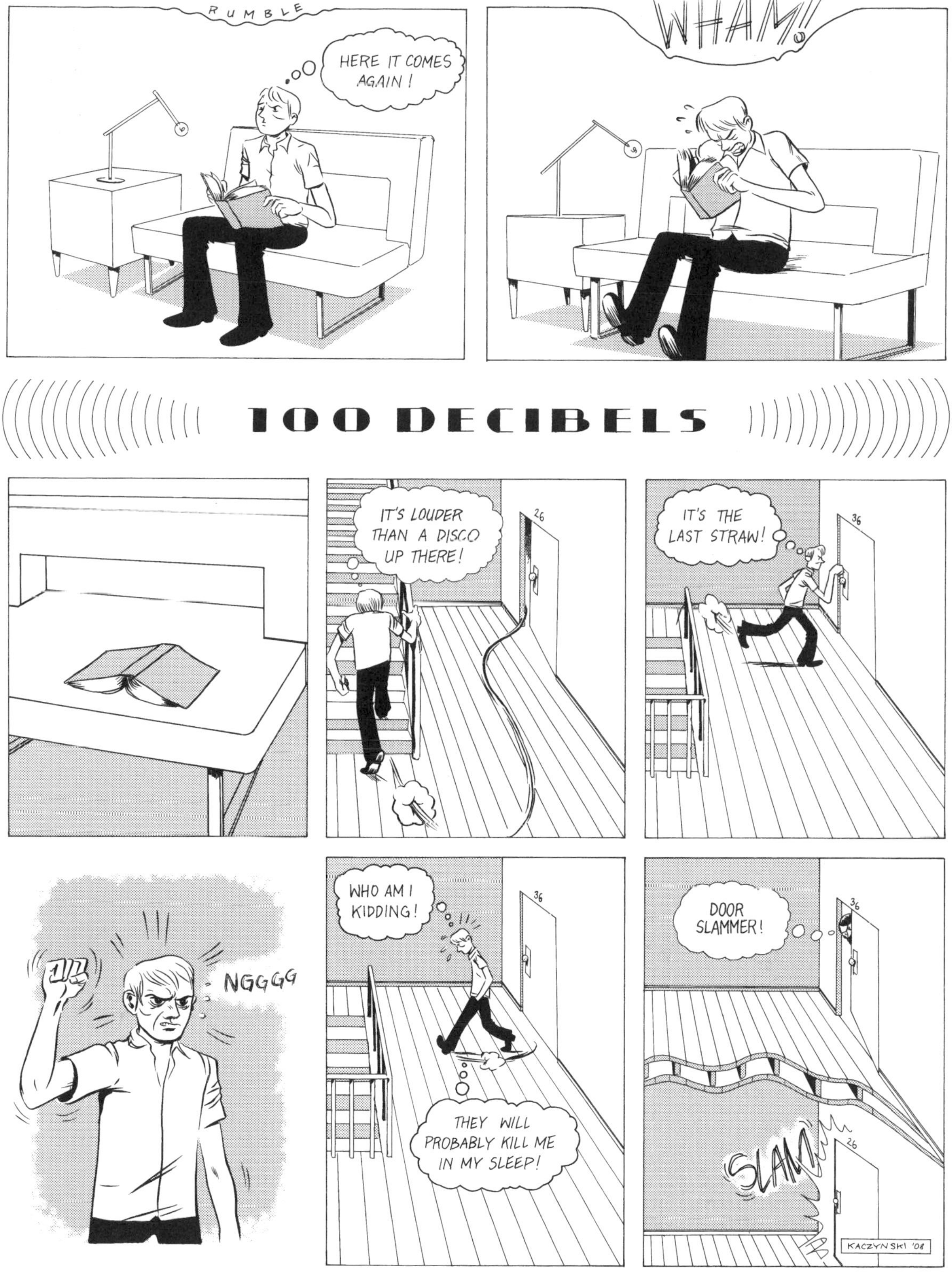
RUMBLE
HERE IT COMES AGAIN!
WHAM!
100 DECIBELS
IT'S LOUDER THAN A DISCO UP THERE!
IT'S THE LAST STRAW!
NGGGG
WHO AM I KIDDING!
THEY WILL PROBABLY KILL ME IN MY SLEEP!
DOOR SLAMMER!
SLAM
KACZYNSKI '08

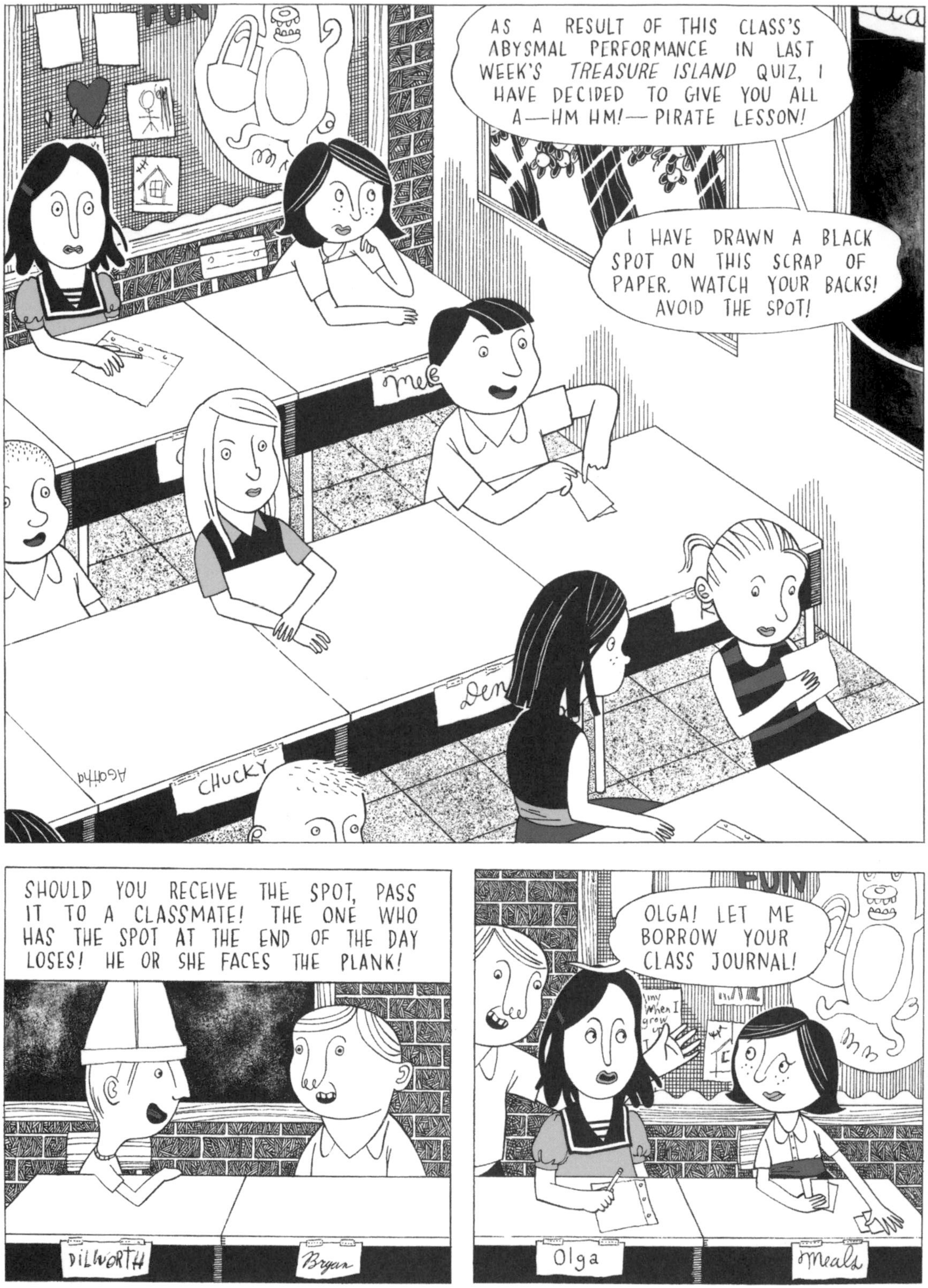
FUN
AS A RESULT OF THIS CLASS'S ABYSMAL PERFORMANCE IN LAST WEEK'S *TREASURE ISLAND* QUIZ, I HAVE DECIDED TO GIVE YOU ALL A—HM HM!—PIRATE LESSON!
I HAVE DRAWN A BLACK SPOT ON THIS SCRAP OF PAPER. WATCH YOUR BACKS! AVOID THE SPOT!
CHUCKY
SHOULD YOU RECEIVE THE SPOT, PASS IT TO A CLASSMATE! THE ONE WHO HAS THE SPOT AT THE END OF THE DAY LOSES! HE OR SHE FACES THE PLANK!
DILWORTH
Bryan
OLGA! LET ME BORROW YOUR CLASS JOURNAL!
Olga
Meals

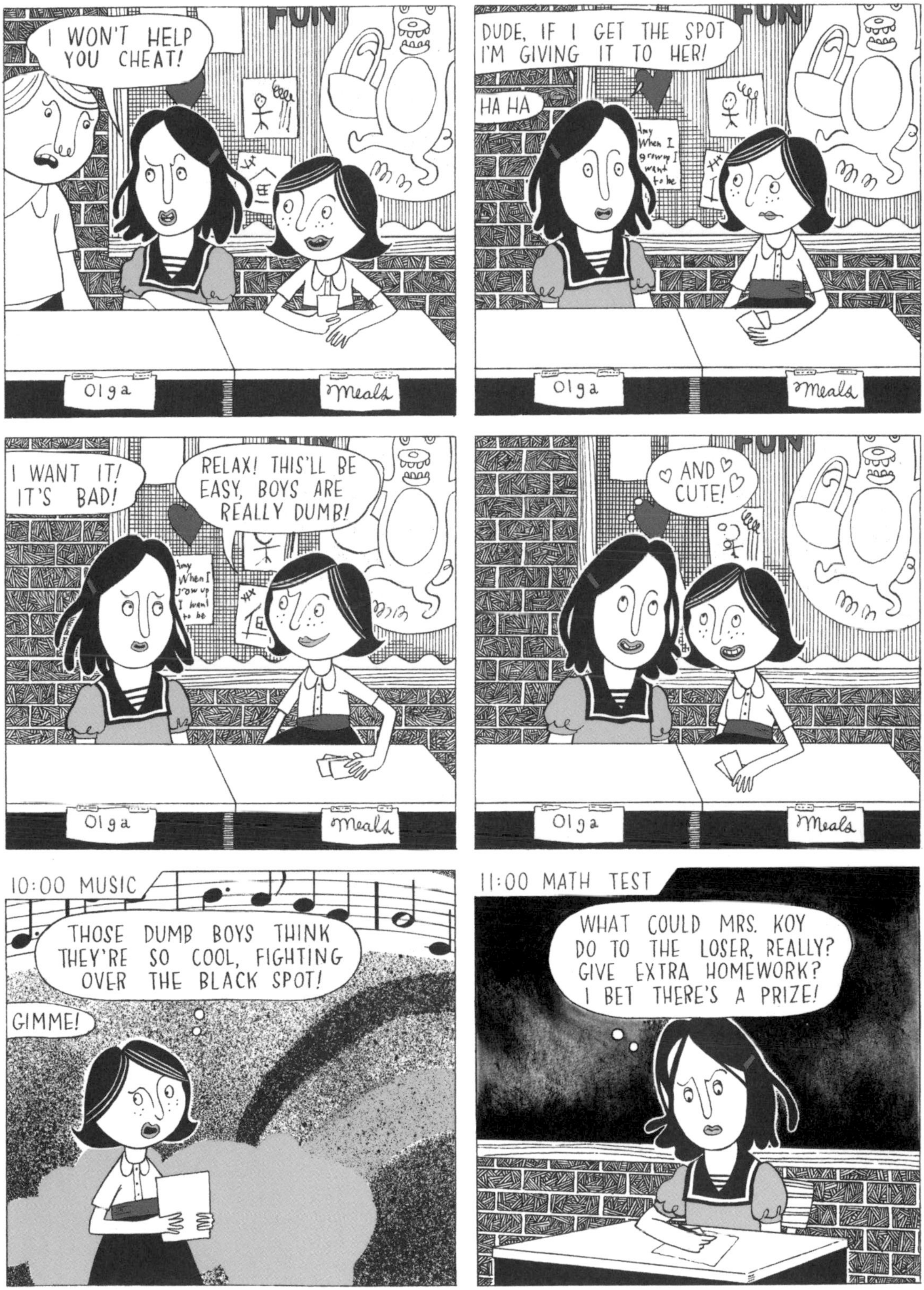
I WON'T HELP YOU CHEAT!
Olga
Meals
DUDE, IF I GET THE SPOT I'M GIVING IT TO HER!
HA HA
Olga
Meals
I WANT IT! IT'S BAD!
RELAX! THIS'LL BE EASY, BOYS ARE REALLY DUMB!
Olga
Meals
AND CUTE!
Olga
Meals
10:00 MUSIC
THOSE DUMB BOYS THINK THEY'RE SO COOL, FIGHTING OVER THE BLACK SPOT!
GIMME!
11:00 MATH TEST
WHAT COULD MRS. KOY DO TO THE LOSER, REALLY? GIVE EXTRA HOMEWORK? I BET THERE'S A PRIZE!

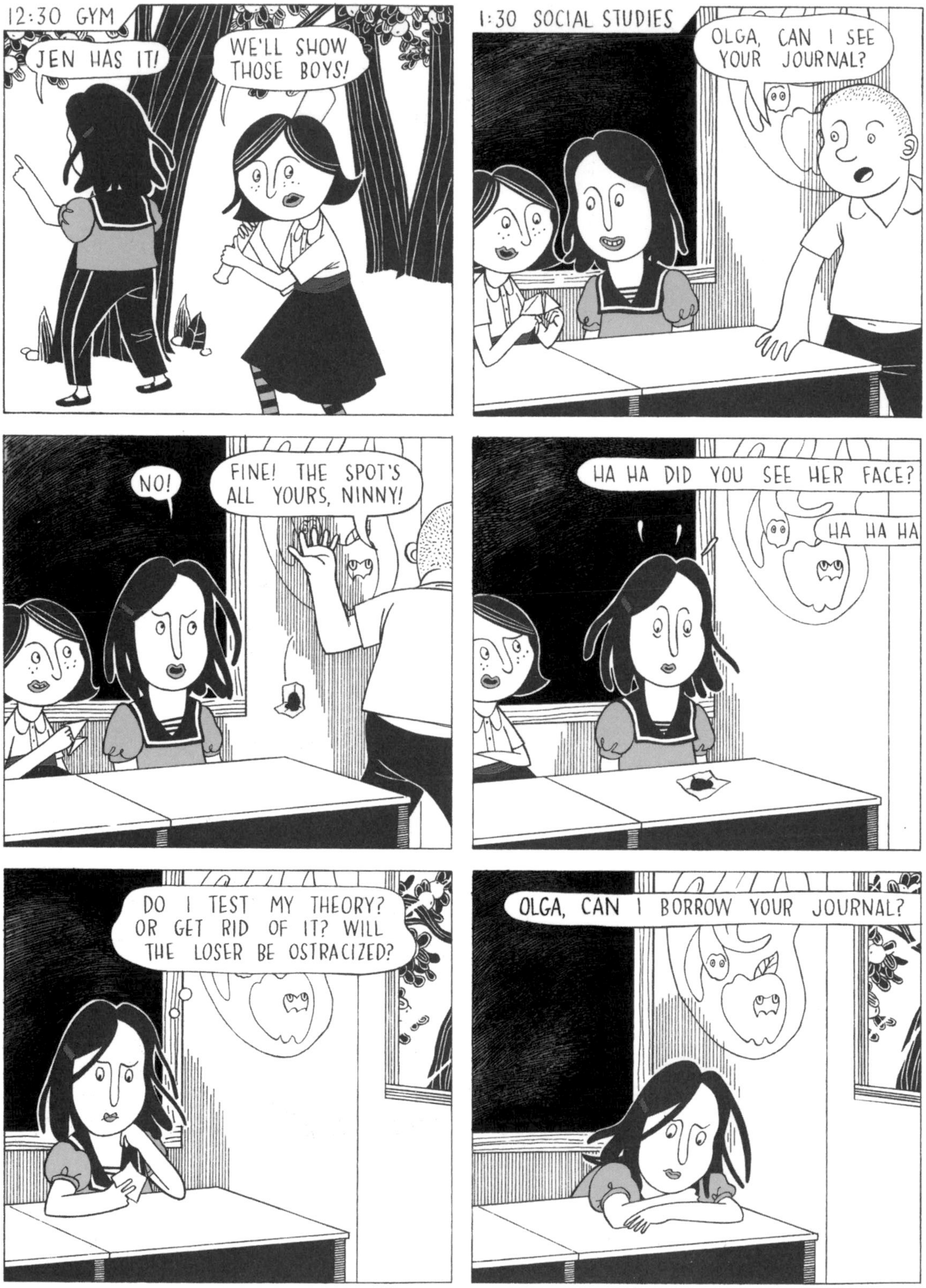
12:30 GYM
JEN HAS IT!
WE'LL SHOW THOSE BOYS!
1:30 SOCIAL STUDIES
OLGA, CAN I SEE YOUR JOURNAL?
NO!
FINE! THE SPOT'S ALL YOURS, NINNY!
HA HA DID YOU SEE HER FACE?
HA HA HA
DO I TEST MY THEORY? OR GET RID OF IT? WILL THE LOSER BE OSTRACIZED?
OLGA, CAN I BORROW YOUR JOURNAL?

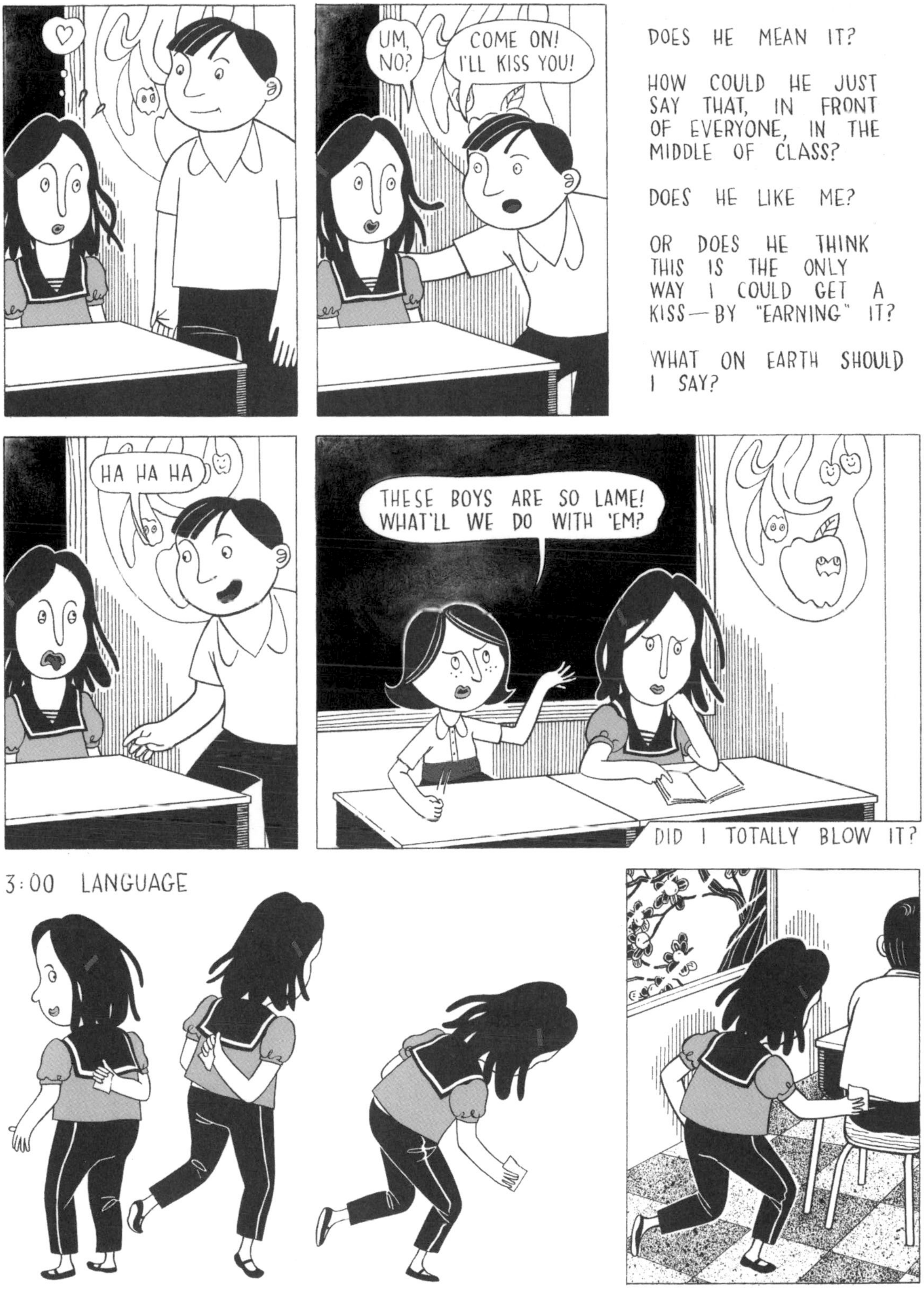
UM, NO?
COME ON! I'LL KISS YOU!
DOES HE MEAN IT?
HOW COULD HE JUST SAY THAT, IN FRONT OF EVERYONE, IN THE MIDDLE OF CLASS?
DOES HE LIKE ME?
OR DOES HE THINK THIS IS THE ONLY WAY I COULD GET A KISS—BY "EARNING" IT?
WHAT ON EARTH SHOULD I SAY?
HA HA HA
THESE BOYS ARE SO LAME! WHAT'LL WE DO WITH 'EM?
DID I TOTALLY BLOW IT?
3:00 LANGUAGE

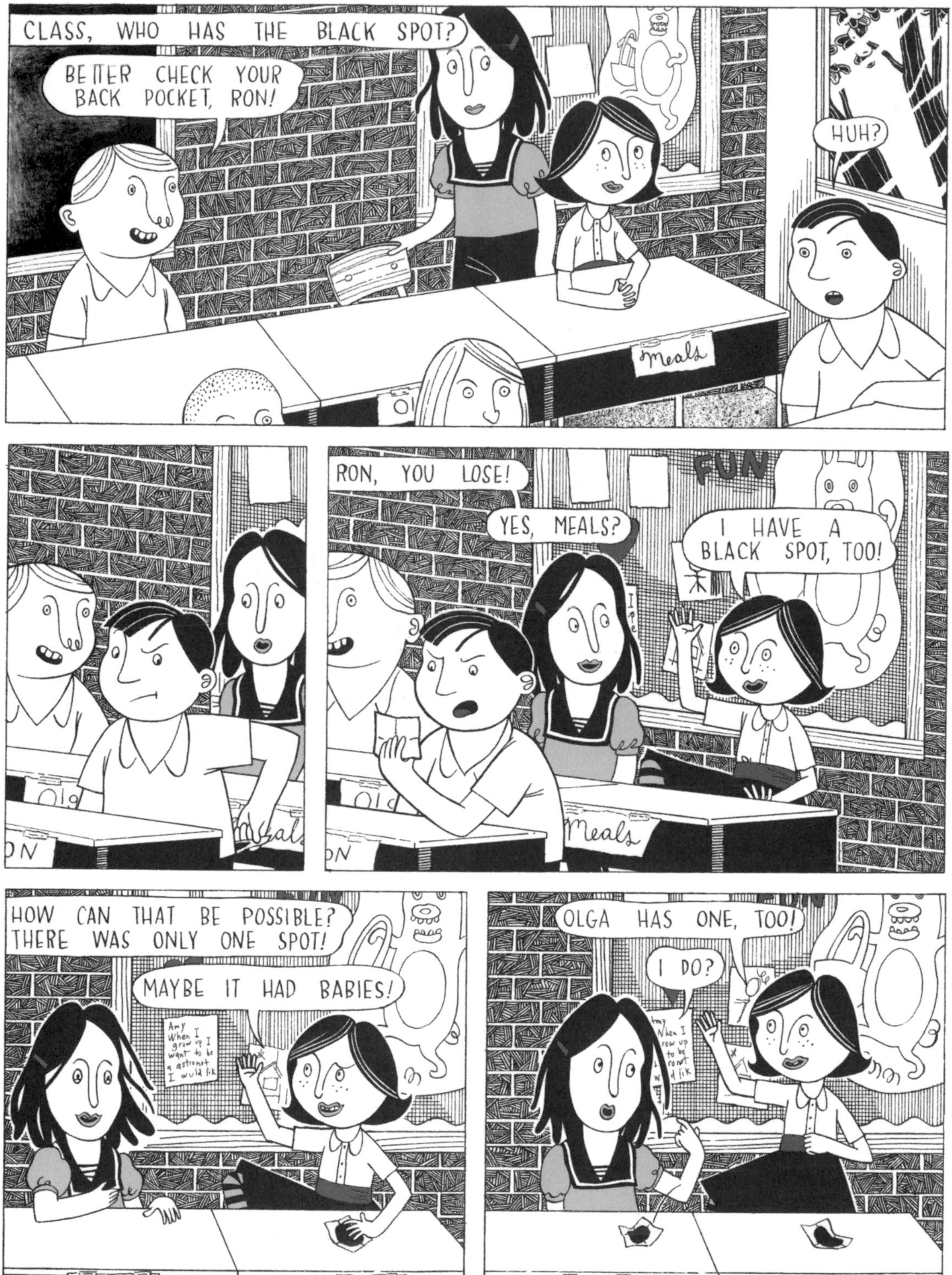
CLASS, WHO HAS THE BLACK SPOT?
BETTER CHECK YOUR BACK POCKET, RON!
HUH?
Meals
RON, YOU LOSE!
YES, MEALS?
I HAVE A BLACK SPOT, TOO!
FUN
Meals
HOW CAN THAT BE POSSIBLE? THERE WAS ONLY ONE SPOT!
MAYBE IT HAD BABIES!
Amy When I grow up I want to be a astronot I wuld lik
Olga
Meals
OLGA HAS ONE, TOO!
I DO?
Olga
Meals

TURN OUT YOUR TONGUES, GIRLS!
WHAT?
Olga
Meals
I CAN ALWAYS TELL WHEN YOUNG PIRATES ARE LYING— WHEN I SEE THEIR TONGUES!
Olga
Meals
NOW!
FUN
Olga
Meals
I SEE! MEALS, YOUR SPOT IS A FAKE! OLGA, YOU ARE A LOSER!
HA HA HA
Olga
Meals
YES, YES... FOR THE—HM HM!—"LOSERS"... WE HAVE CANDY!
Olga
for Yannie
Sara ♡

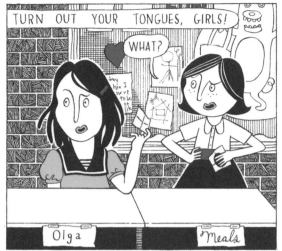

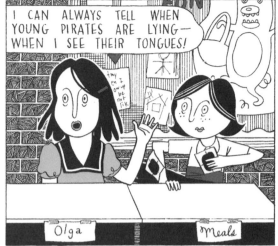

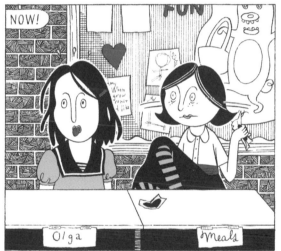

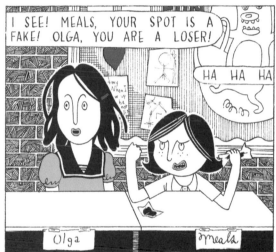

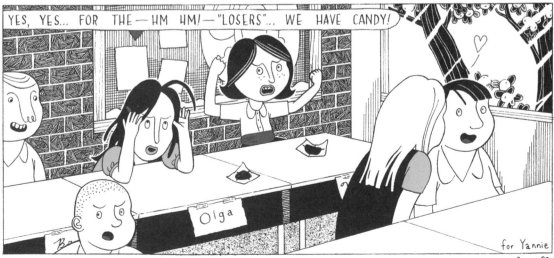

YOU CAN RECOGNIZE THE MOMENT ALMOST INSTANTLY. THOSE ALREADY ASLEEP ARE JARRED AWAKE.

WHAT YOU NOTICE IS THE LACK OF SOUND. THE CONSTANT DIN OF CIVILIZATION HAS GROUND TO A HALT. EVEN THE FRIDGE STOPPED PURRING REASSURINGLY. IS THIS JUST A NORMAL FLUCTUATION OF THE POWER GRID?

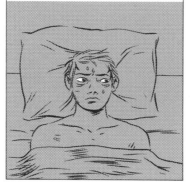

THEN YOU NOTICE THE INSECTS. SCREECHING SWARMS... OBLIVIOUS TO YOUR PRESENCE. HOW MANY ARE THERE? THEY WERE HERE BEFORE MANKIND. THEY WILL STILL BE HERE AFTER HUMANS GO EXTINCT.

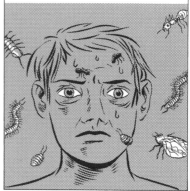

THE CARDIOVASCULAR SYSTEM RESPONDS. BLOOD RUSHES THROUGH THE VEINS WITH DEADENING VIOLENCE ACTIVATING OBSCURE GLANDS AND LONG FORGOTTEN SENSORY ORGANS.

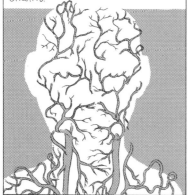

WHITE NOISE

THE IMPERCEPTIBLE TECTONIC DRIFT COMES INTO SHARP RELIEF... CONTINENTAL SHELVES CRASH INTO EACH OTHER... ANCIENT REMAINS SHIFT UNEASILY BENEATH EARTH'S CRUST...

GRIND

YOU CAN EVEN HEAR THE FAINT RADIO HUM OF DISTANT SUPERNOVAS TRAVELLING FOR AEONS THROUGH DEAD SPACE AHEAD OF THE SILENT SCREAMS OF ALIEN WORLDS...

ENGULFED IN COUNTLESS SOLAR HOLOCAUSTS...

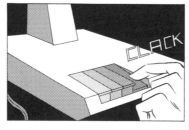

CLACK

WHHHRRR

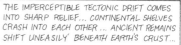

WHHHRRRRR

ZZZZZ

T. KACZYNSKI '08

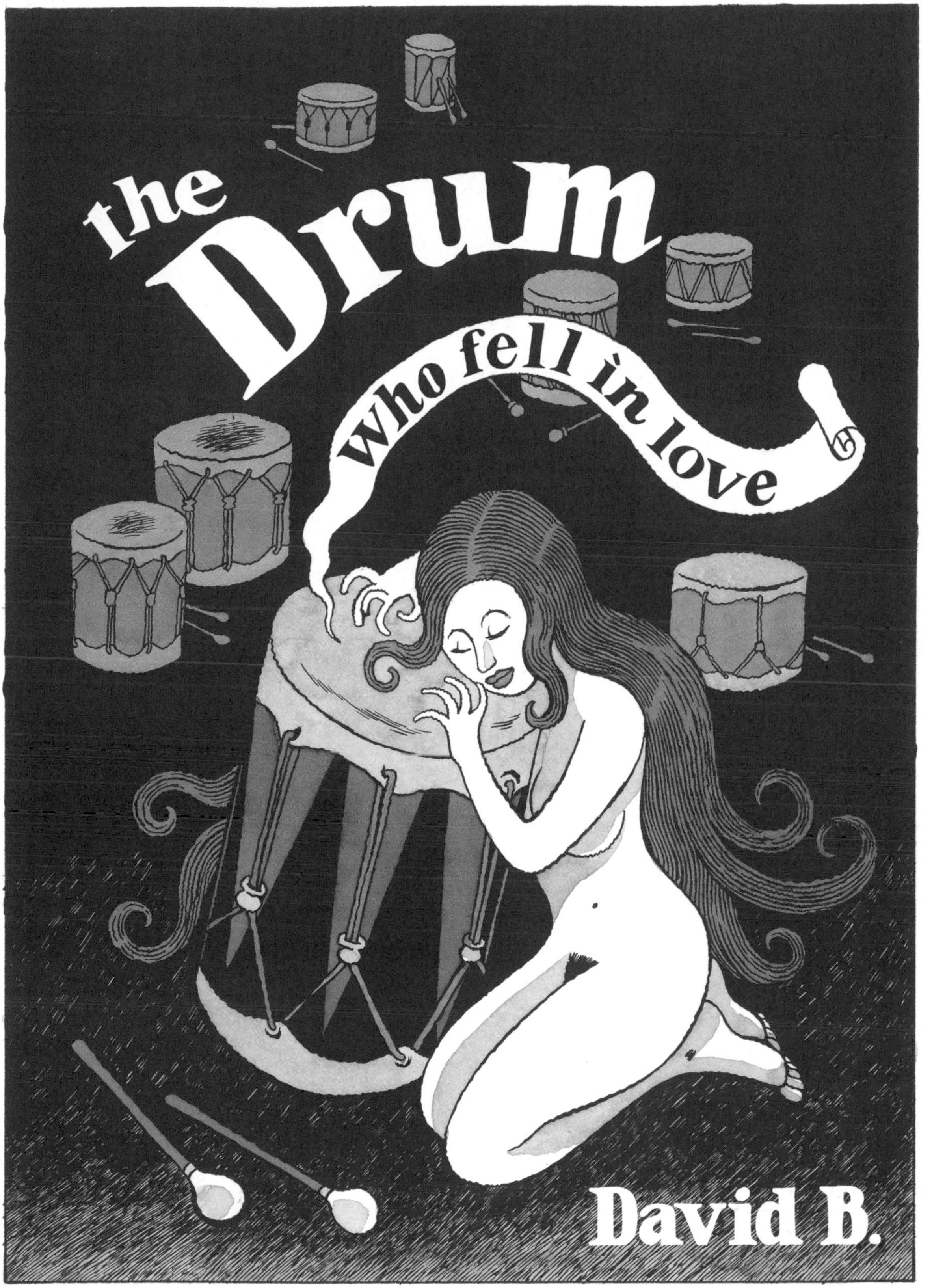
the Drum
Who fell in love
David B.

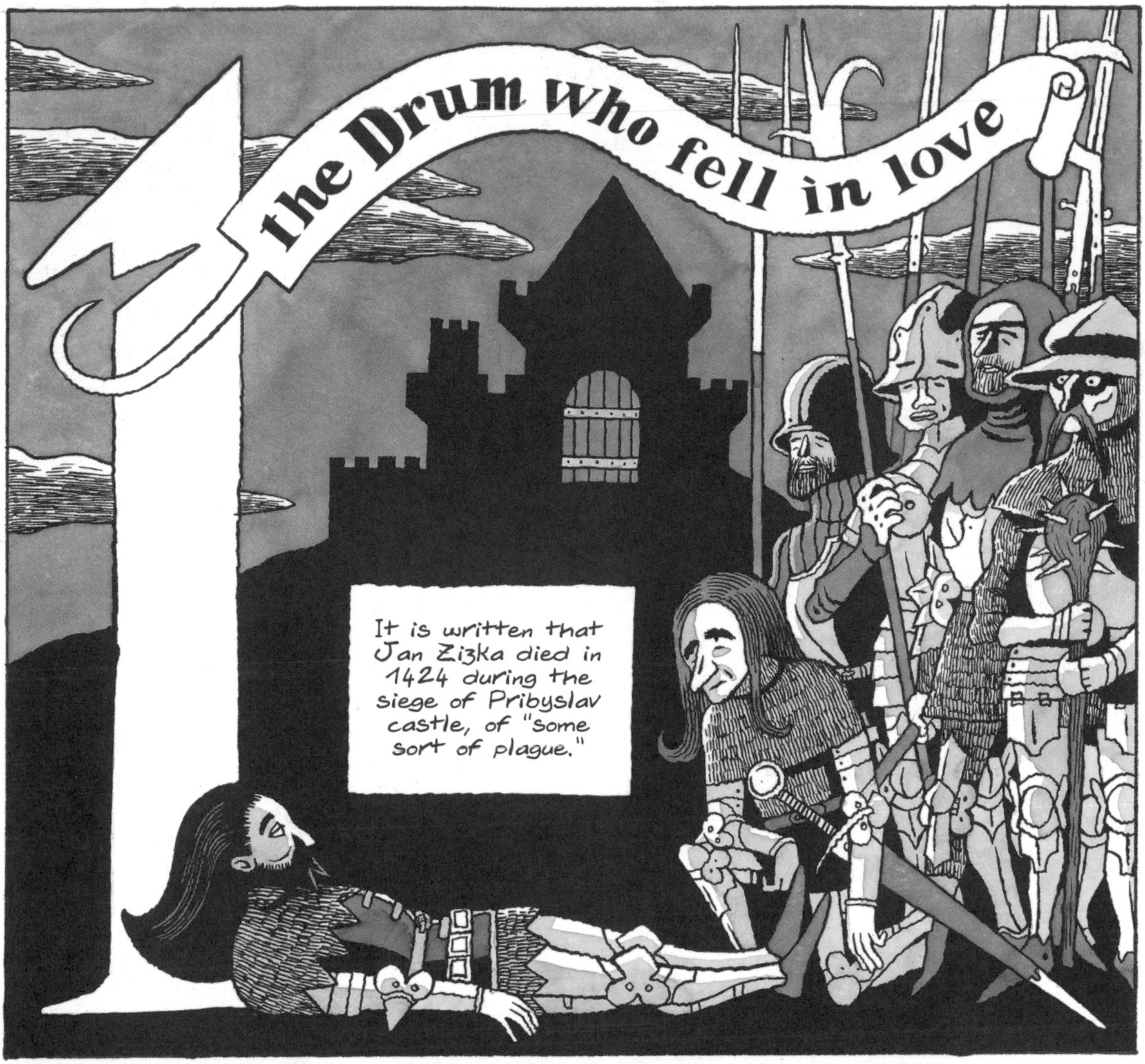
the Drum who fell in love
It is written that Jan Zizka died in 1424 during the siege of Pribyslav castle, of "some sort of plague."

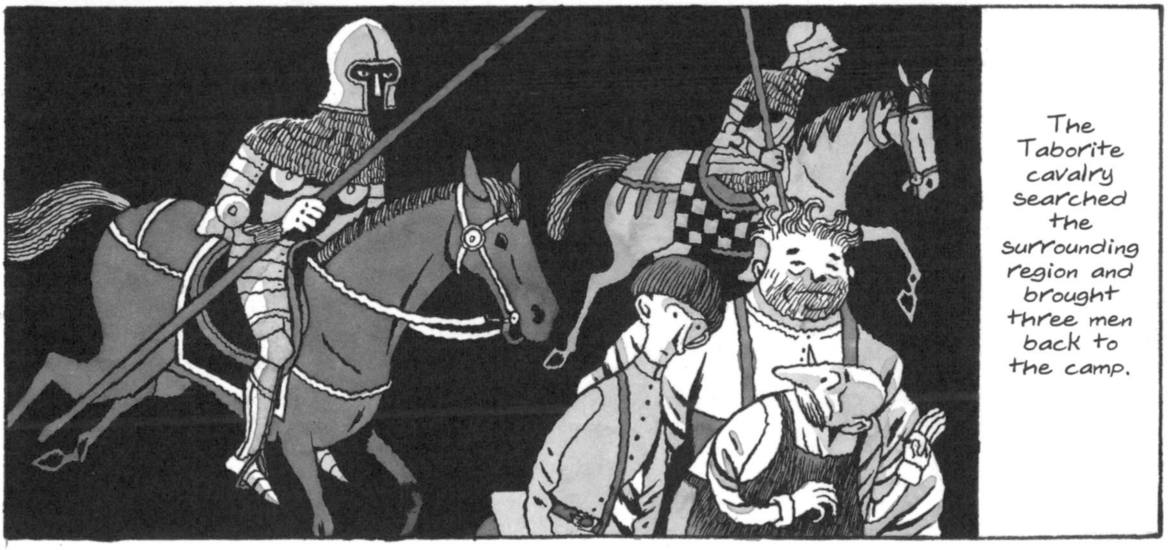
The Taborite cavalry searched the surrounding region and brought three men back to the camp.

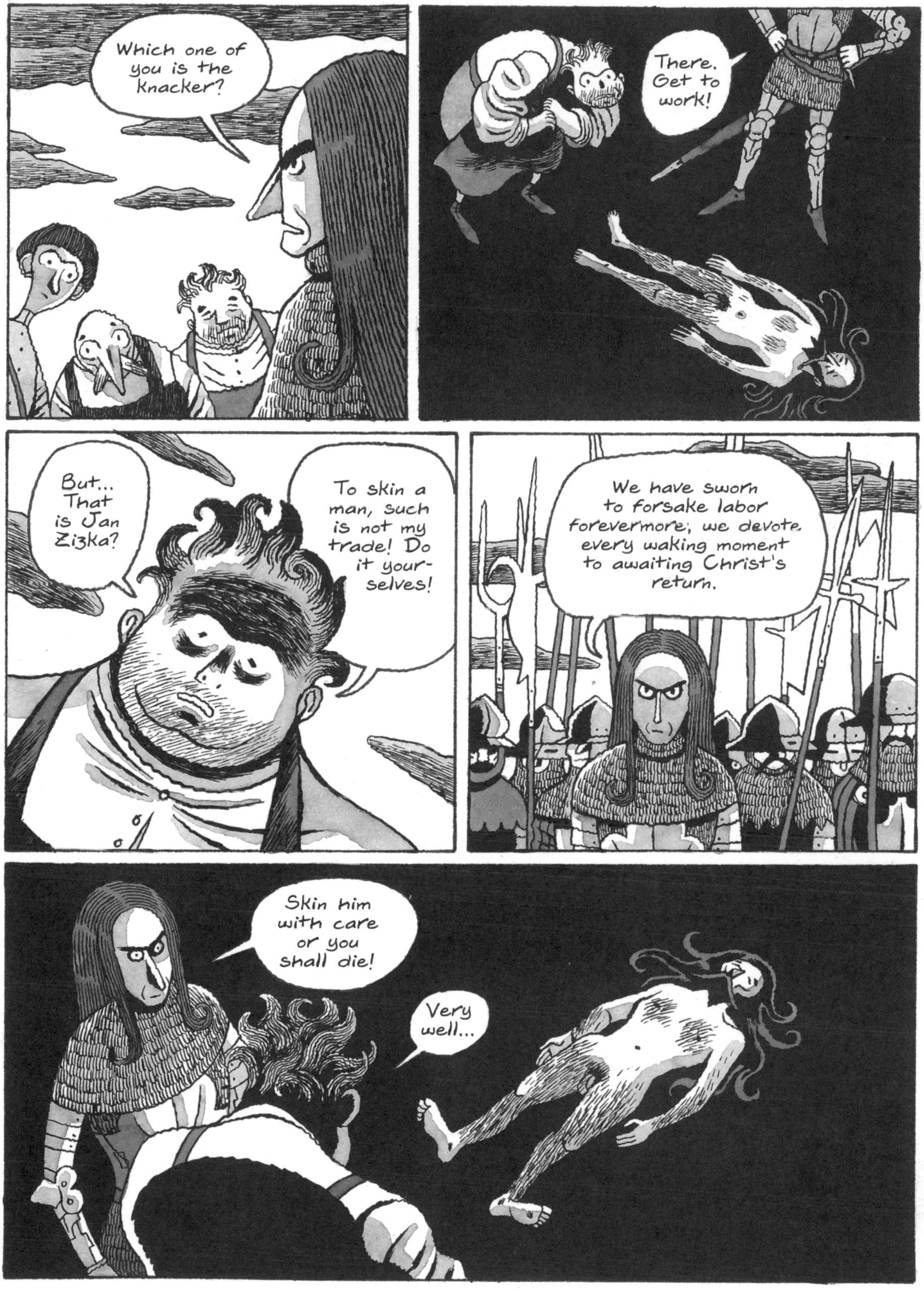
Which one of you is the knacker?
There. Get to work!
But... That is Jan Zizka?
To skin a man, such is not my trade! Do it your-selves!
We have sworn to forsake labor forevermore; we devote every waking moment to awaiting Christ's return.
Skin him with care or you shall die!
Very well...

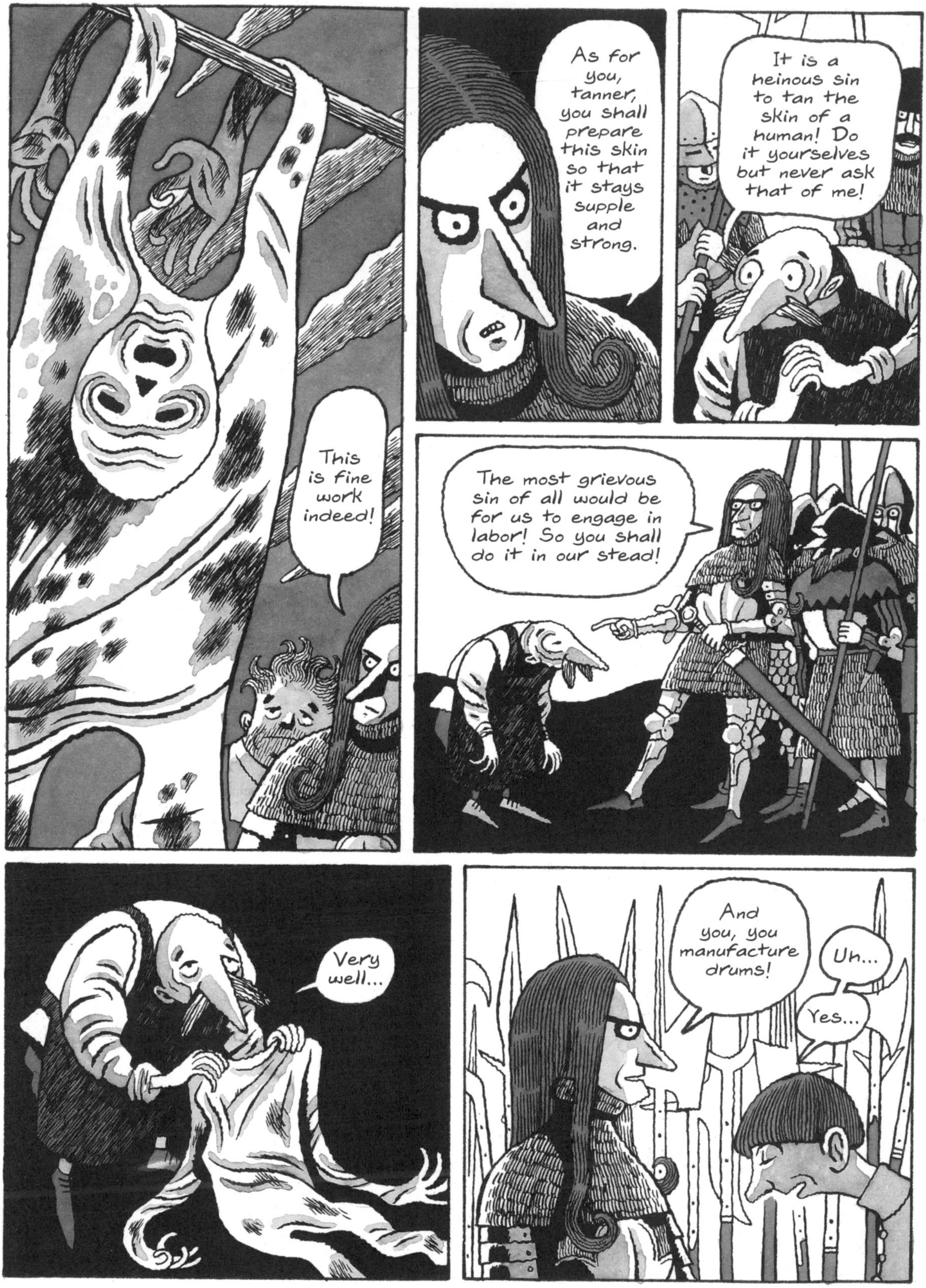
This is fine work indeed!
As for you, tanner, you shall prepare this skin so that it stays supple and strong.
It is a heinous sin to tan the skin of a human! Do it yourselves but never ask that of me!
The most grievous sin of all would be for us to engage in labor! So you shall do it in our stead!
Very well...
And you, you manufacture drums!
Uh...
Yes...

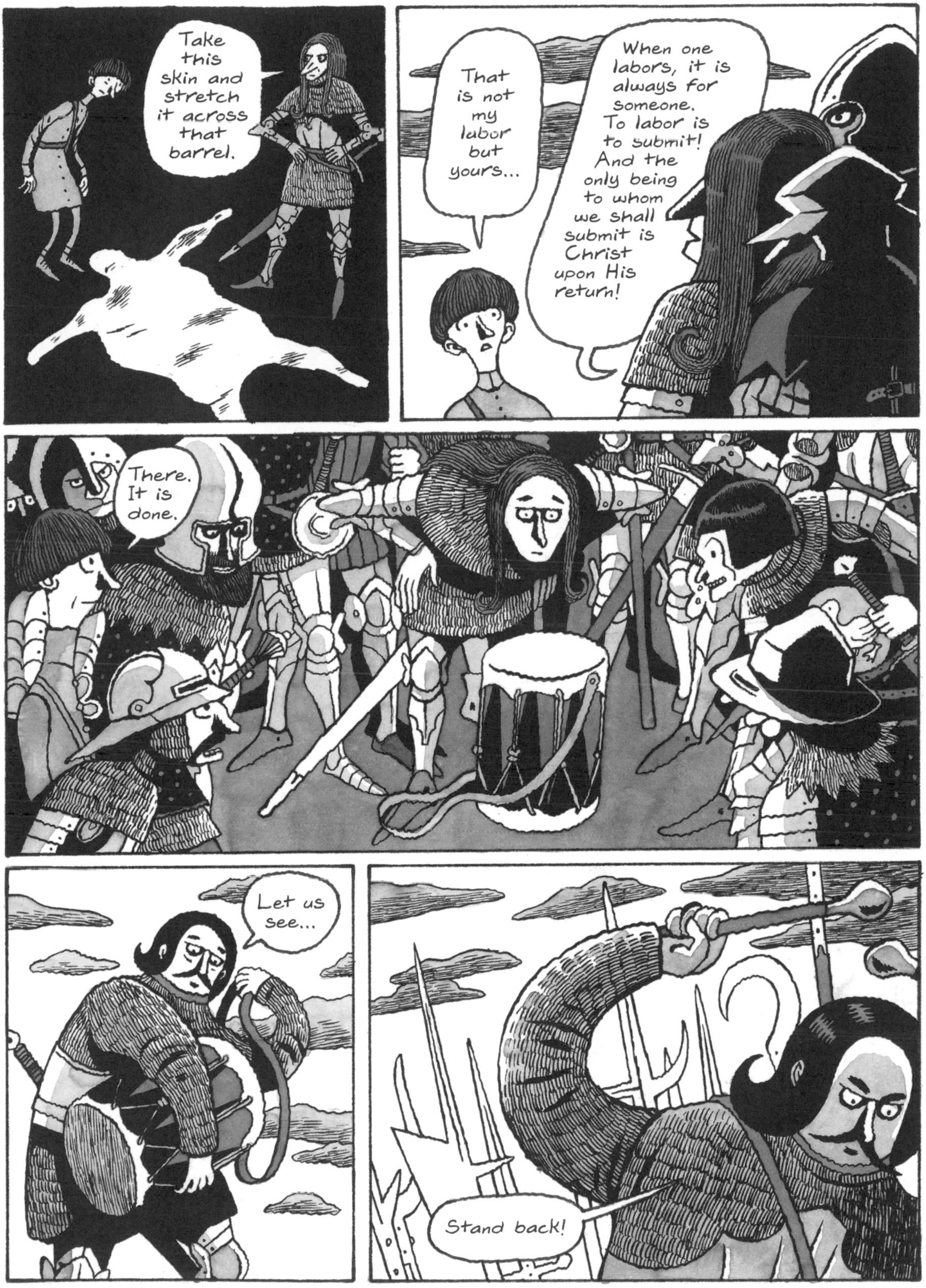
Take this skin and stretch it across that barrel.
That is not my labor but yours...
When one labors, it is always for someone. To labor is to submit! And the only being to whom we shall submit is Christ upon His return!
There. It is done.
Let us see...
Stand back!

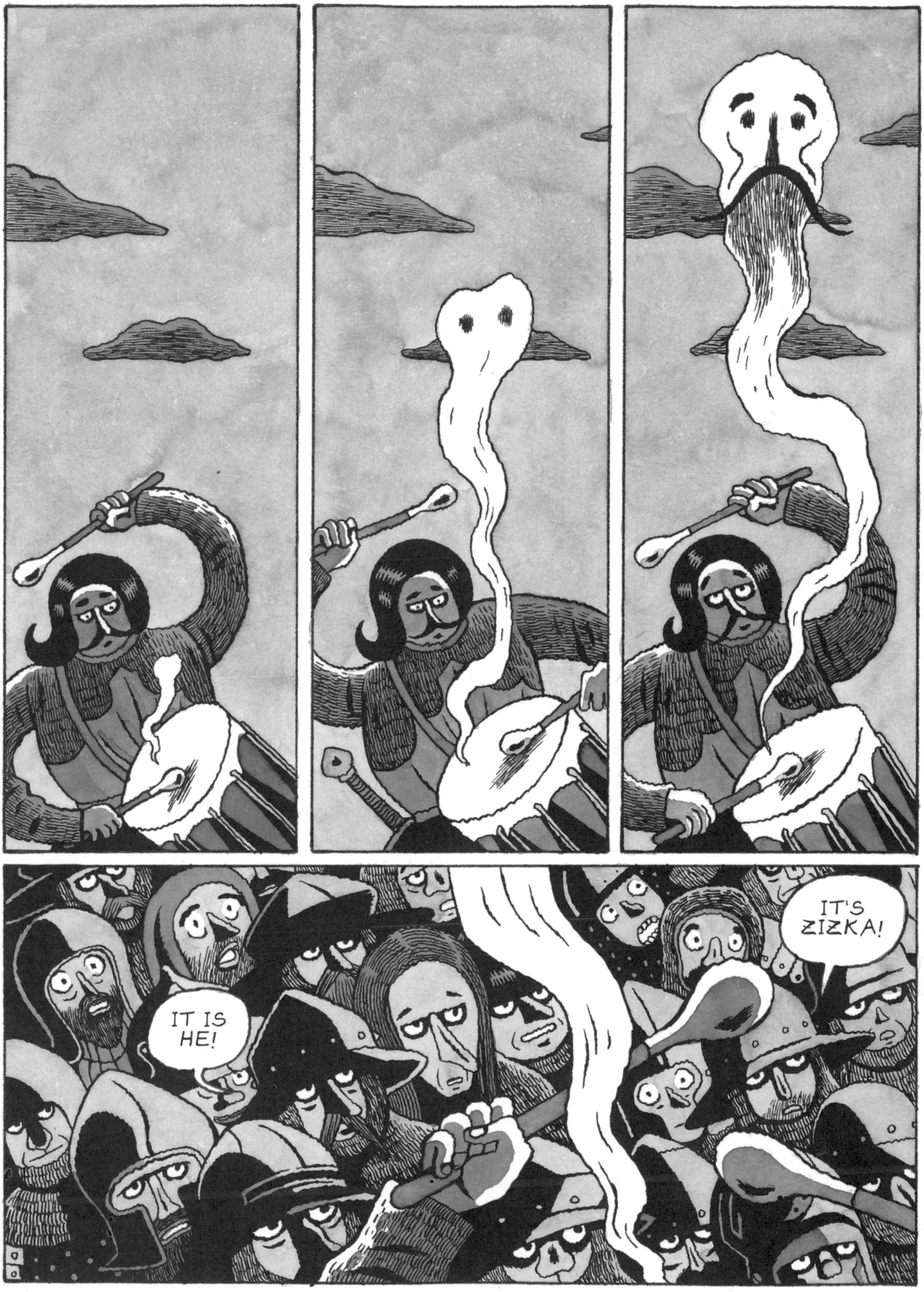
IT IS HE!
IT'S ZIZKA!

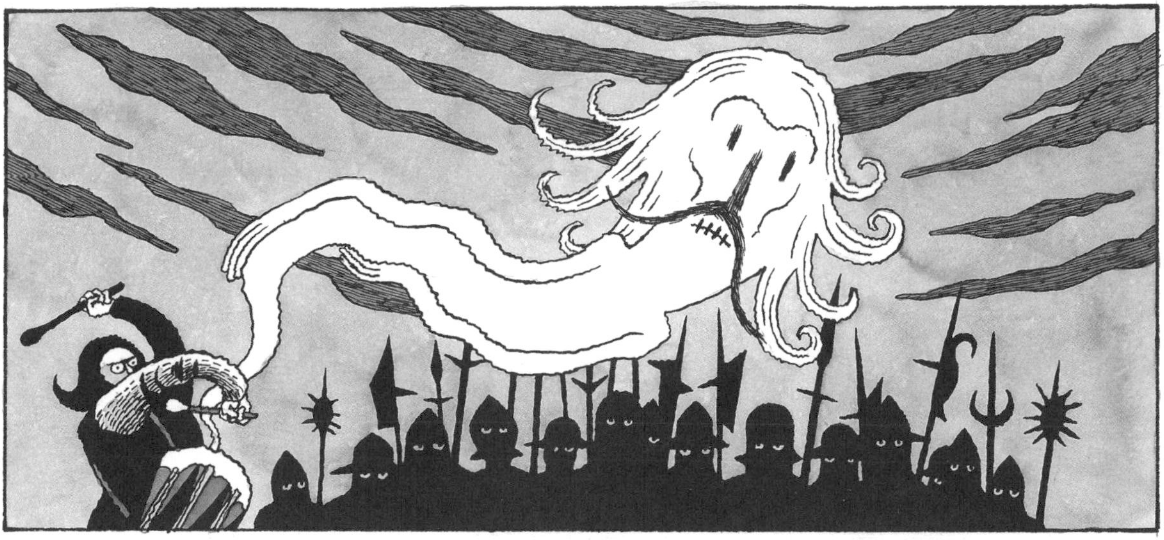

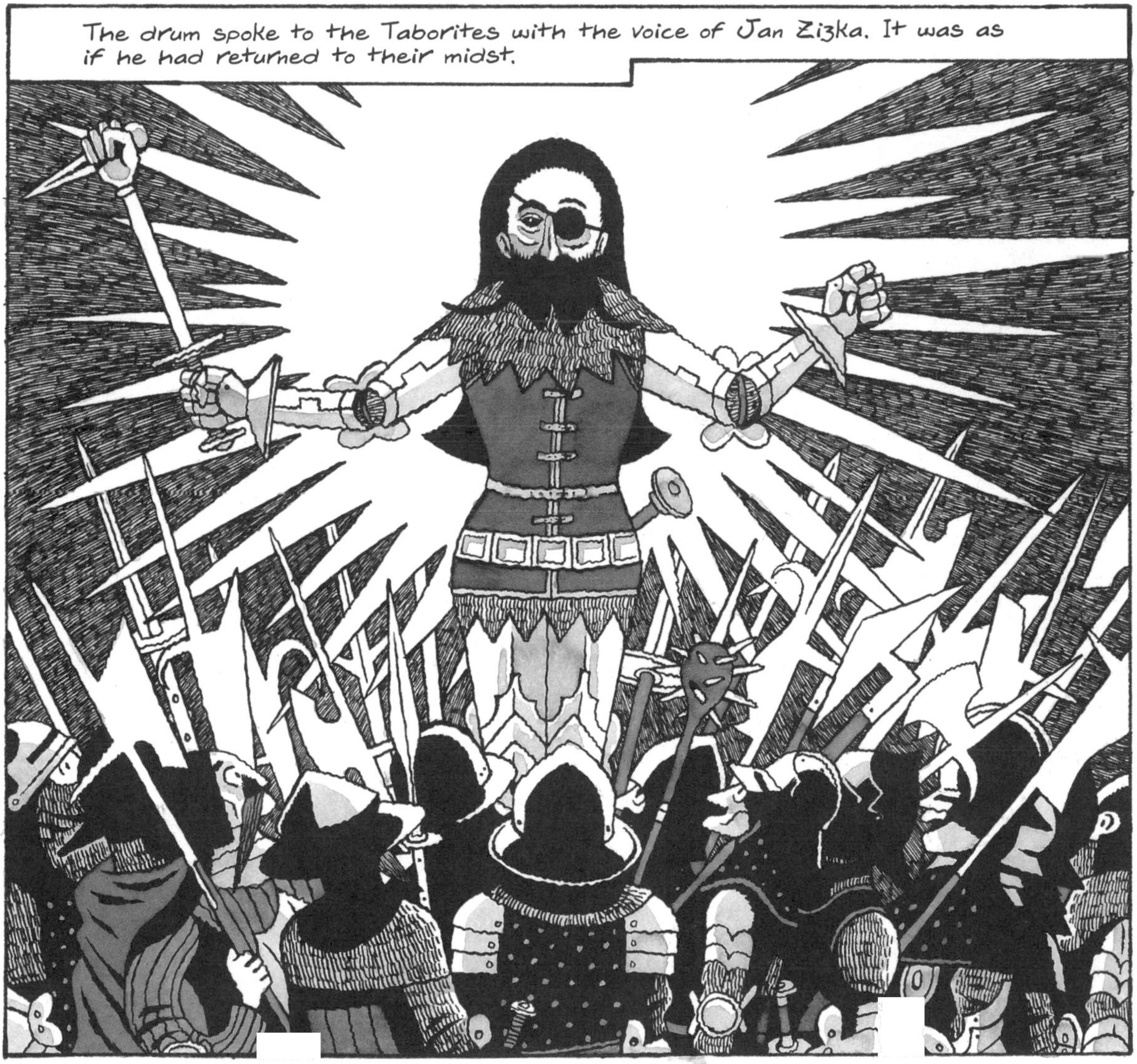
The drum spoke to the Taborites with the voice of Jan Zizka. It was as if he had returned to their midst.

Once again Zizka led the army through battles without end, and those men of his who refused to labor had never labored so hard in their lives.

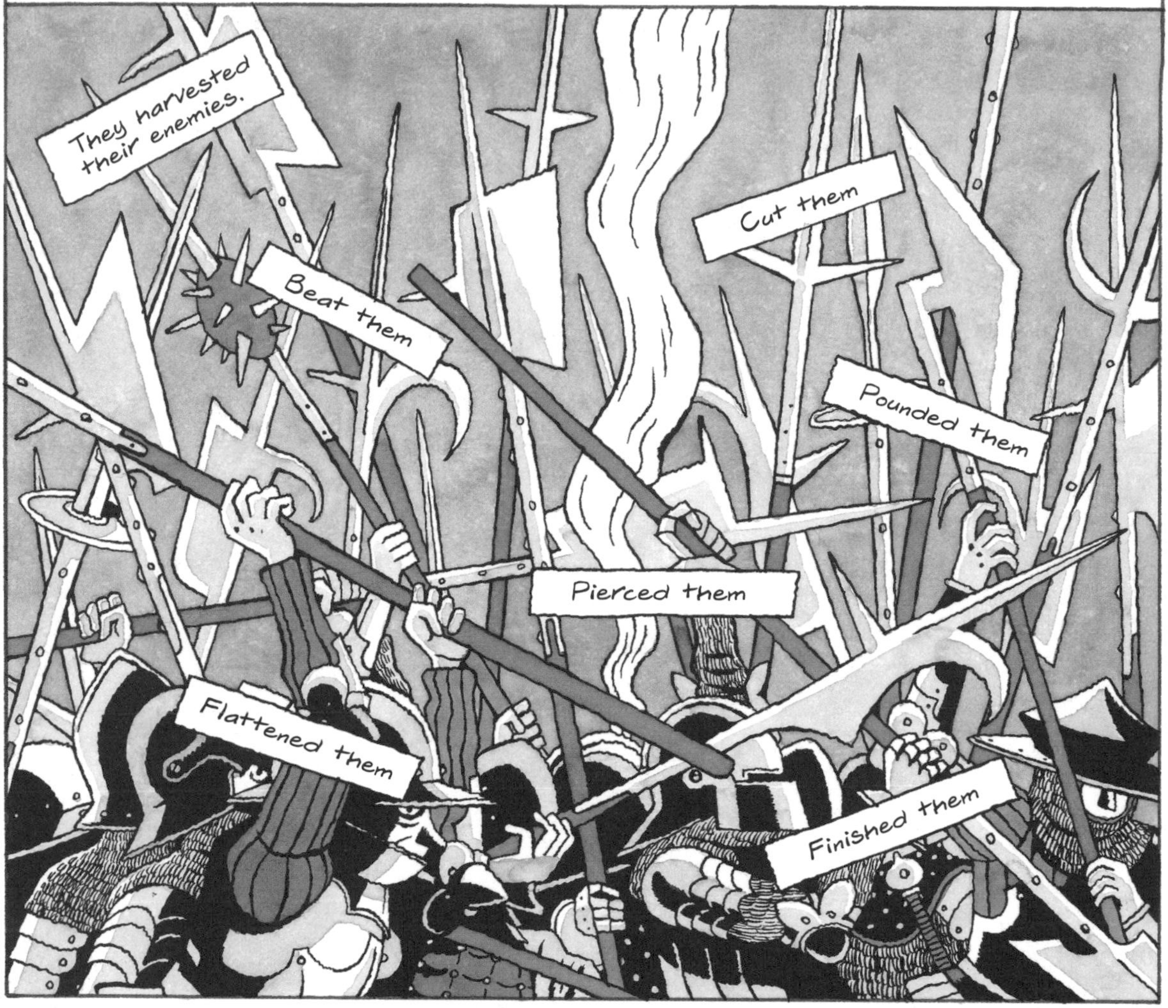
They harvested their enemies.
Beat them
Cut them
Pounded them
Pierced them
Flattened them
Finished them

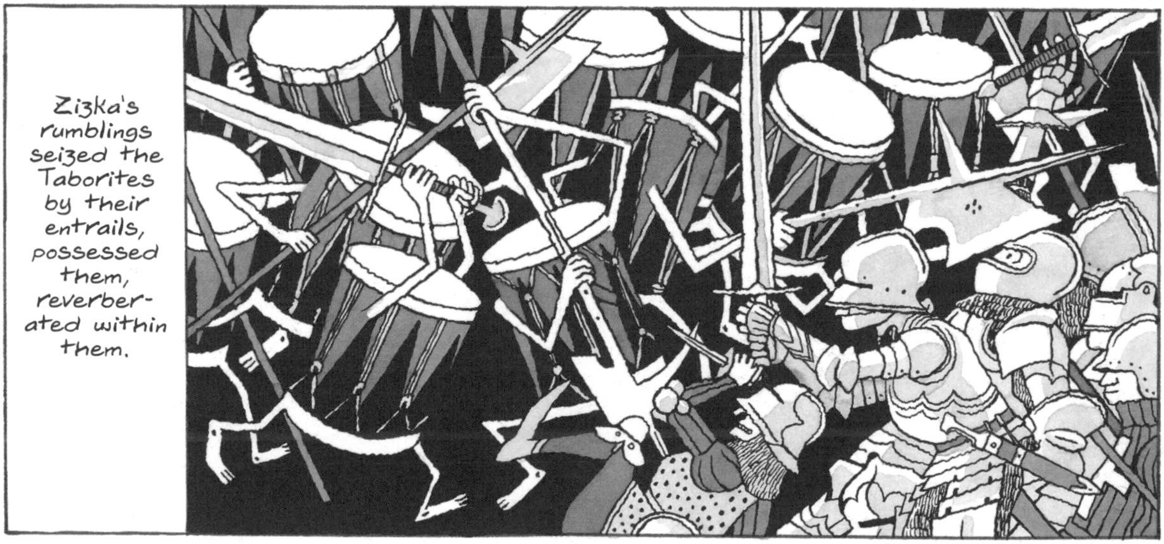
Zizka's rumblings seized the Taborites by their entrails, possessed them, reverberated within them.

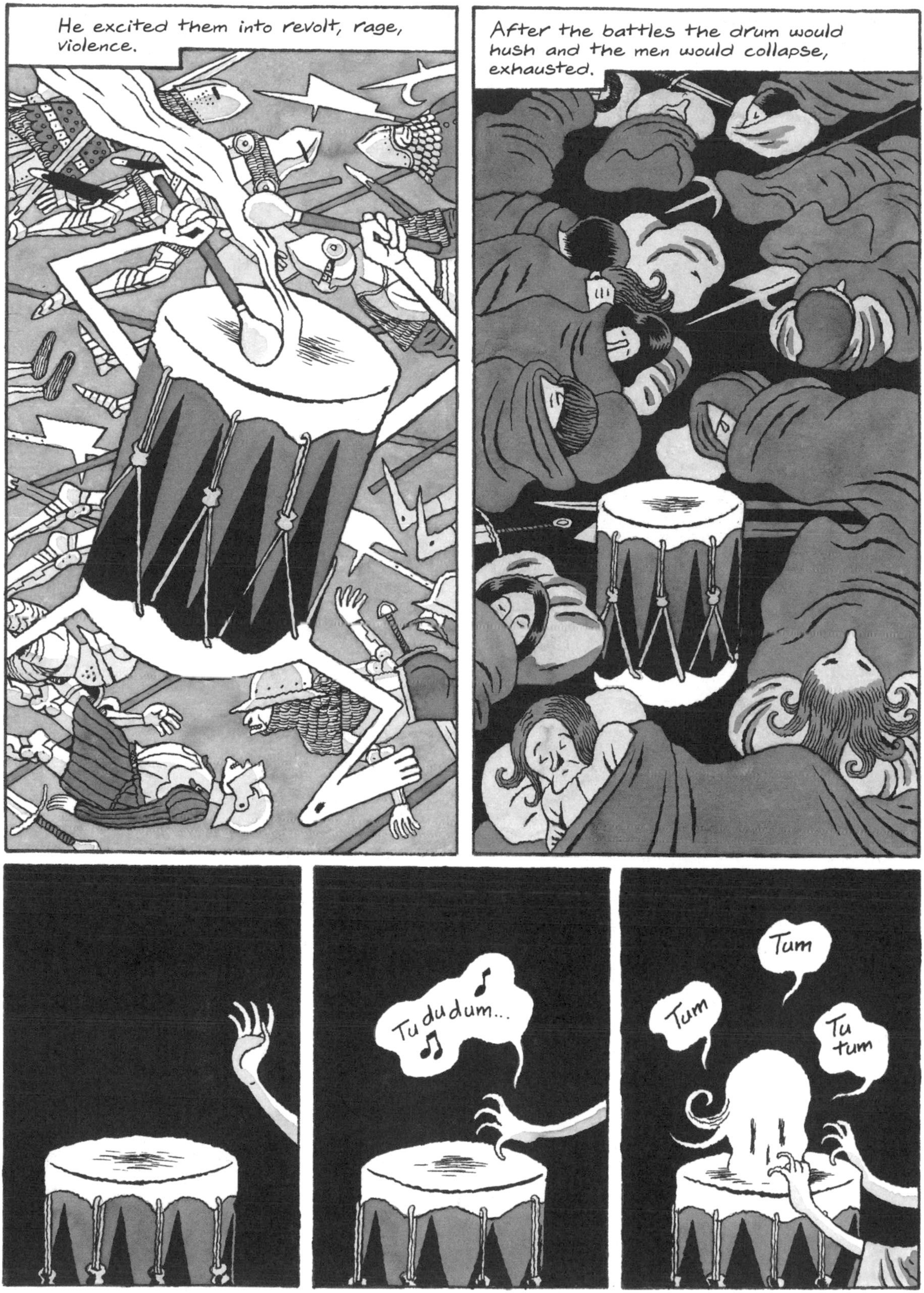
He excited them into revolt, rage, violence.
After the battles the drum would hush and the men would collapse, exhausted.
Tu du dum...
Tum
Tum
Tu tum

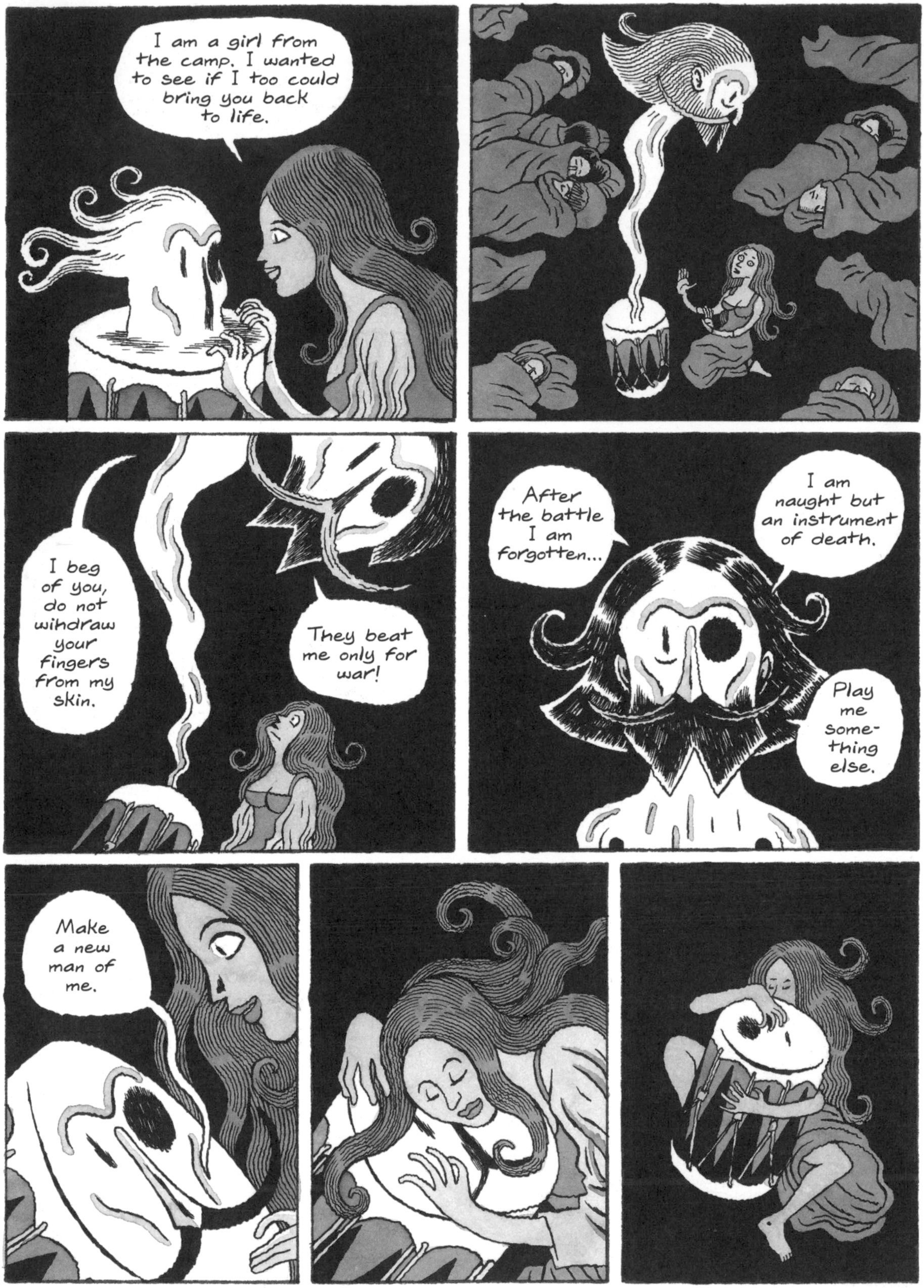
I am a girl from the camp. I wanted to see if I too could bring you back to life.
I beg of you, do not wihdraw your fingers from my skin.
They beat me only for war!
After the battle I am forgotten...
I am naught but an instrument of death.
Play me some-thing else.
Make a new man of me.

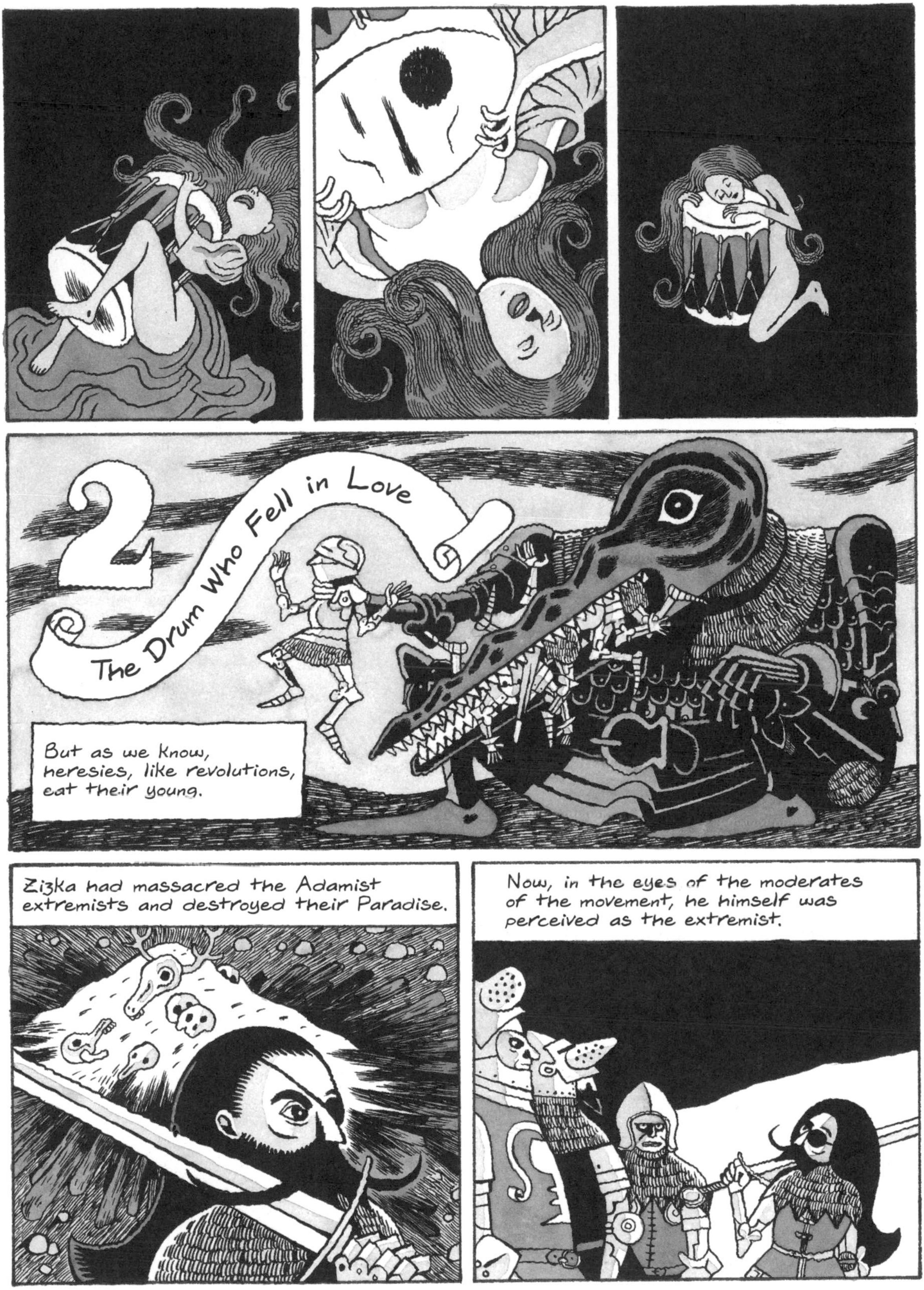
2
The Drum Who Fell in Love
But as we know, heresies, like revolutions, eat their young.
Zizka had massacred the Adamist extremists and destroyed their Paradise.
Now, in the eyes of the moderates of the movement, he himself was perceived as the extremist.

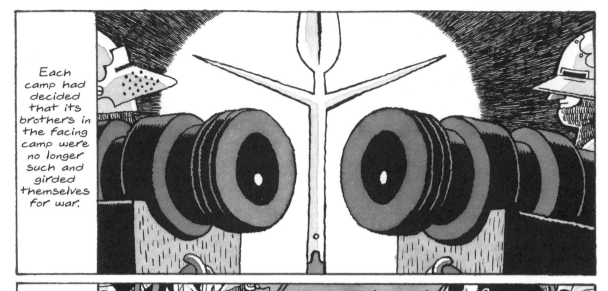

Each camp had decided that its brothers in the facing camp were no longer such and girded themselves for war.

On May 30, 1434, the two armies faced off at the Battle of Lipany.

Dum

Dudum dudu dum

Dudum

AIM FOR THE DRUMMER!

Borek de Miletinek, leader of the moderates.

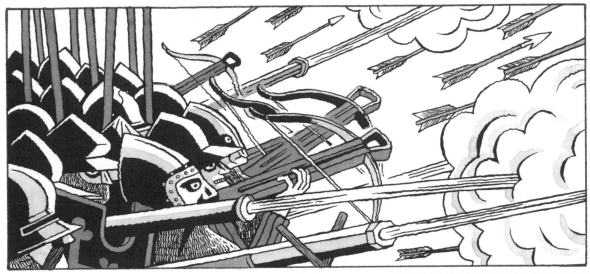

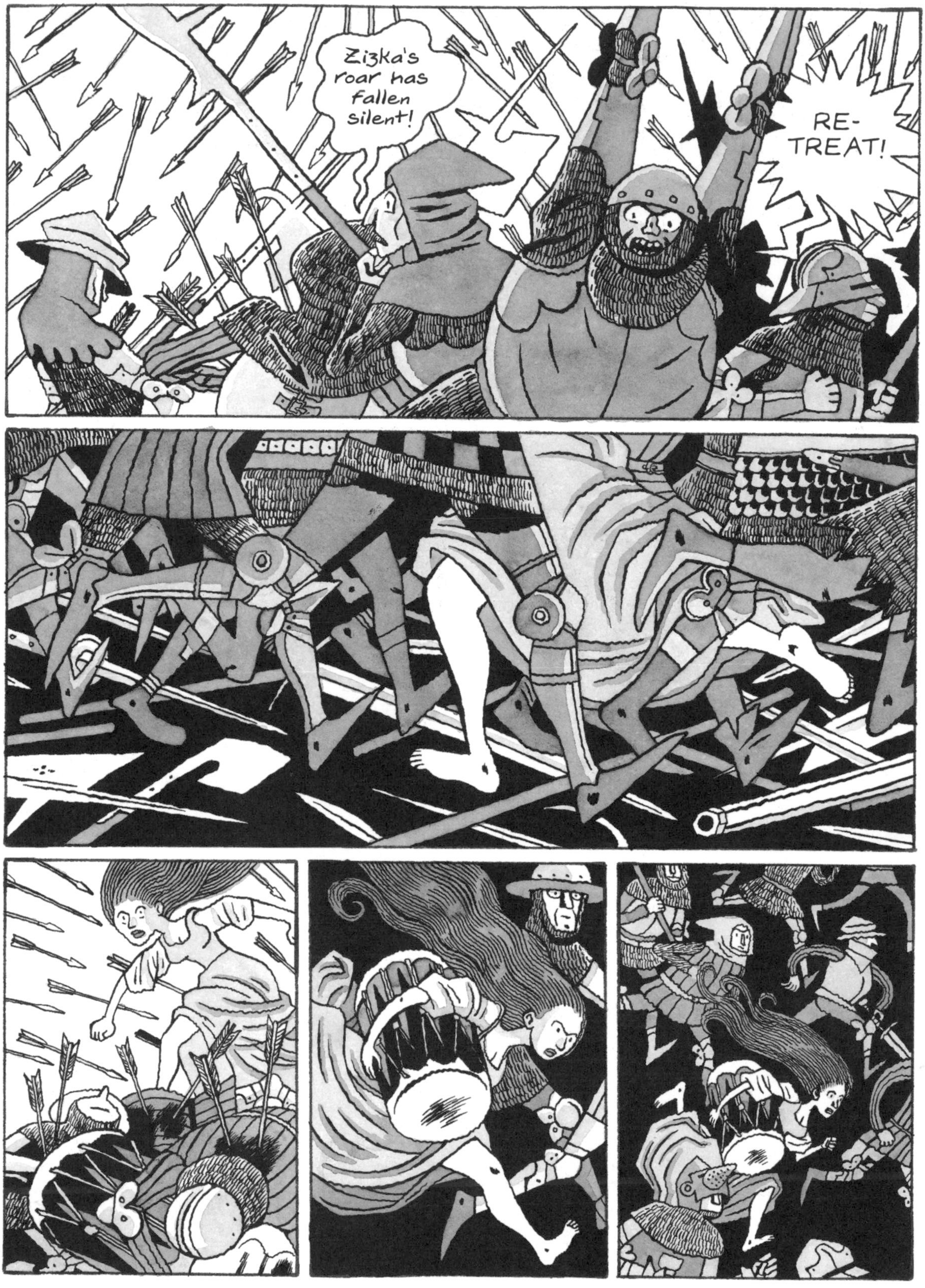
Zizka's roar has fallen silent!
RE-TREAT!

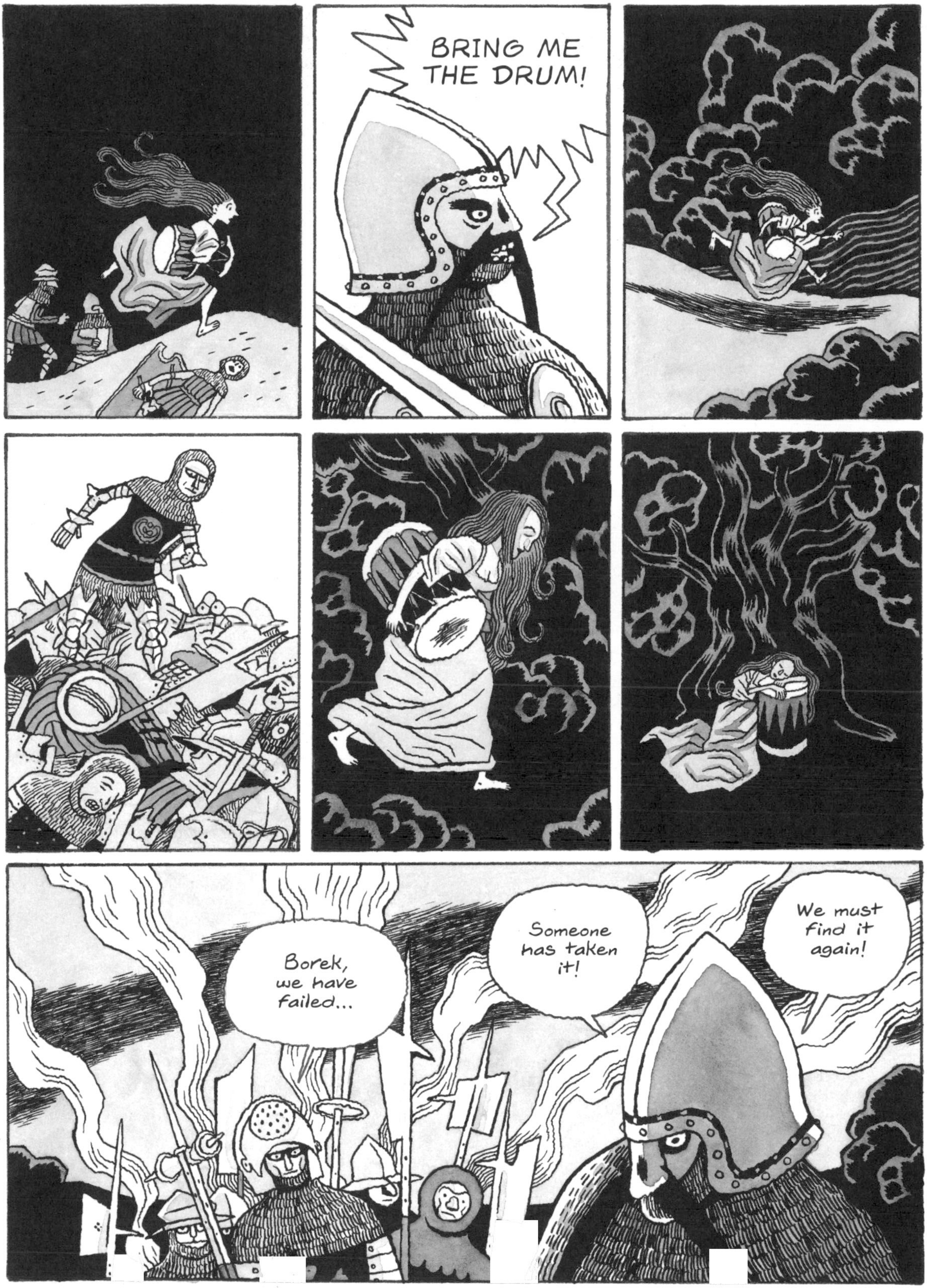
BRING ME THE DRUM!
Borek, we have failed...
Someone has taken it!
We must find it again!

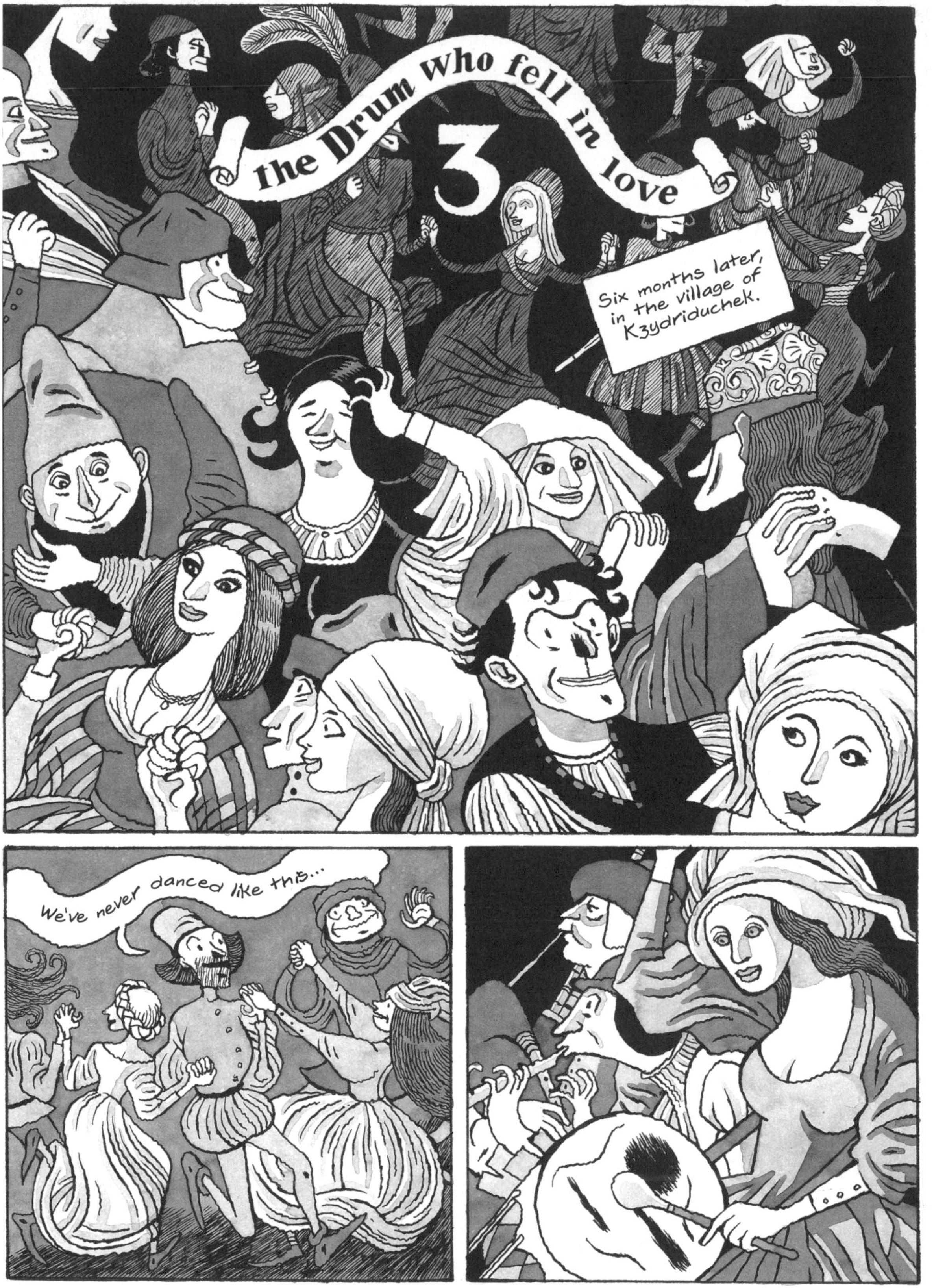
the Drum Who fell in love
3
Six months later, in the village of Kzydriduchek.
We've never danced like this...

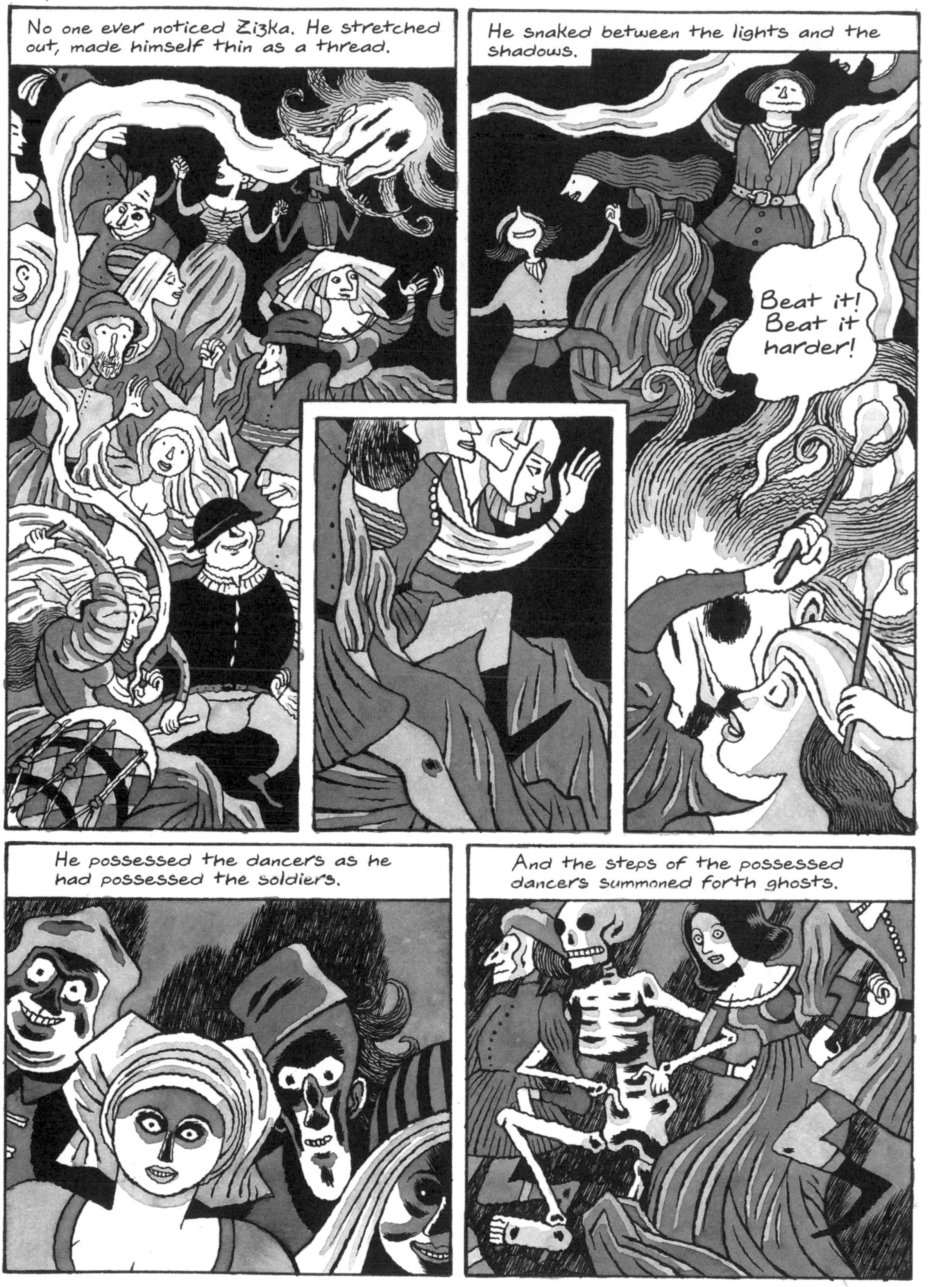
No one ever noticed Zizka. He stretched out, made himself thin as a thread.
He snaked between the lights and the shadows.
Beat it! Beat it harder!
He possessed the dancers as he had possessed the soldiers.
And the steps of the possessed dancers summoned forth ghosts.

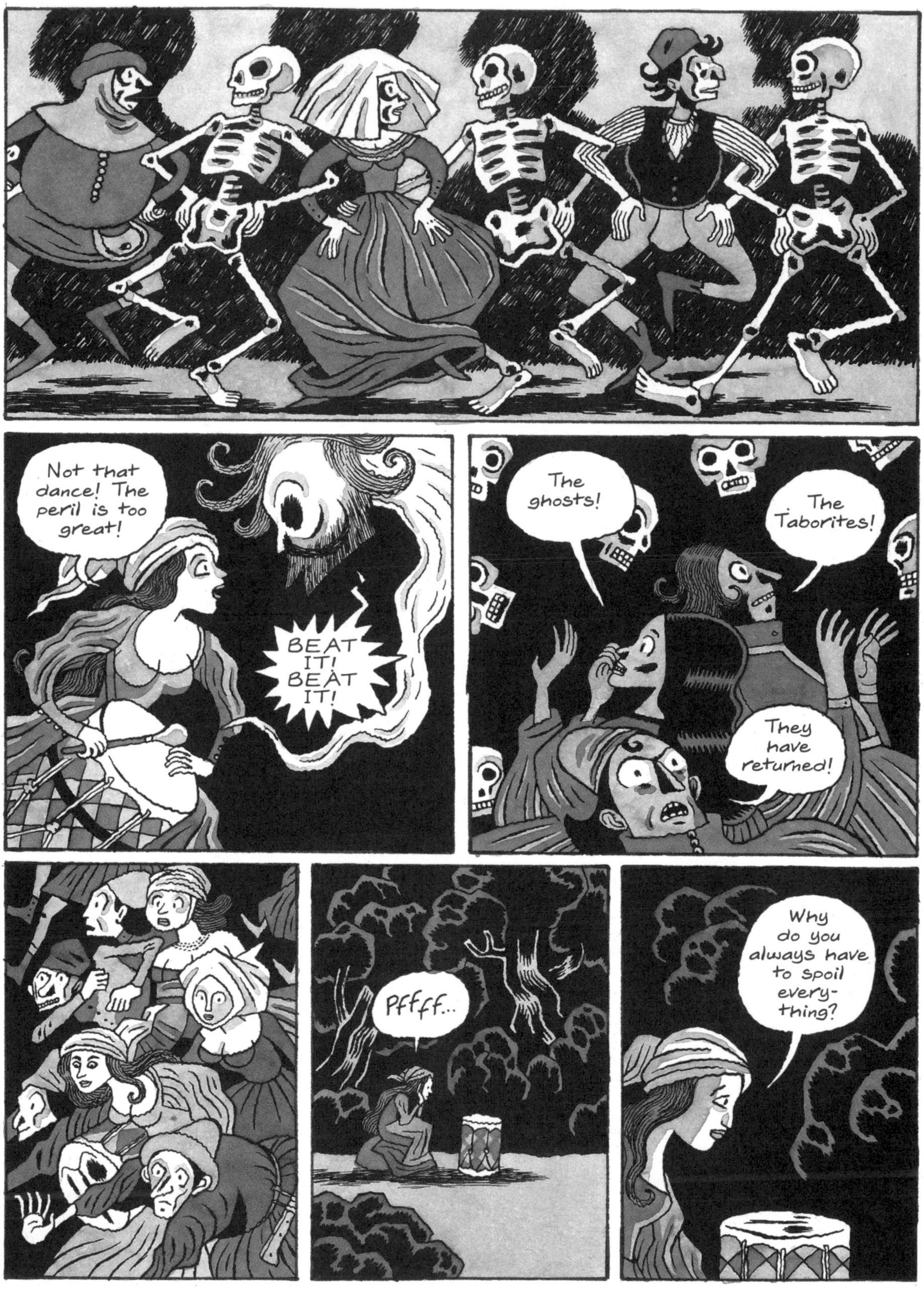
Not that dance! The peril is too great!
BEAT IT! BEAT IT!
The ghosts!
The Taborites!
They have returned!
Pffff...
Why do you always have to spoil every-thing?

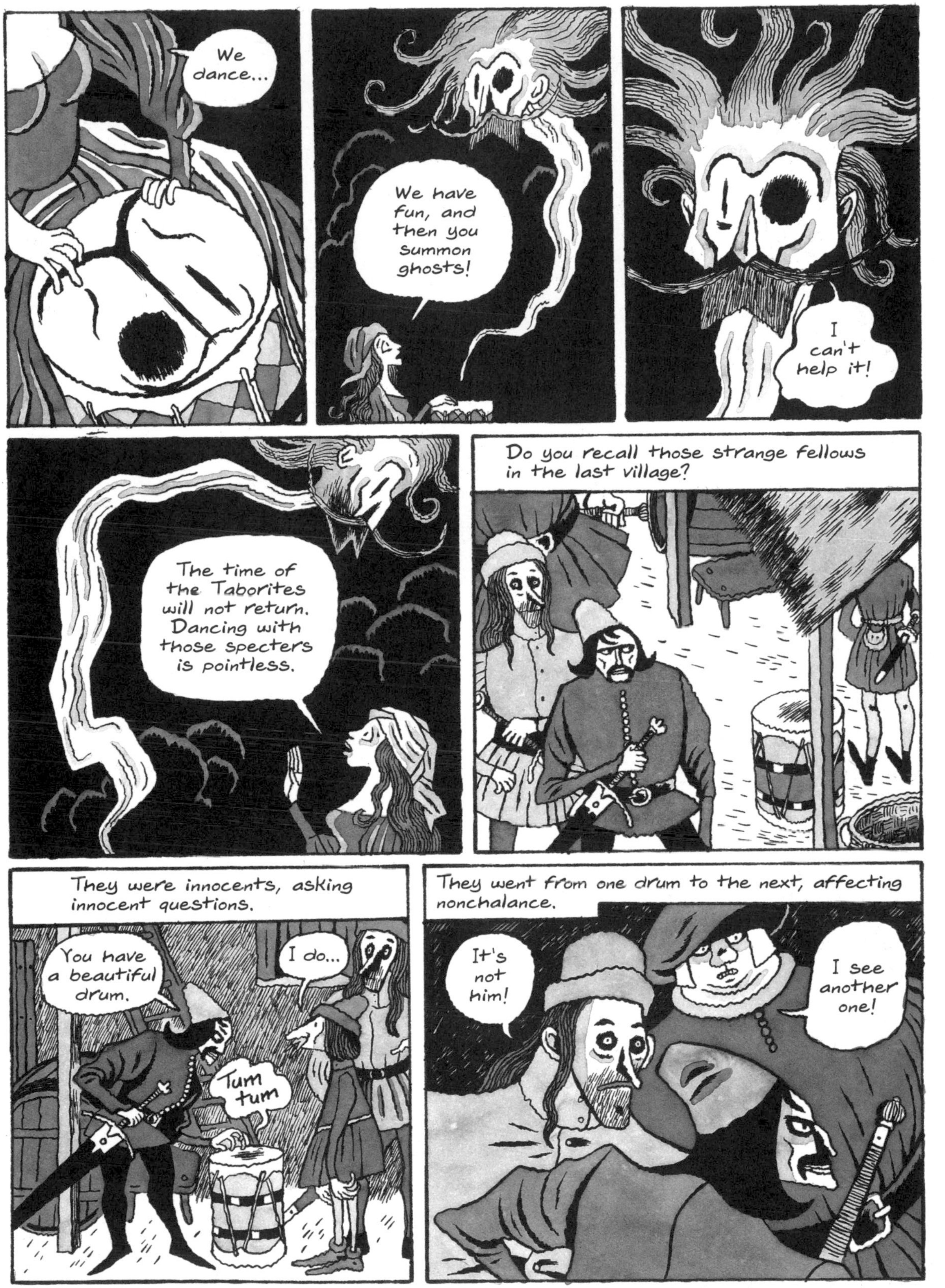
We dance...
We have fun, and then you summon ghosts!
I can't help it!
The time of the Taborites will not return. Dancing with those specters is pointless.
Do you recall those strange fellows in the last village?
They were innocents, asking innocent questions.
You have a beautiful drum.
I do...
Tum tum
They went from one drum to the next, affecting nonchalance.
It's not him!
I see another one!

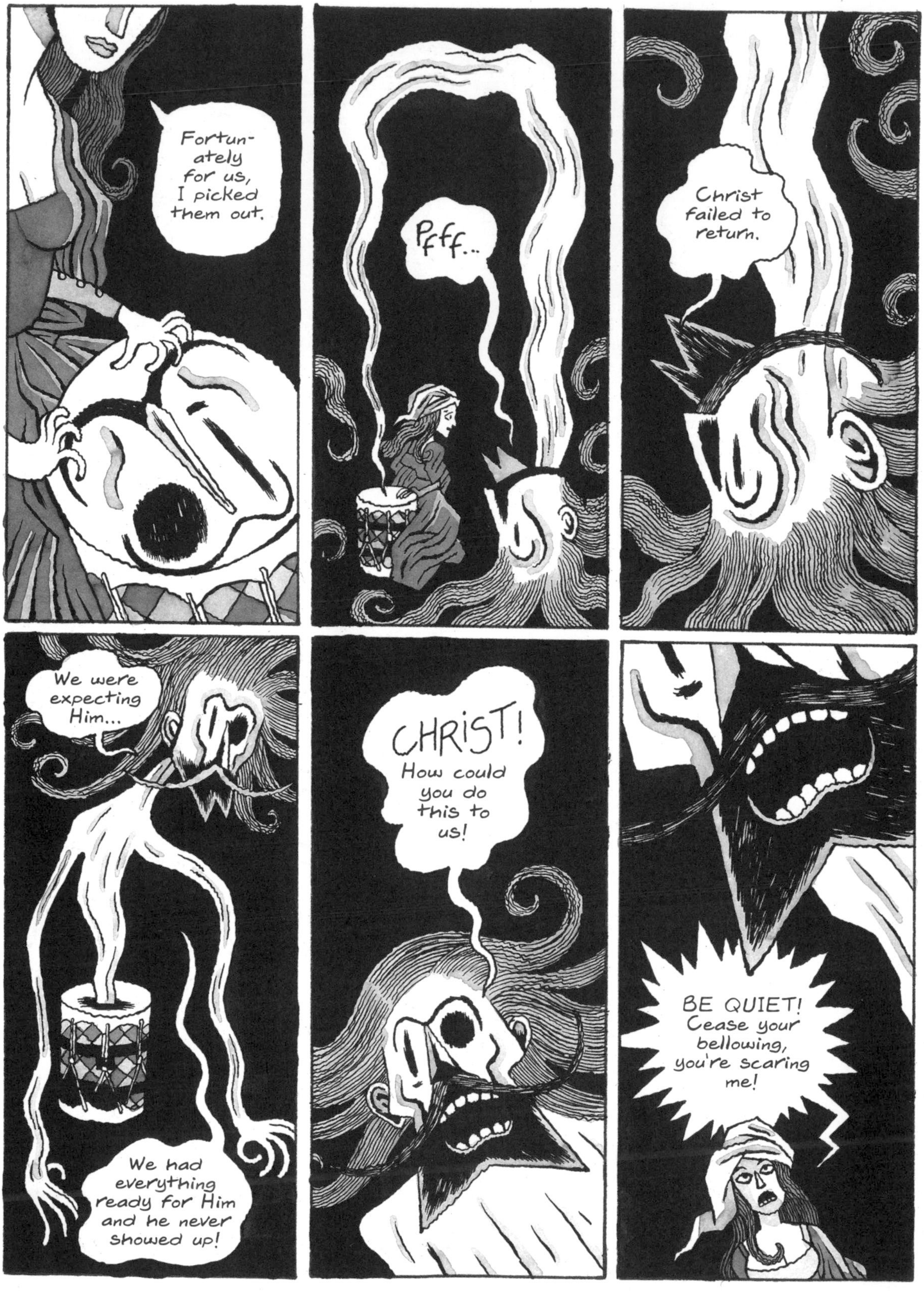
Fortunately for us, I picked them out.
Pfff...
Christ failed to return.
We were expecting Him...
We had everything ready for Him and he never showed up!
CHRIST! How could you do this to us!
BE QUIET! Cease your bellowing, you're scaring me!

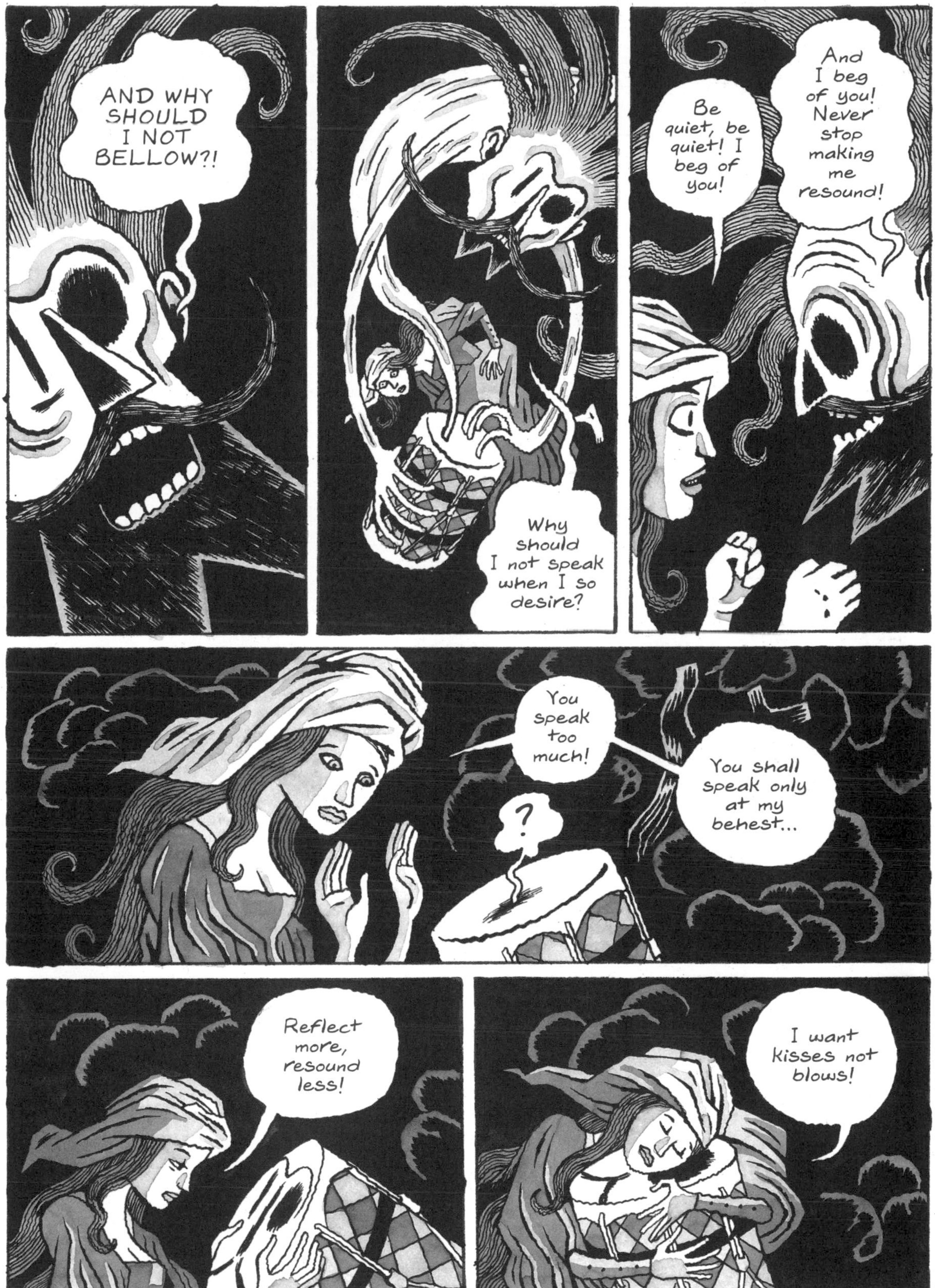
AND WHY SHOULD I NOT BELLOW?!
Why should I not speak when I so desire?
Be quiet, be quiet! I beg of you!
And I beg of you! Never stop making me resound!
You speak too much!
You shall speak only at my behest...
?
Reflect more, resound less!
I want kisses not blows!

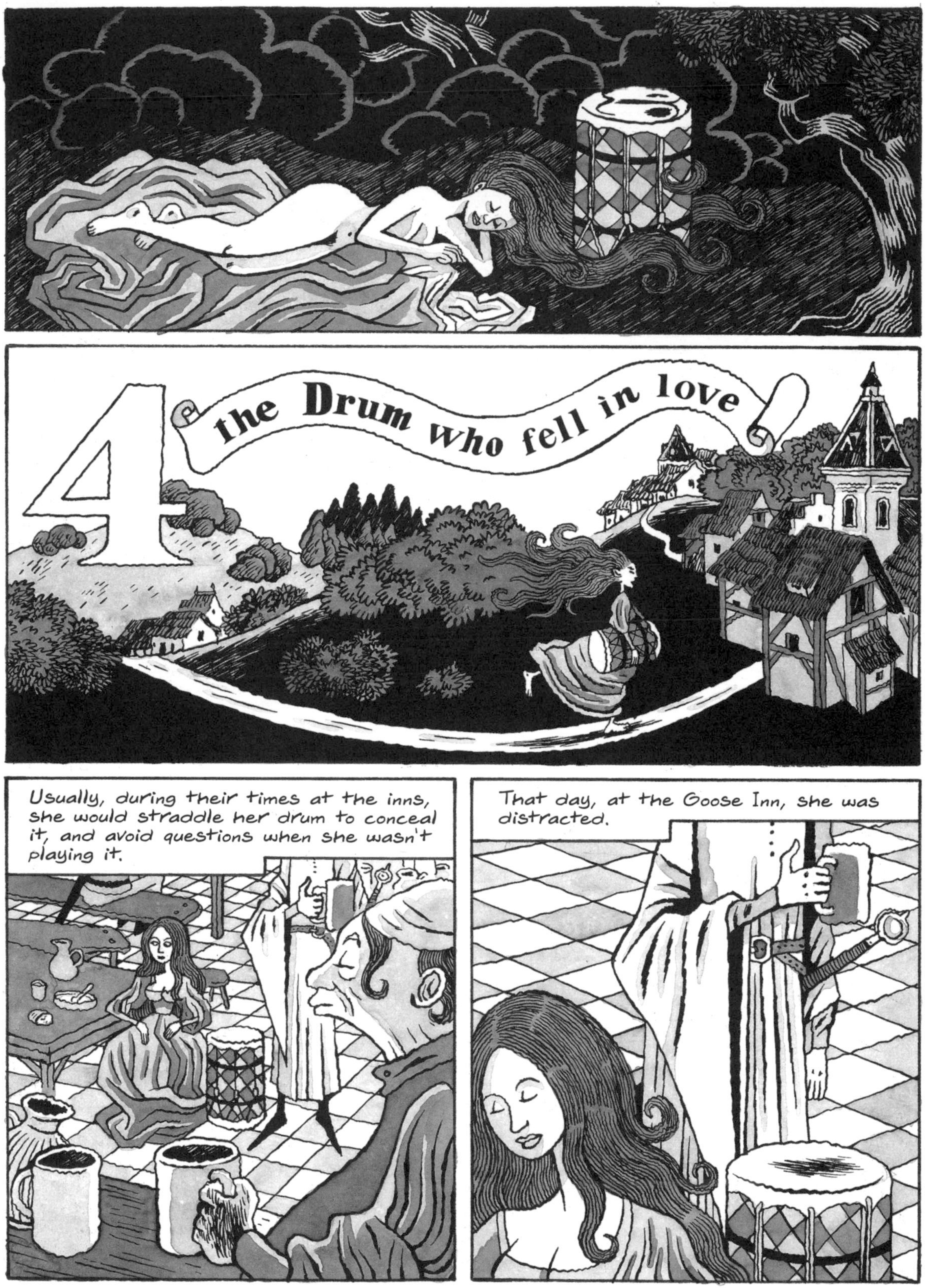
4
the Drum who fell in love
Usually, during their times at the inns, she would straddle her drum to conceal it, and avoid questions when she wasn't playing it.
That day, at the Goose Inn, she was distracted.

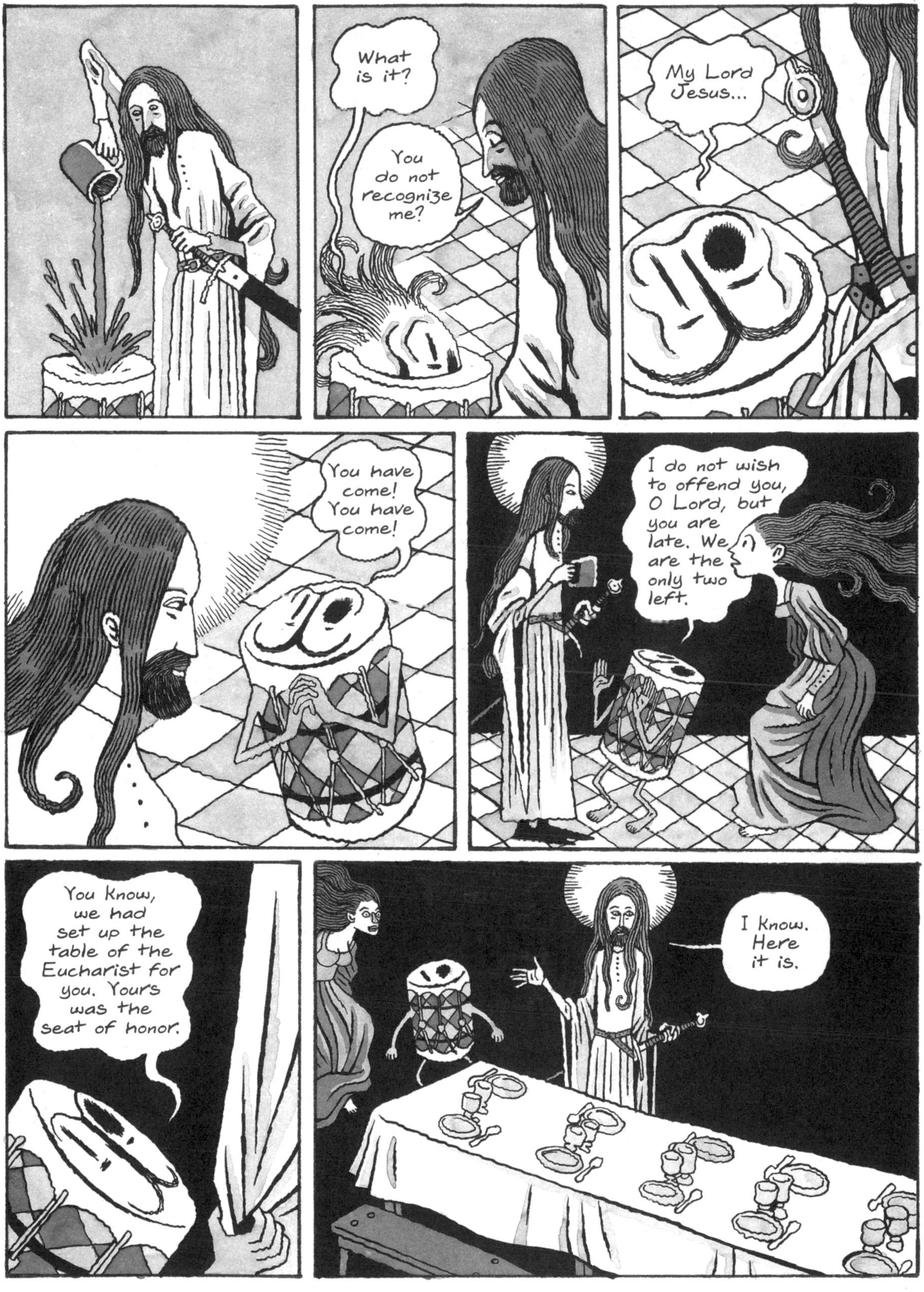
What is it?
You do not recognize me?
My Lord Jesus...
You have come! You have come!
I do not wish to offend you, O Lord, but you are late. We are the only two left.
You know, we had set up the table of the Eucharist for you. Yours was the seat of honor.
I know. Here it is.

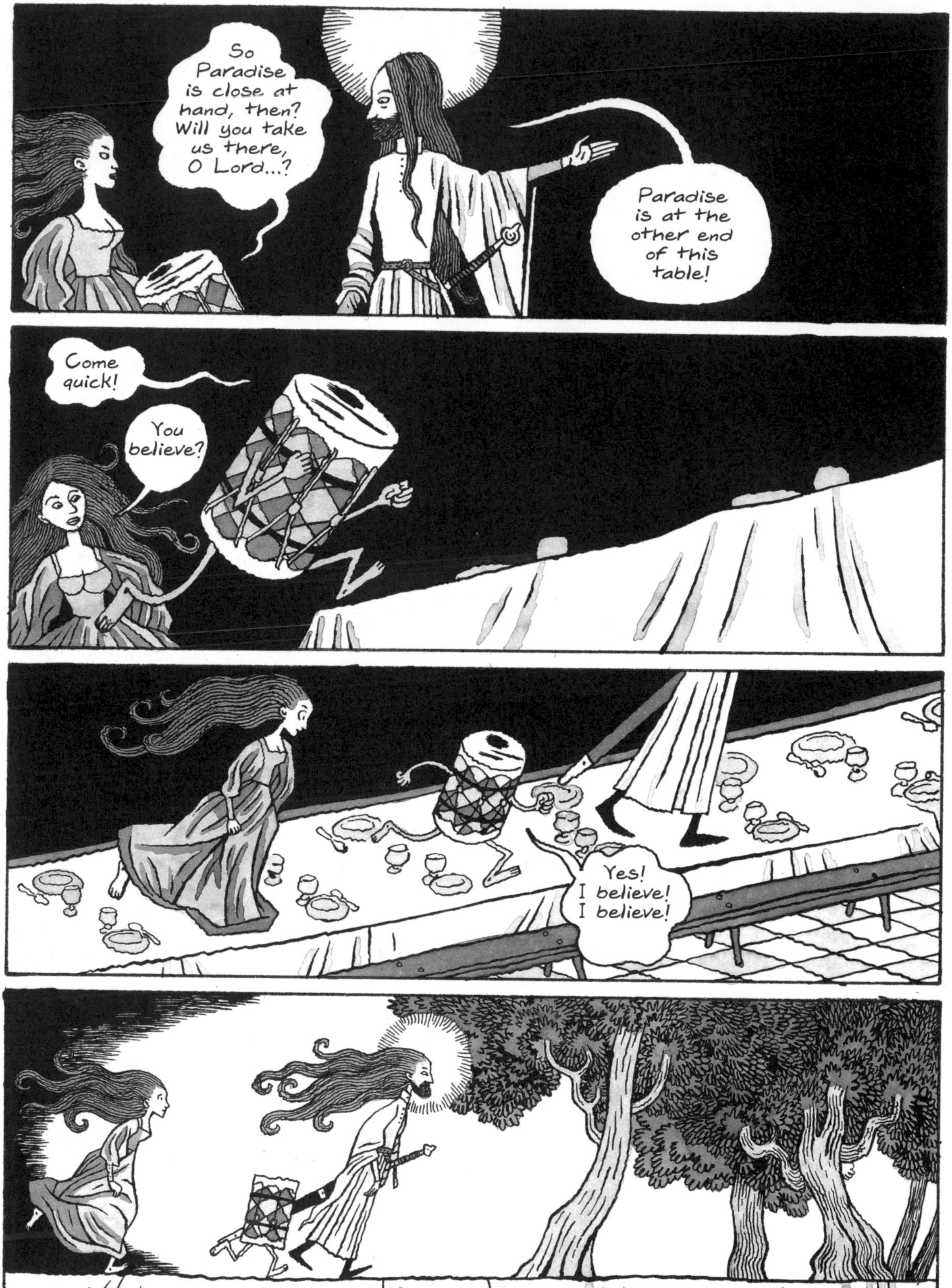
So Paradise is close at hand, then? Will you take us there, O Lord...?
Paradise is at the other end of this table!
Come quick!
You believe?
Yes! I believe! I believe!

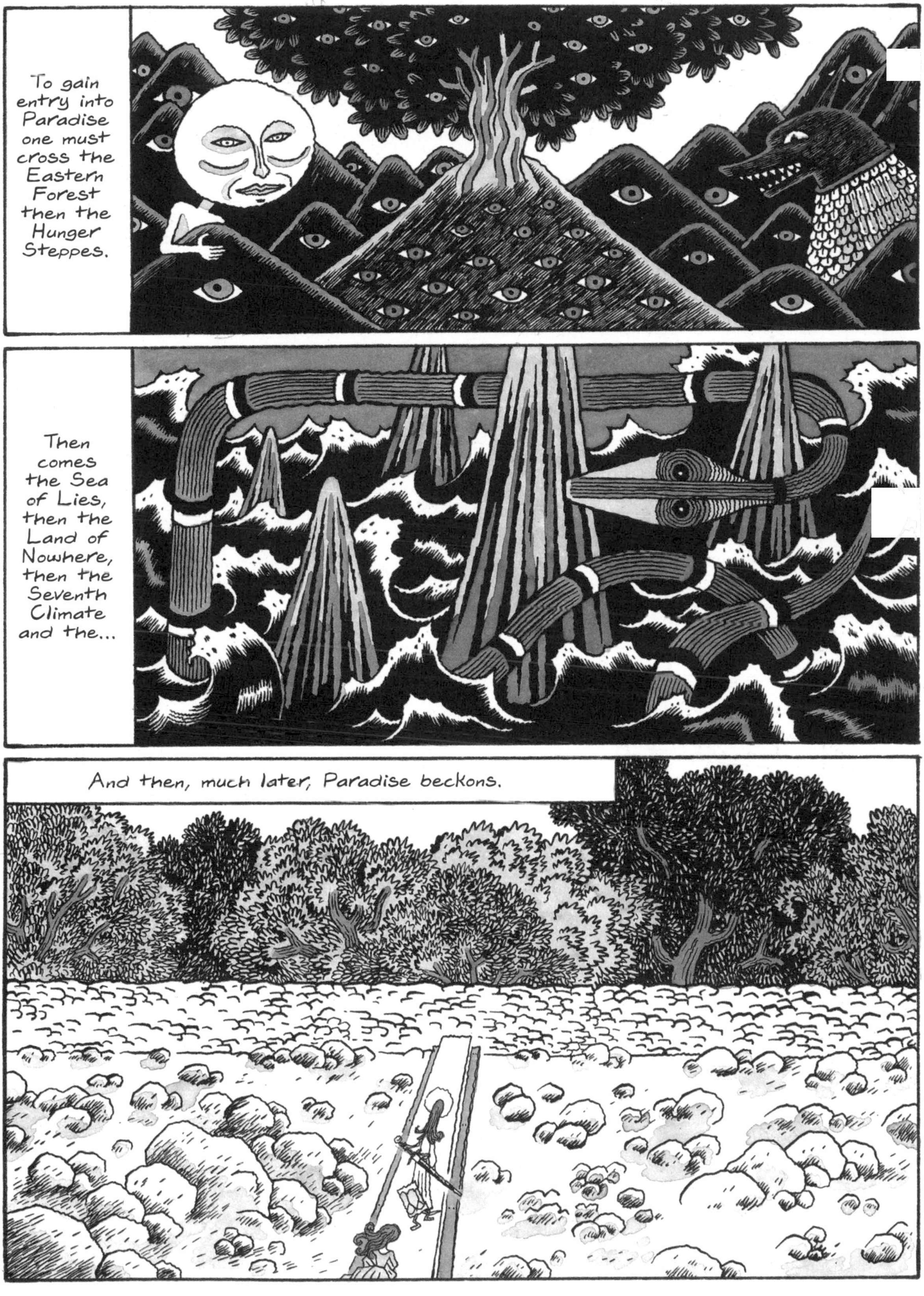
To gain entry into Paradise one must cross the Eastern Forest then the Hunger Steppes.
Then comes the Sea of Lies, then the Land of Nowhere, then the Seventh Climate and the...
And then, much later, Paradise beckons.

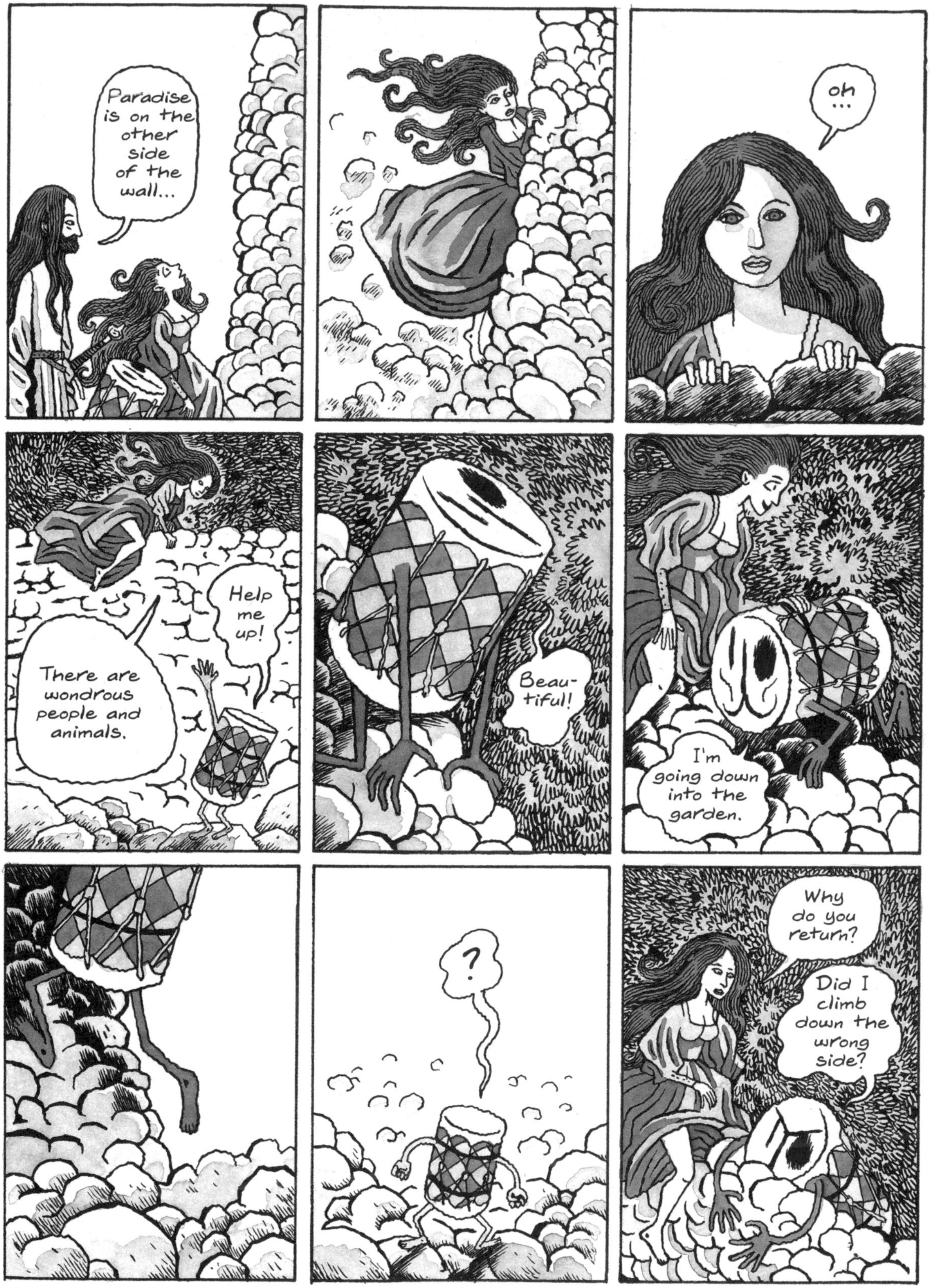
Paradise is on the other side of the wall...
oh ...
Help me up!
There are wondrous people and animals.
Beau-tiful!
I'm going down into the garden.
?
Why do you return?
Did I climb down the wrong side?

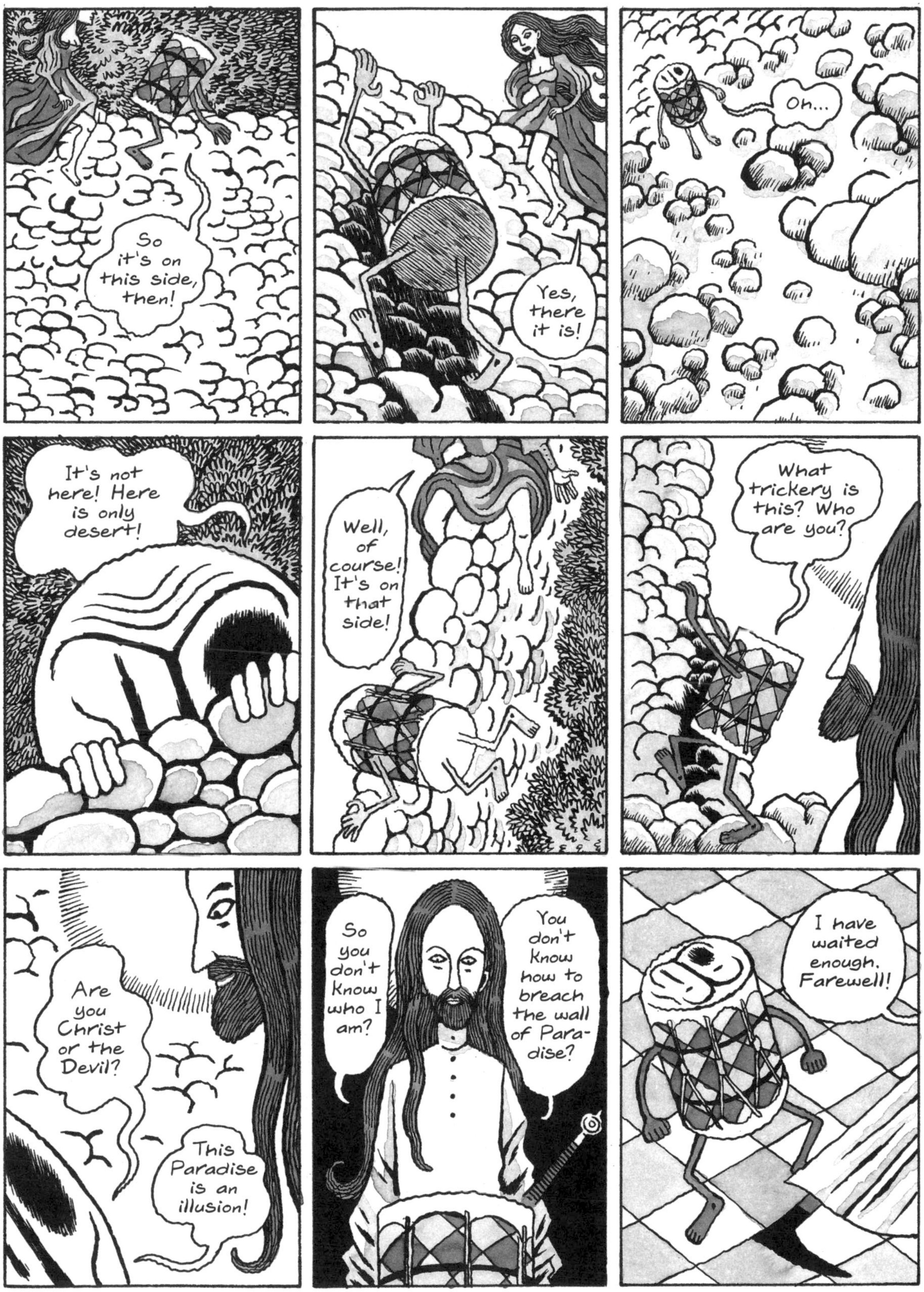
So it's on this side, then!
Yes, there it is!
Oh...
It's not here! Here is only desert!
Well, of course! It's on that side!
What trickery is this? Who are you?
Are you Christ or the Devil?
This Paradise is an illusion!
So you don't know who I am?
You don't know how to breach the wall of Paradise?
I have waited enough. Farewell!

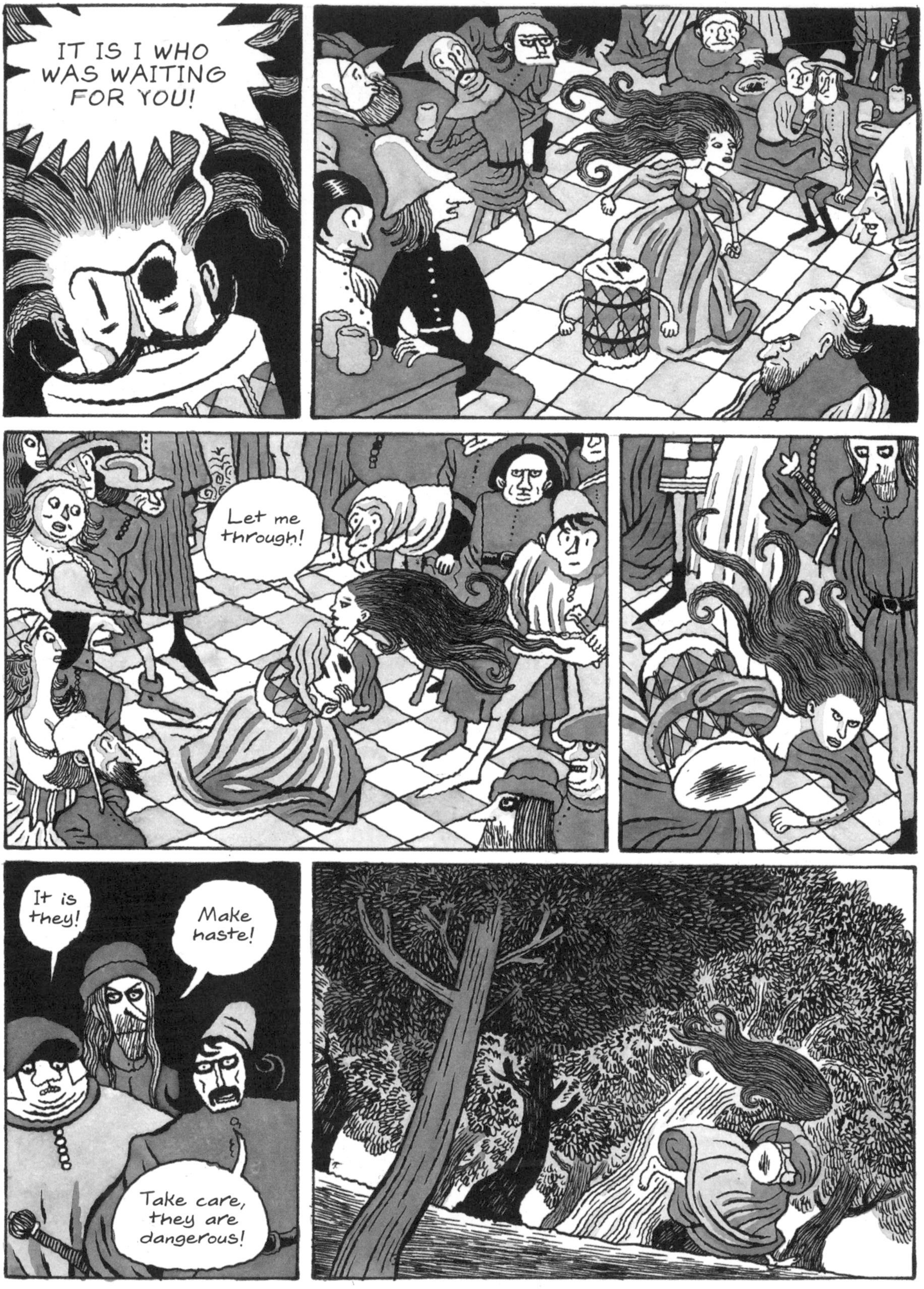
IT IS I WHO WAS WAITING FOR YOU!
Let me through!
It is they!
Make haste!
Take care, they are dangerous!

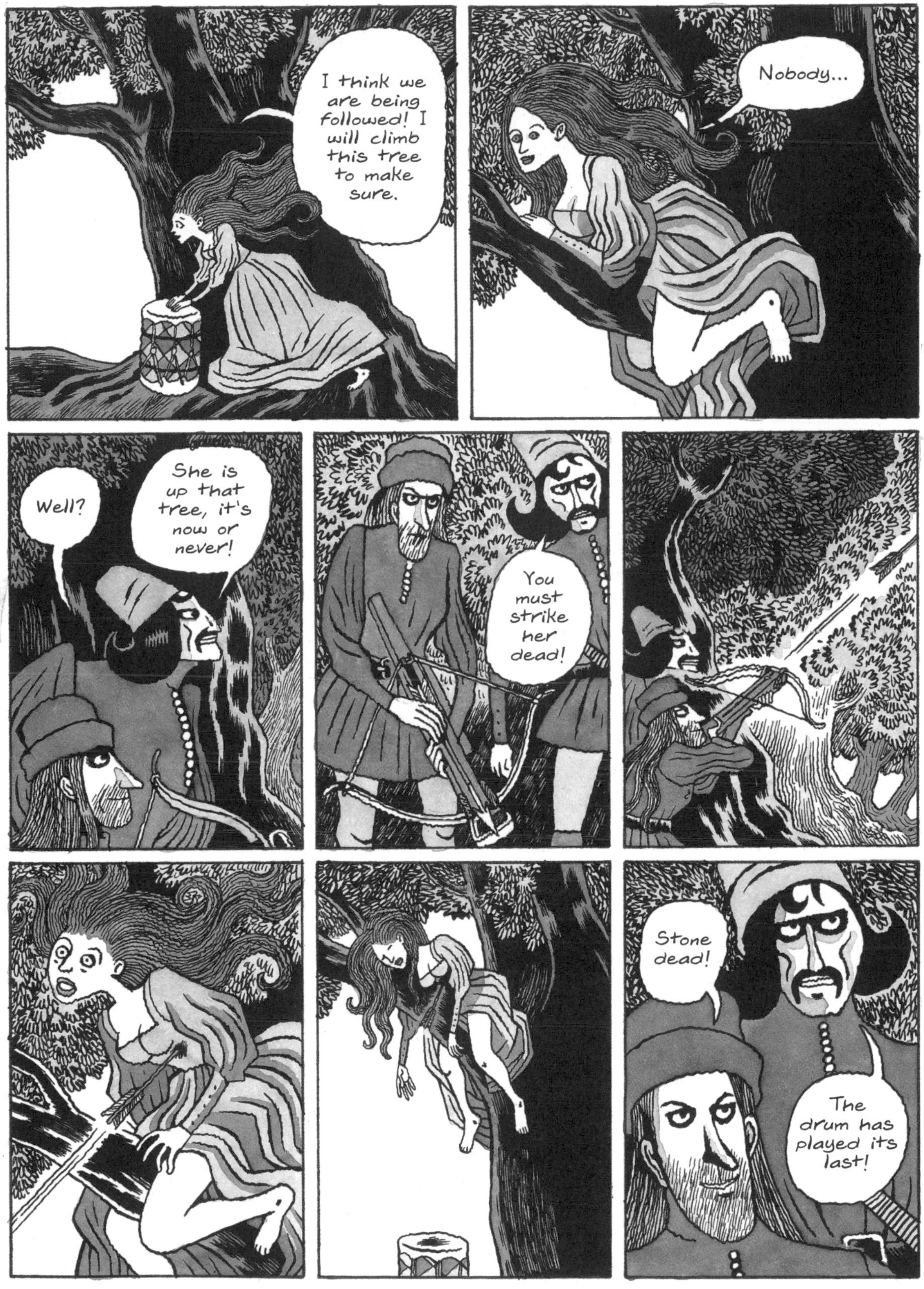
I think we are being followed! I will climb this tree to make sure.
Nobody...
Well?
She is up that tree, it's now or never!
You must strike her dead!
Stone dead!
The drum has played its last!

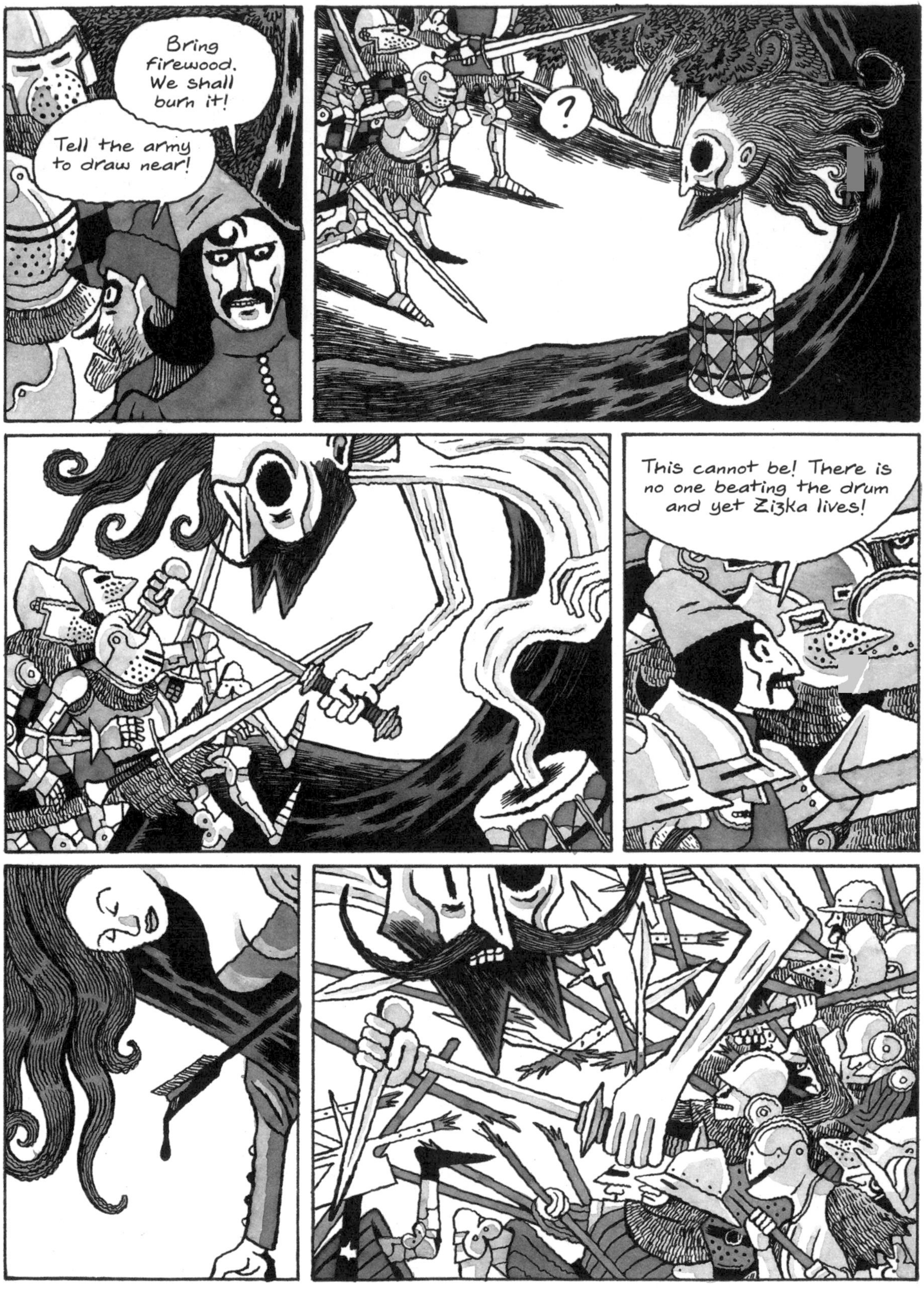

Bring firewood. We shall burn it!
Tell the army to draw near!
?
This cannot be! There is no one beating the drum and yet Zizka lives!

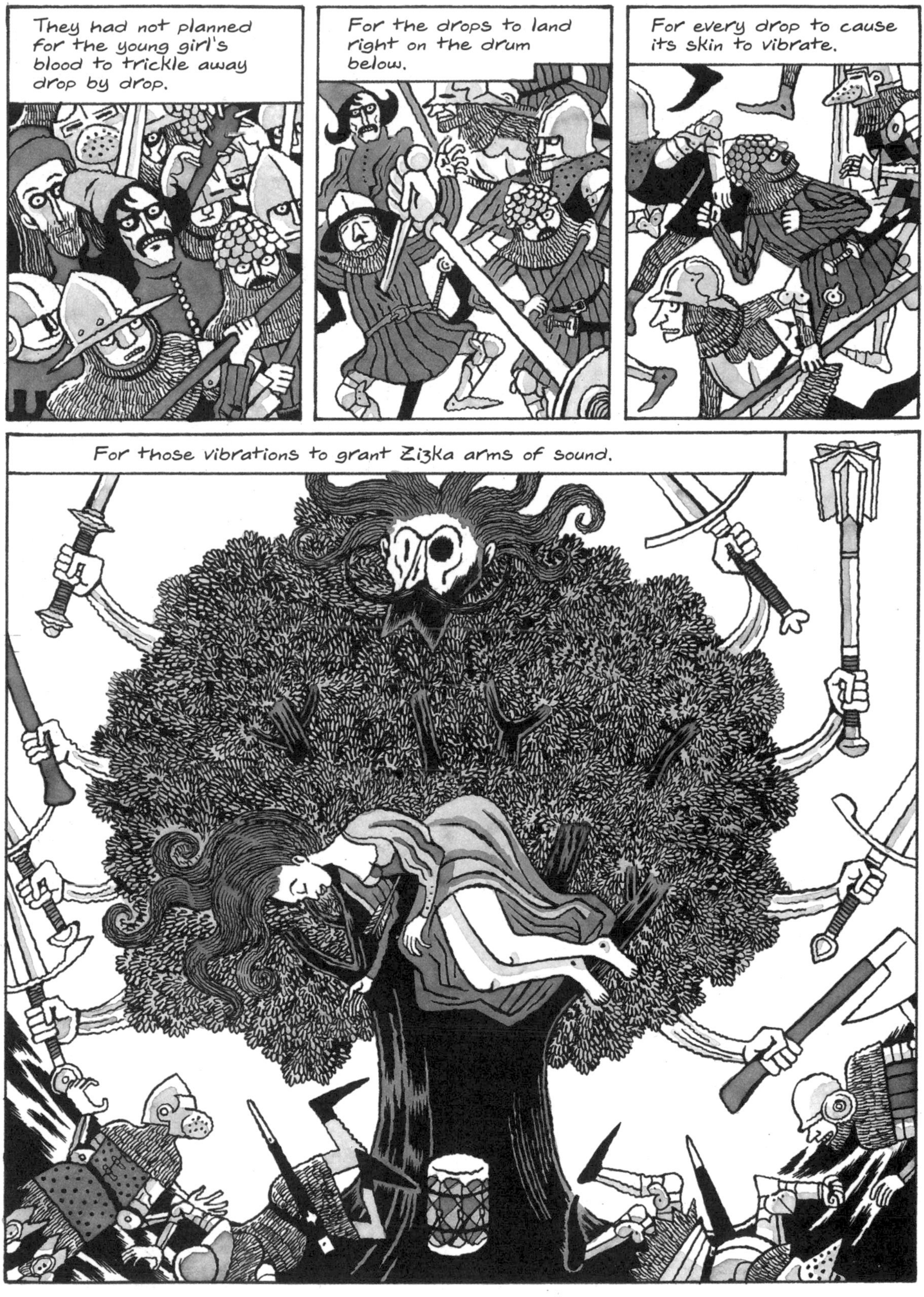
They had not planned for the young girl's blood to trickle away drop by drop.
For the drops to land right on the drum below.
For every drop to cause its skin to vibrate.
For those vibrations to grant Zizka arms of sound.

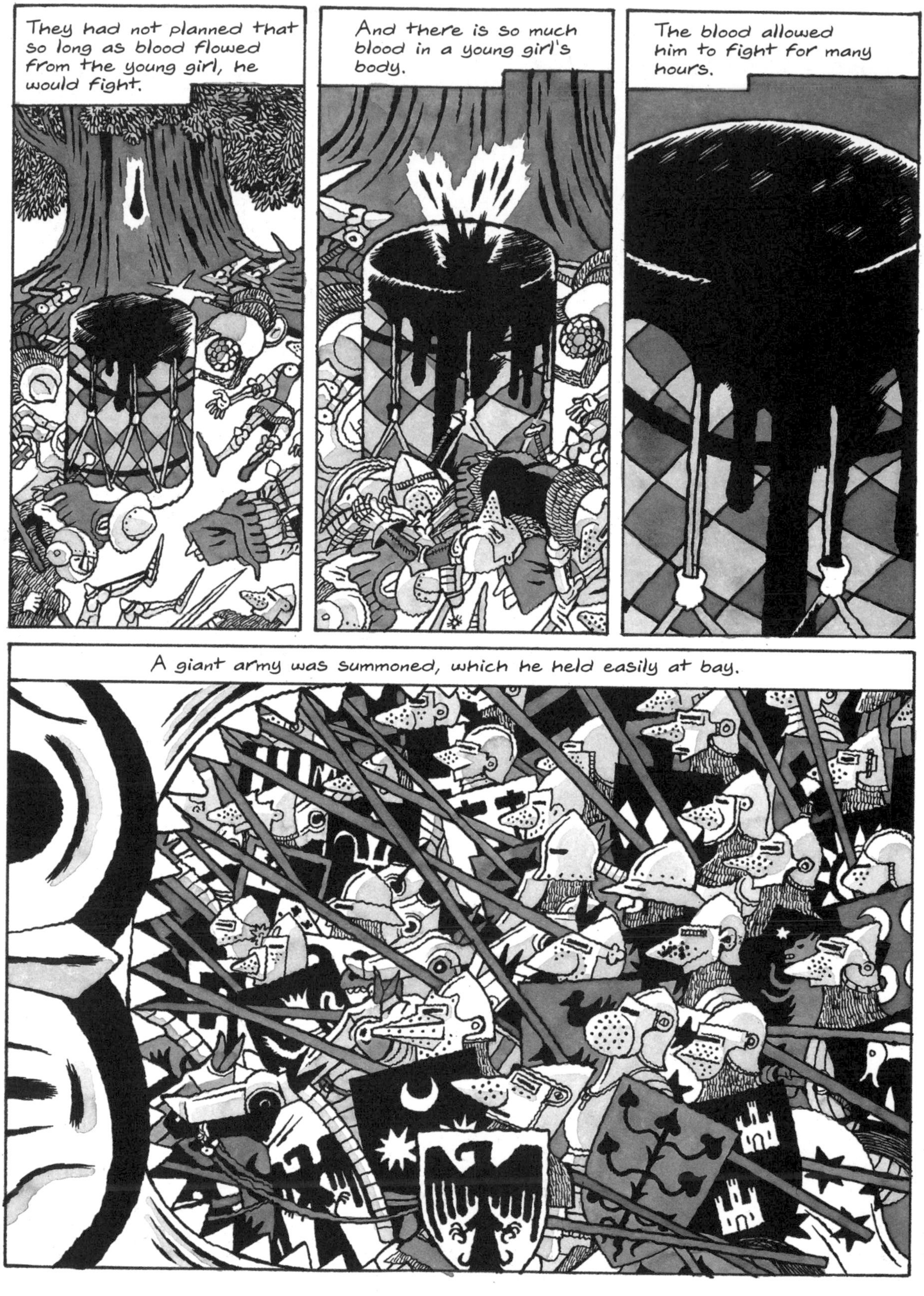
They had not planned that so long as blood flowed from the young girl, he would fight.
And there is so much blood in a young girl's body.
The blood allowed him to fight for many hours.
A giant army was summoned, which he held easily at bay.

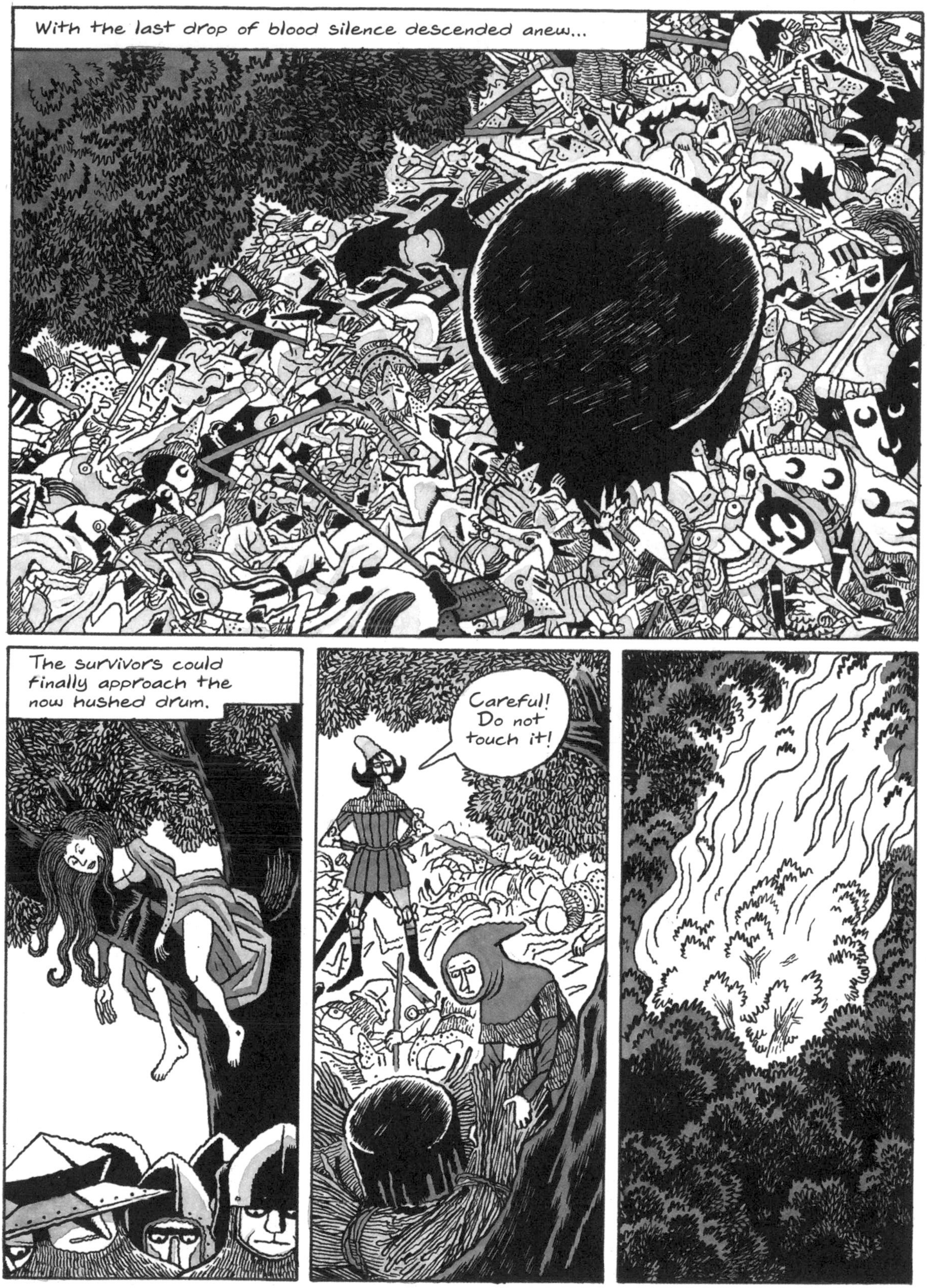
With the last drop of blood silence descended anew...
The survivors could finally approach the now hushed drum.
Careful! Do not touch it!

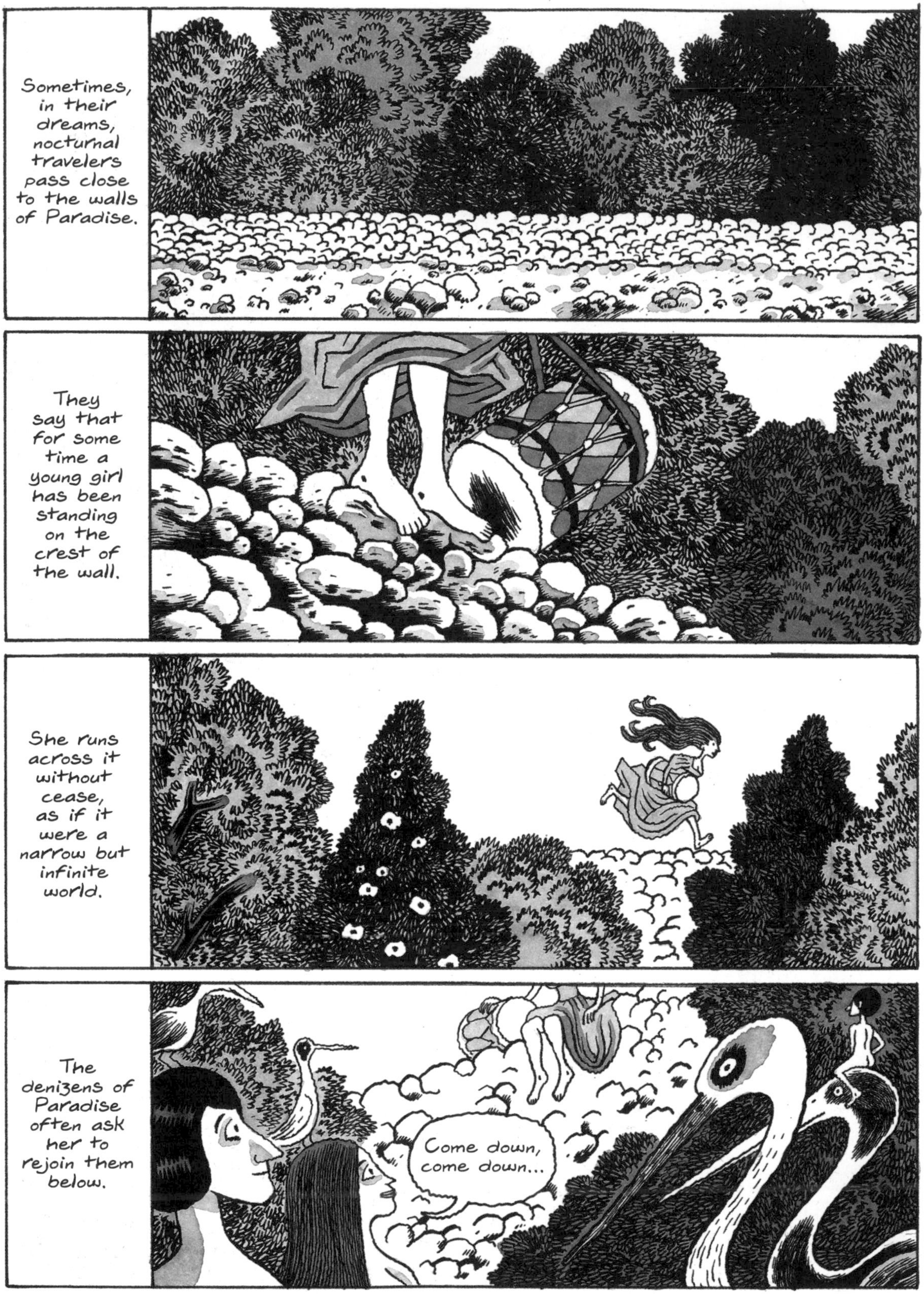
Sometimes, in their dreams, nocturnal travelers pass close to the walls of Paradise.
They say that for some time a young girl has been standing on the crest of the wall.
She runs across it without cease, as if it were a narrow but infinite world.
The denizens of Paradise often ask her to rejoin them below.
Come down, come down...

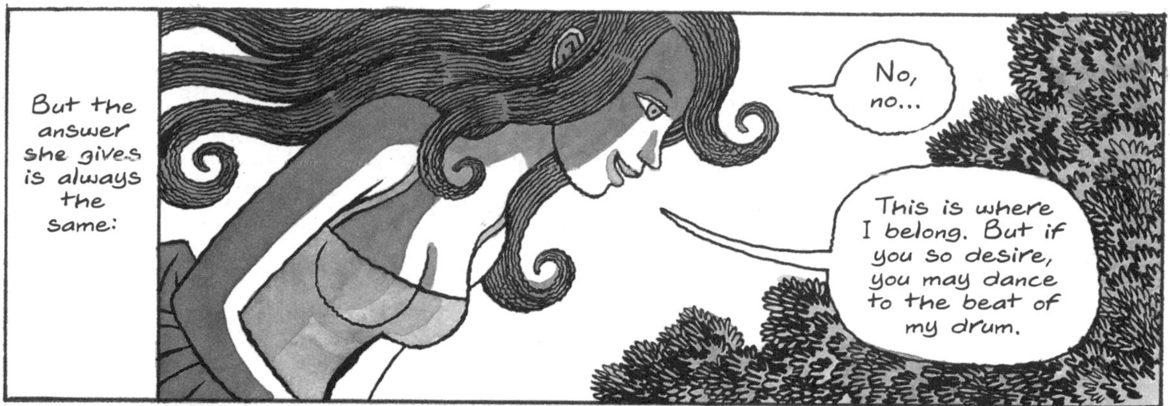
But the answer she gives is always the same:
No, no...
This is where I belong. But if you so desire, you may dance to the beat of my drum.

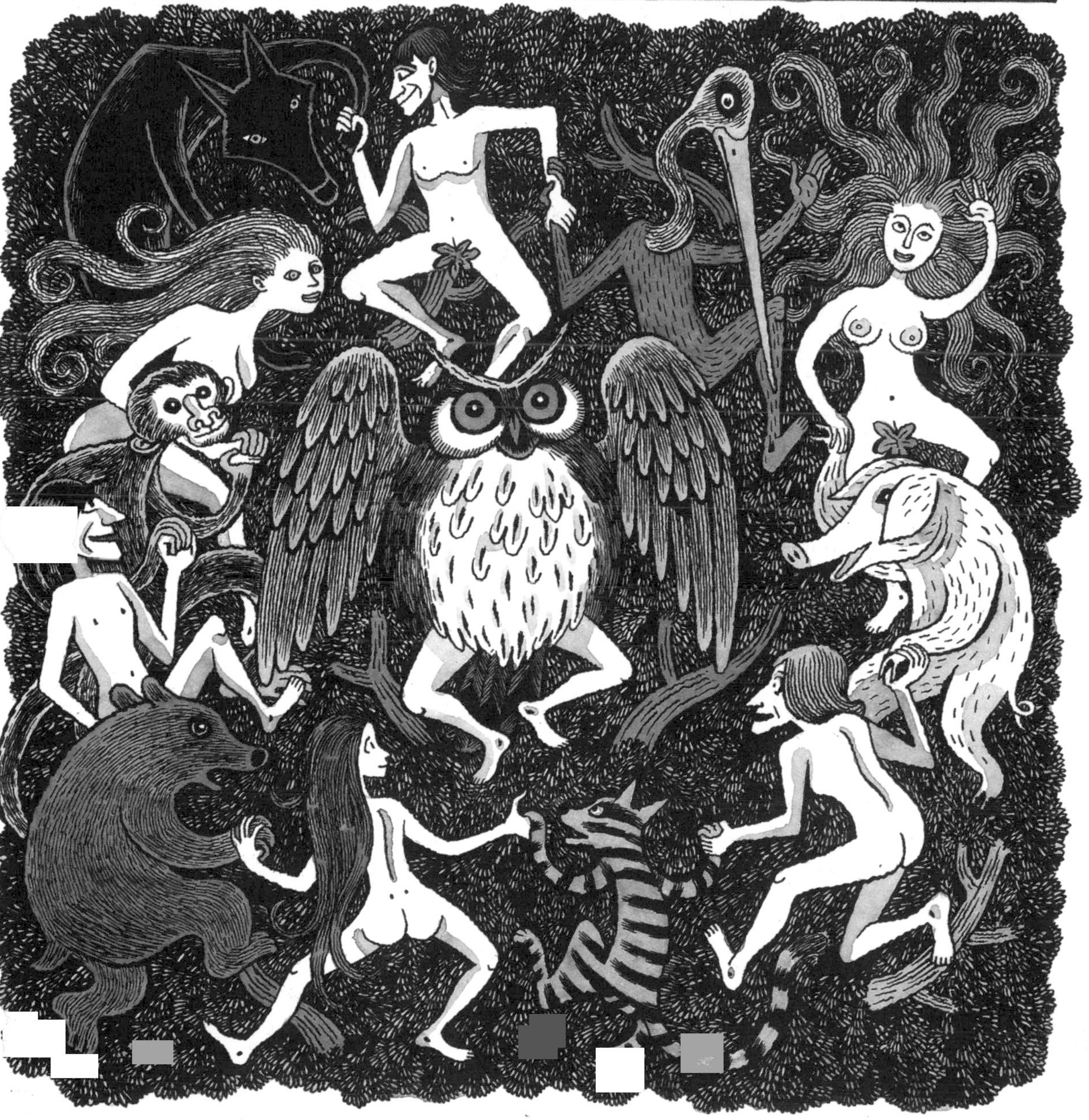

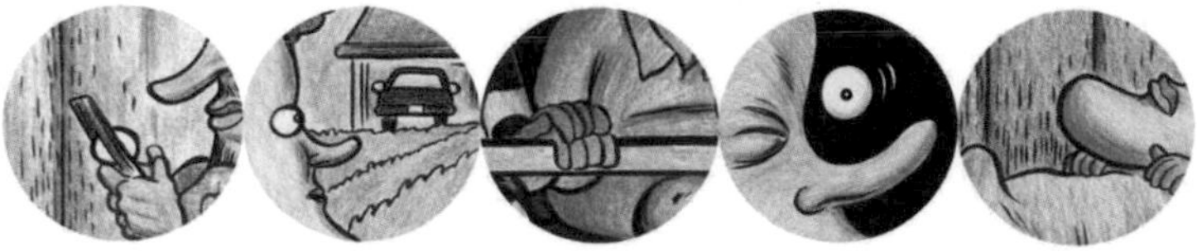

The SPOILS of the FAIR

I've lived here for a while, about four years, but there are still boxes that I've yet to unpack. This isn't an isolated fact. Since I left my parents' house in Southern Ohio, I've always managed to leave something for later, never fully giving over to wherever I'd set myself down. I moved each year and the un-unpacked boxes moved with me.

Granted, in the four years I've lived here, in the same apartment, the amount of permanently packed boxes has dwindled, but there are still two boxes left, shoved behind a door. Occasionally I note the boxes, then promptly forget them.

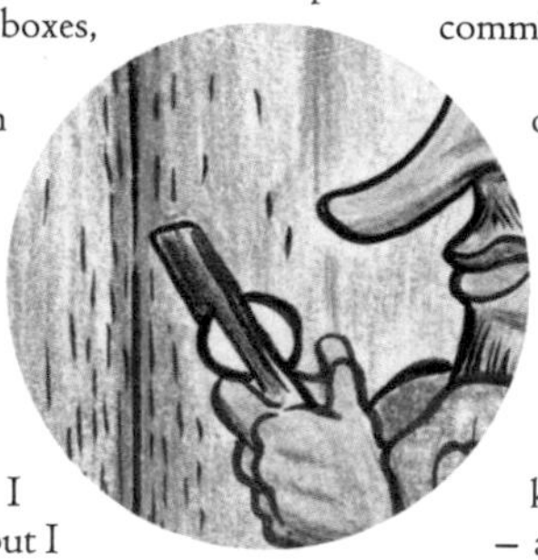

Another reality in my everyday living: I am scatterbrained. This has gotten worse over the years. When I was fifteen or sixteen I noticed my head feeling differently and I started to freely associate words and events a bit too freely for normal conversation. Also I started masturbating a lot more, but I think that was because of Christie Klein.

I usually speak with a solid point in mind, but some word will have an interesting neighbor in my head, and a new idea will take precedence. In listening to the few of my conversations recorded on well-meaning videos of family events, I feel a mix of embarrassment and gratitude that my family has yet to institutionalize me.

Still, my brain comes in handy sometimes. When I am faced with a deadline or an actual decision, television can go only so far as a distraction. But my brain houses an endless repertoire of buried to-do lists and dutifully produces obstacles to combat the looming commitment.

So, in the face of finishing an overdue manuscript, this is how I found myself on the floor, digging through a box, this past Friday evening.

The top layer of the box was filled mainly with brain-friendly items: objects of nominal significance that kept my brain on task. The task – as I'd defined it – was removing each object, staring at it blankly for a moment, then placing it in one of a growing number of piles in a semicircle around me.

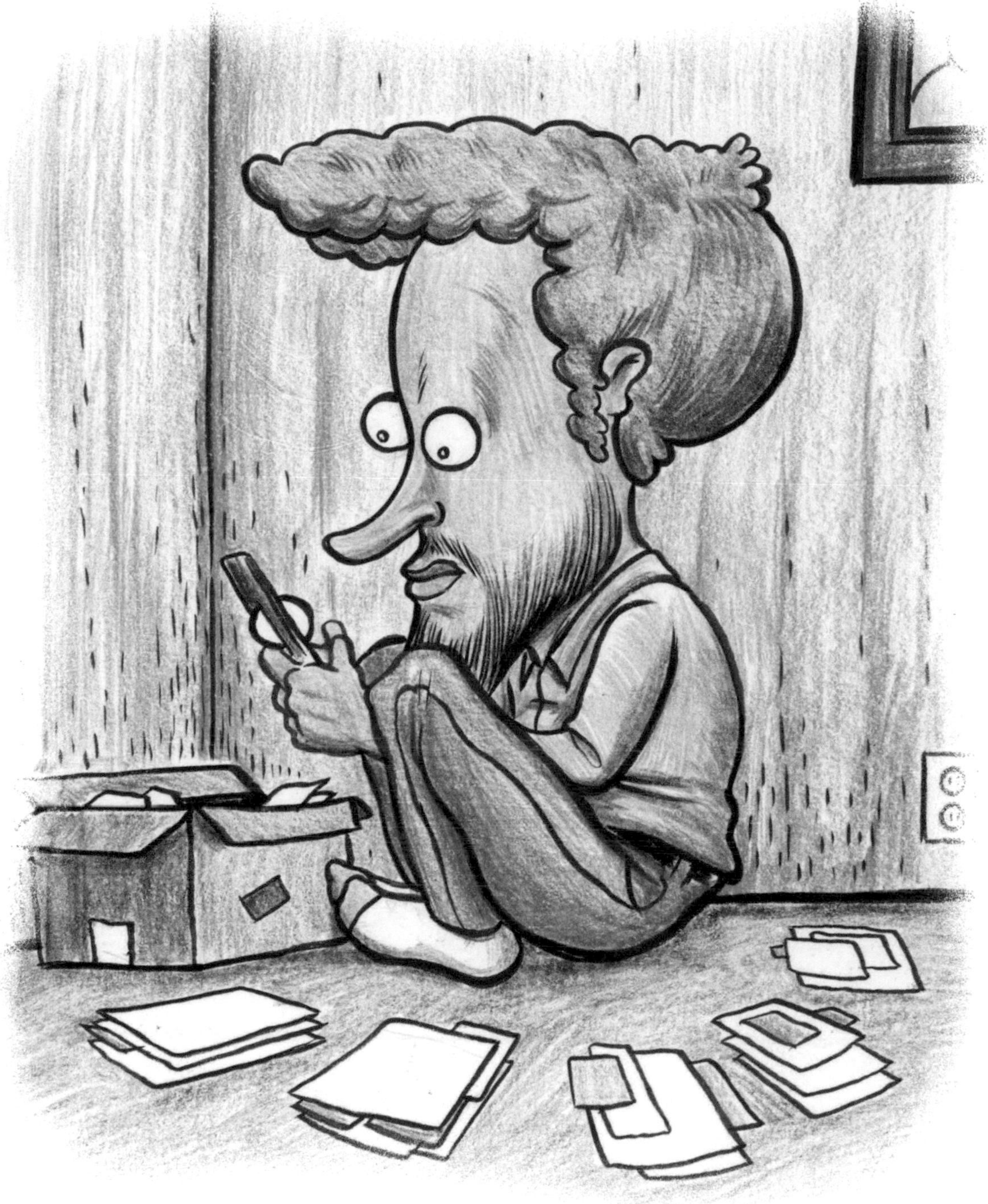

Ticket stubs and programs had their pile, scraps of paper carrying scribbled notes formed another pile. And so forth. What to do with these piles afterward was really of no concern at the time.

Then the production hit an obstacle: Christie Klein. Or, rather, a soccer ball shift knob.

The soccer ball shift knob is supposed to replace the ball atop your car's gear shift. Apparently the default ball is too painfully boring or too woefully devoid of personal expression for an appreciable section of the population. Thus, the production of the soccer ball shift knob.

The soccer ball shift knob was still in its packaging.

I held the prize and slouched, sighing a little. My brain did its work, derailed, and I was fifteen in Southern Ohio again, which is, for very understandable reasons, a really unpopular tourist destination in space-time.

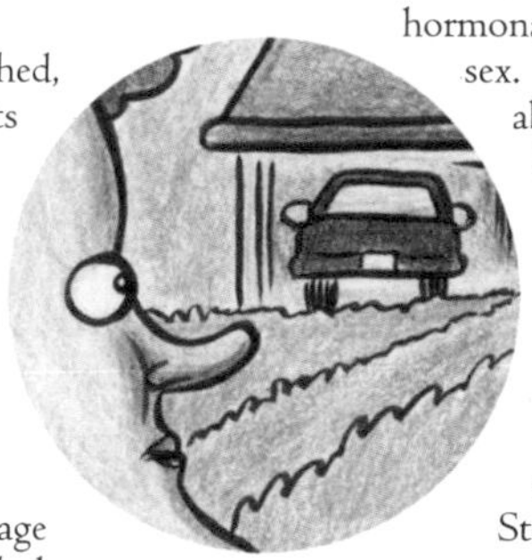

But this is when and where I knew Christie Klein.

Christie Klein was average height for a girl of fifteen, with long brunette hair, the ends all perfectly straight. She wore a melting smile and, though she had only moved to our town, Grantswood, two years earlier, she had already become one of the most popular girls in our school. She rode horses and lived with her impossibly attractive parents on hilltop farmland outside of town. Their house was new and warm, and riding my bicycle up her long, ascending driveway always punctuated her family's affluence, and my family's lack. I would drop my bike in the grass a bit before reaching the house, embarrassed to stand it next to the maroon car I knew would be hers in a few months.

Christie tanned easily and was often a gold-copper to my wilting peach. She and I could not have been more ill-suited for one another, dermatologically or otherwise, but I had asked her to the county fair, and she'd accepted. And in the few weeks between the invitation and its consummation, we became boyfriend and girlfriend, much to the under-the-breath disgust of the high school hierarchy.

I had kissed a girl at that point, but only one, and even that was during a bonfire-side game of spin-the-bottle. I was Catholic, and scared, and brimming with lust. Christie Klein wore satin panties. And she only went to church at Christmas.

Though her parents weren't often home, and even though, in the short period of time before the fair, we had ample opportunity and hormonal motive to do so, we did not have sex. We never got past awkwardly aborted nudity and nervous darts beneath underwear.

On the day we were to attend the fair, Christie arrived at my house wearing a black and white sweater and her hair down. The sweater had an "A" in the upper right hand corner, and a "Z" in the lower left. Standing before her, our sexless sexual history was simultaneously omnipresent and completely erased. I was nervous to the point of nausea. She was effortlessly awe-inspiring in the way only a fifteen year-old girl can be to a fifteen year-old boy.

Christie meeting me at my house was only for the sake of formality. She and her mother were essentially living at the fair in a trailer near the horse barns. Going to the fair with me, for her, was the equivalent of going to her living room, only with brighter lights and blaring big hair heavy metal.

In the perfection of the Midwest autumn, the air around us and leaves beneath us were crisp and definite. Our hands pressed together, forming a pocket of warmth, as we

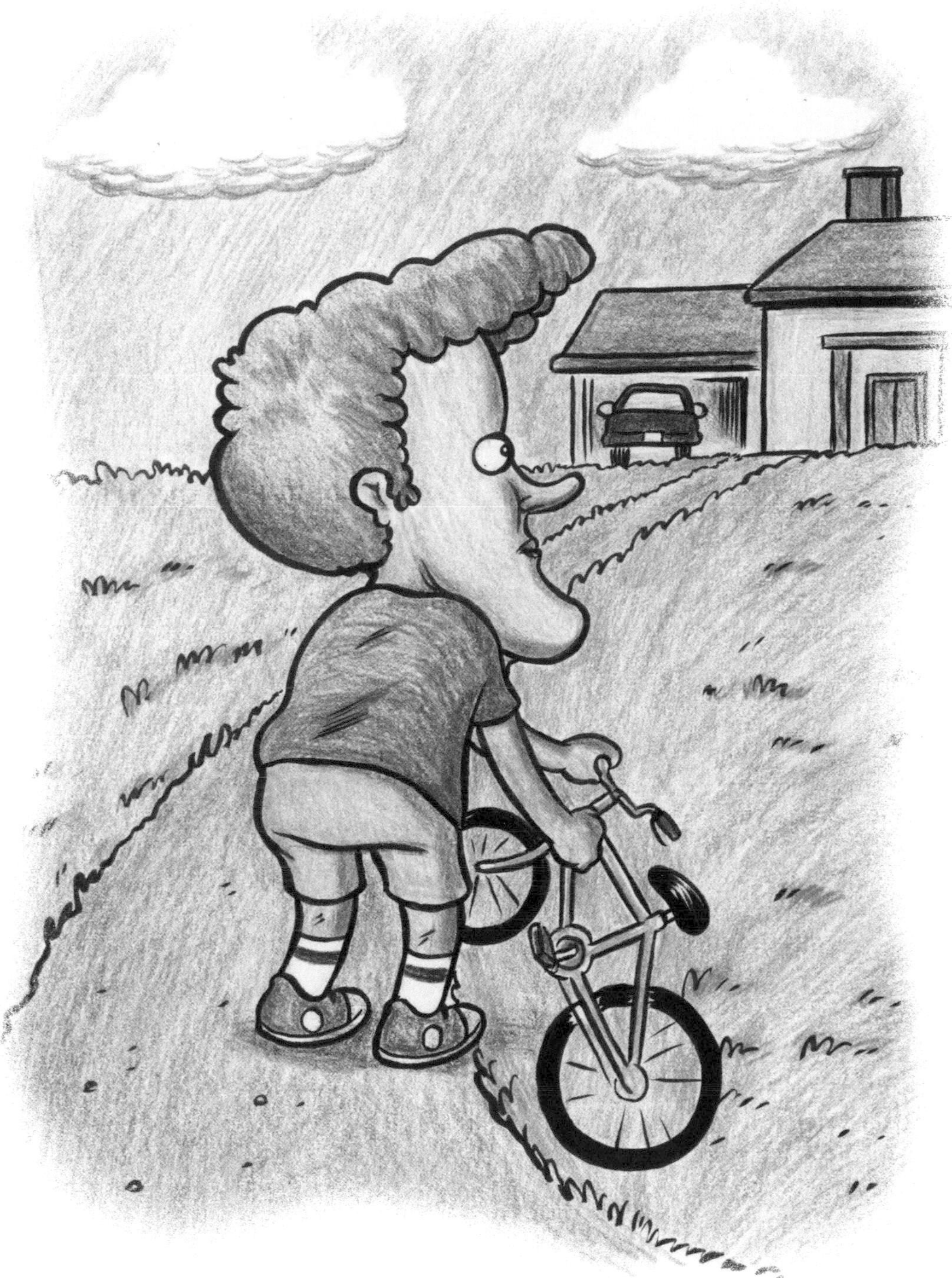

went about all the requisite activities. Caramel apples. Perusing the pig barn. Perusing the rabbit barn. Def Leppard serenades on "the Gravitron." Attempting to win something for her at the machine gun game. Attempting to win something for her at the water gun game. Attempting to win something for her at ski ball. Settling instead for miniature golf, where there were no prizes, just little holes and windmills. And later, some pizza.

Finally there was the Ferris wheel. The Ferris wheel was the only ride of romance at the fair, and was populated by only two species: little girls with their fathers and young, sexually frustrated couples like us.

We didn't talk much on the Ferris wheel. Her hand was on top of mine, mine on top of the cold metal bar in front of us. Eventually the ride slowed and began letting the current round of riders off. We had just missed being the first car unloaded and thus had the longest stint in the circular start-stop of disembarking.

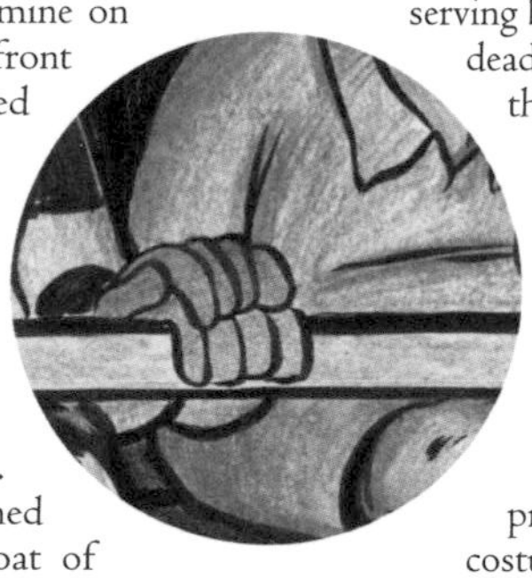

At the wheel's apex everything was slow and silent. The light of the fairgrounds pushed dully against the pure black coat of the country night, and we seemed to hang up there longer than one would expect. Christie's shoulder was warm against me. She looked at me out of the corner of her eye, then turned and kissed my cheek. It was the only thing beyond handholding we'd done that night, and all the more significant for it. Eventually, the wheel lurched, we began our descent, and after walking her back to her trailer by the horse barns, we said goodnight.

I'm sure I didn't sleep well that night. Though I was boiling with the compulsion, I couldn't even masturbate, for fear it would somehow have bruised this new feeling. I fell asleep face down in the pillow, vocalizing two-person dialogue fantasies. Me and Christie. Me and my jealous friends. Me and God. Christie and her friends. Me and me.

The entire week of the fair we had no school, and so I spent the next day lounging around the house, eating cake my mother had purchased at one of the baked goods auctions, and trying to keep my chest and head from exploding, and my hand from masturbating. Eventually I was given the relief of serving pork tenderloins.

My mother, a municipal judge, was constantly campaigning and volunteering. The county fair was a goldmine of potential voters, and my sisters and I were smiling, animated trophies of her accomplishments as a mother. So this was how I got into the pork tenderloin serving business, which was fine by me, as dead pig and elderly farmers truly are the perfect antidotes for a rampant hard-on.

That evening Christie had to show horses. I could talk with her briefly before and after one of her events, but there was considerable dead time between, when she and her mother needed to prepare the horses and Christie's costumes. So chiefly I busied myself with attempting to right the failures of the night before: I set about trying to win Christie a prize.

Nearly at the end of my admittedly meager fifteen year-old's finances, fortune made peace with me at ski-ball. The police car lights above my alley whipped to life and sirens went off. I was puffing with pride and could feel confidence and adrenalin rushing out from my chest to my limbs. But I had to choose quickly! The barker-changemaster pointed to my area of selection. I had the choice between a stuffed diamond back rattlesnake and a soccer ball shift knob.

So I reasoned this way:

No girls I knew, Christie included, were

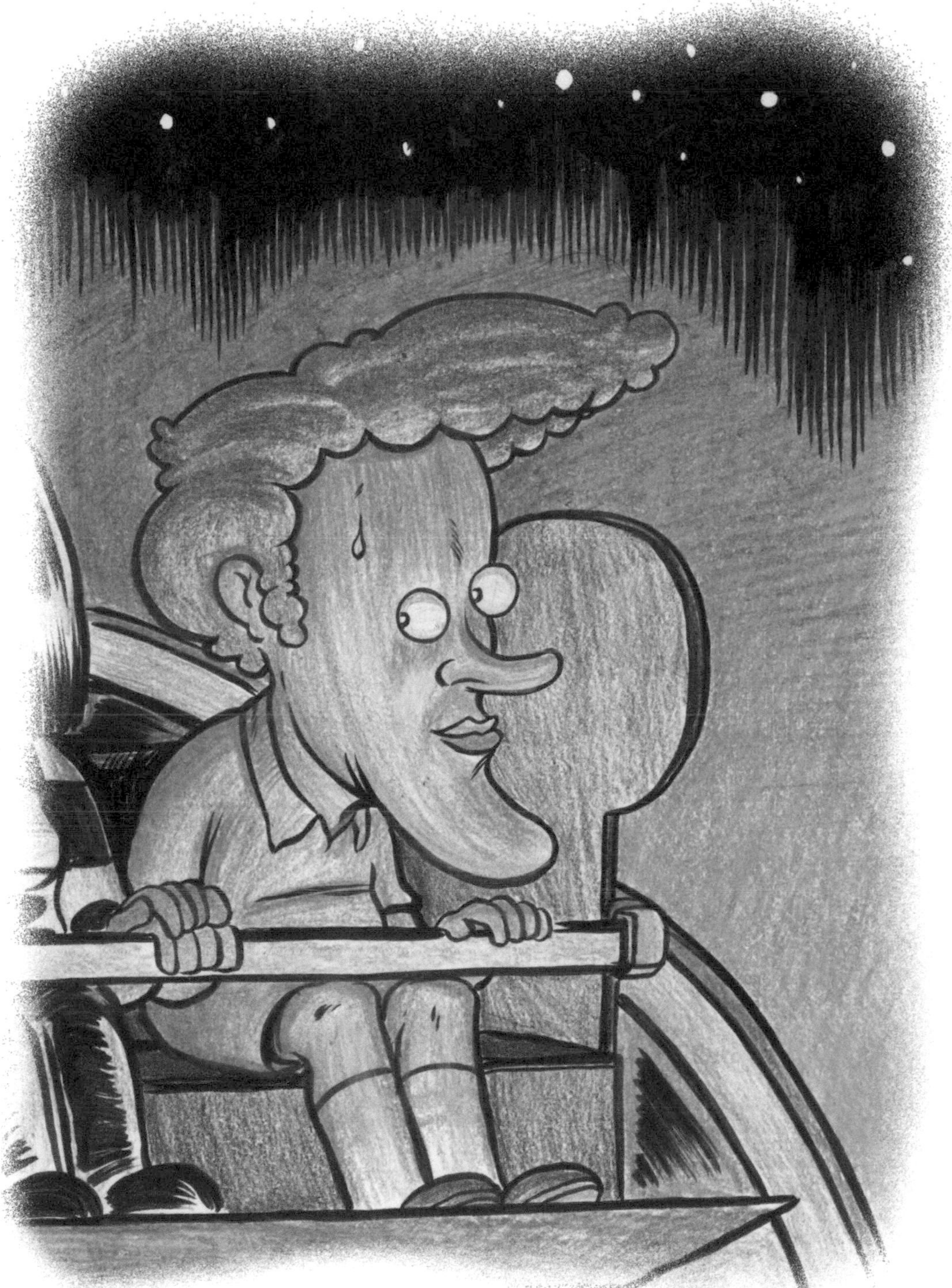

fans of snakes in general, stuffed or otherwise, which made the already appealing soccer ball shift knob all the more clear as the correct choice. Christie would soon be getting her license and her promised car was a stick shift. The soccer tie-in seemed obvious and decently romantic, as we had kissed once, two weeks prior, on the soccer field behind our school building.

(Again, I was at the beginning of a mental shift to being scatterbrained, or, as I was diagnosed some ten years after that fair, hypomanic, so somehow all this made complete sense. It did not occur to me for even an instant that these connections I was making would not occur immediately (perhaps ever) to a single other person on the face of the planet. It did not occur to me that this horrible, cheap piece of plastic and metal appeared dirty and shoddily painted (and perhaps even used?), all before being removed from its generic packaging. Or at least those things did not occur to me at that moment.)

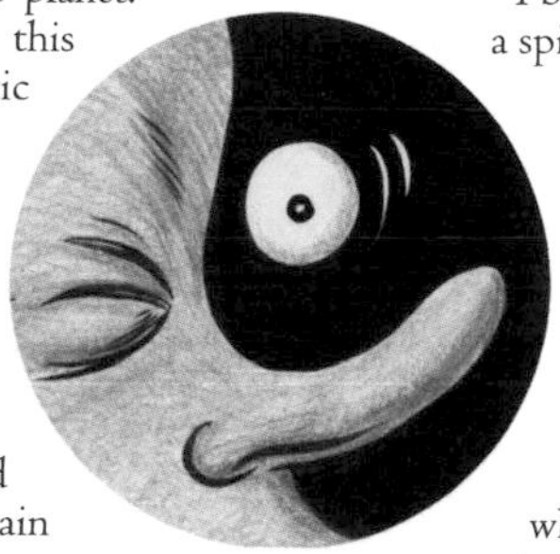

I took up my prize and walked, convinced, toward the main gates of the fairgrounds.

On my way out, I noticed my friend, Jesse, and another boy, Harmon, involved in some low-grade dispute. Harmon was horribly obese and was perpetually ridiculed for this. This constant mockery – in concert with what I had learned peripherally was a poor home life – had crafted a rather nasty disposition. That is to say: Harmon was sort of an asshole. But I made it a point to leave him alone as I myself had been bullied on and off a few years earlier, and felt a sort of camaraderie with him and other outcasts.

But still:

I was fifteen and cocksure and nobody had beaten me up in years. And I had just won a prize for my girlfriend. And this guy was messing with my friend. So I walked into the situation.

"Why don't you fuck off, man boobs?!" I said.

Harmon was visibly wounded and surprised, as he'd never heard anything remotely like that from me. I can't say I was even sorry in the moment, I was just that filled with acidic teenage juices. Harmon muttered some malformed comeback and sulked off. I exchanged high fives with Jesse and continued toward the gate.

"Hey!"

I barely noticed it at first, it was just a spike in the noise field of the fair.

"Hey!"

I assumed this wasn't directed at me, not being followed by my name or some mutated version thereof. Horshmeer. Hornch. Pauly. Paula.

"Hey!"

I finally turned to see who was shouting. This was a mistake. A thick-necked boy and his identical twin moved toward me, followed by a beanstalk with a goatee. The thick-neck continued the lead with his slurring twang.

"Hey, why're you messin' with that big kid?" It was immediately clear these three didn't know Harmon or Harmon's name.

"He was shoving my friend," I responded. I hoped this would appease them.

"He wuhddn' doin' nuthin'. He was just foolin' around."

Nope. No dice. This guy just wanted to fight. God had put him on this earth to kick some ass.

"Well... he was..." I stammered. I didn't know where to go with this, so I figured I'd just go, "I'm just leaving, so..." I turned and started

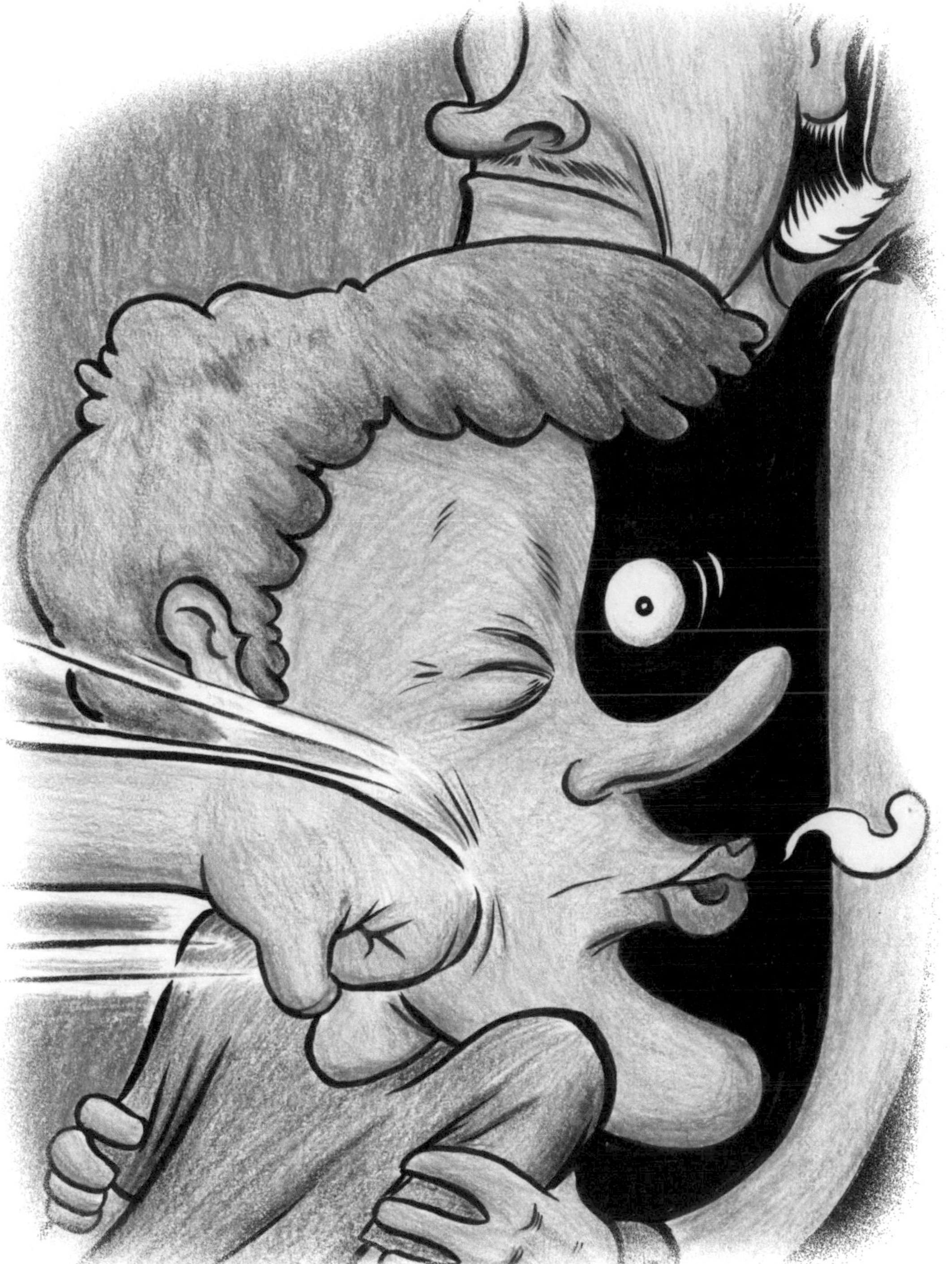

to walk away.

A pair of hands grabbed me and whirled me around. It was the beanstalk. He held my arms to my side.

The thick-necked talker was working himself into a frenzy. "You wanna push somebody around? Huh? You wanna push somebody around?"

Great. Now we'd gotten to saying things twice.

He was shifting his weight back and forth from one foot to another. "Maybe you wanna push me around? Huh? You wanna push me around?"

There were easily a hundred people watching at this point. A friend told me the next day he'd seen the whole thing hanging upside down in a nearby ride called "the Orbiter."

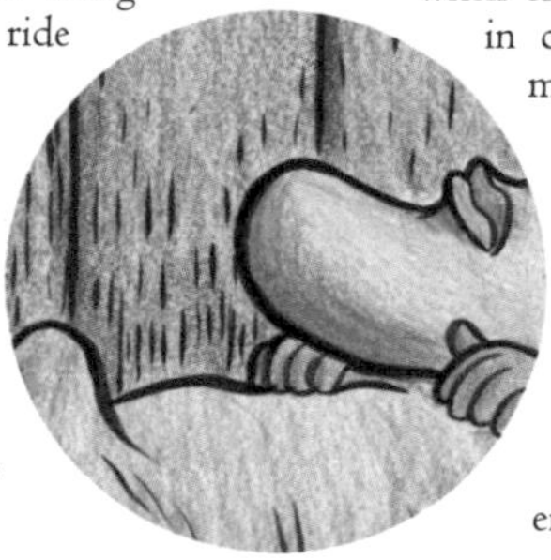

I think I might have responded with something along the lines of no, really, I didn't want to push anyone around, but those sort of details didn't really matter. No, he was going to pummel me. I was going to be pummeled. We were locked in the inevitable.

To the thick-neck's credit, he was a very skilled boxer. There was his hand next to his body, and then there was my head snapping back, again and again, with the beanstalk as a vice grip around me. There was only the occasional blur of his fist traveling, otherwise it was a well-executed, painful magic trick. He was just that good.

Of course, that glowing evaluation of his pugilism came only afterward, as a way of masking the fact that it hurt, my lip was bloodied, and I was humiliated violently in front of more people than were in my entire graduating class. The thick-neck's girlfriend eventually pulled him away from me, screaming the fairly obvious fact that perhaps I didn't want to fight after all. I took the lull in action as my cue, turned, and shuffled out the gates.

During the short walk home, I wiped the blood off, and on entering our kitchen said an abbreviated hello to my parents, keeping my head down. I went to my room and got in bed. I never told my parents what happened. I knew no one could fully understand. I had been sure of myself and been punished for it. This is the joy of being reared Catholic.

In my twin bed, in that late Southern Ohio September, I thought of Christie.

I still think of her from time to time.

I remained infatuated with her long after she moved to Pennsylvania, the summer before our senior year. I visited her a few times: later, when she attended a college near mine in central Ohio. After college, she moved to Cincinnati, not far from my hometown, and became a real estate agent.

We've exchanged a few e-mail updates, but there is ultimately no real point to this. We don't resemble those fifteen year-olds. We were ill-fitted then; now she occupies an entirely different genus.

I'm not even sure if she still rides horses. But I know I never gave her the shift knob.

And sitting here, in my current apartment, holding that cheap thing never given to its intended recipient, part of me wanted to throw it out, part of me wanted to call Christie. I have a trashcan and her phone number, I could have done either.

But then, faced with a real decision, my mind did its job, flipped a silent switch, and I turned to something else, throwing my careful semicircle of piles back into the box, moving the door back into place as I left the room.

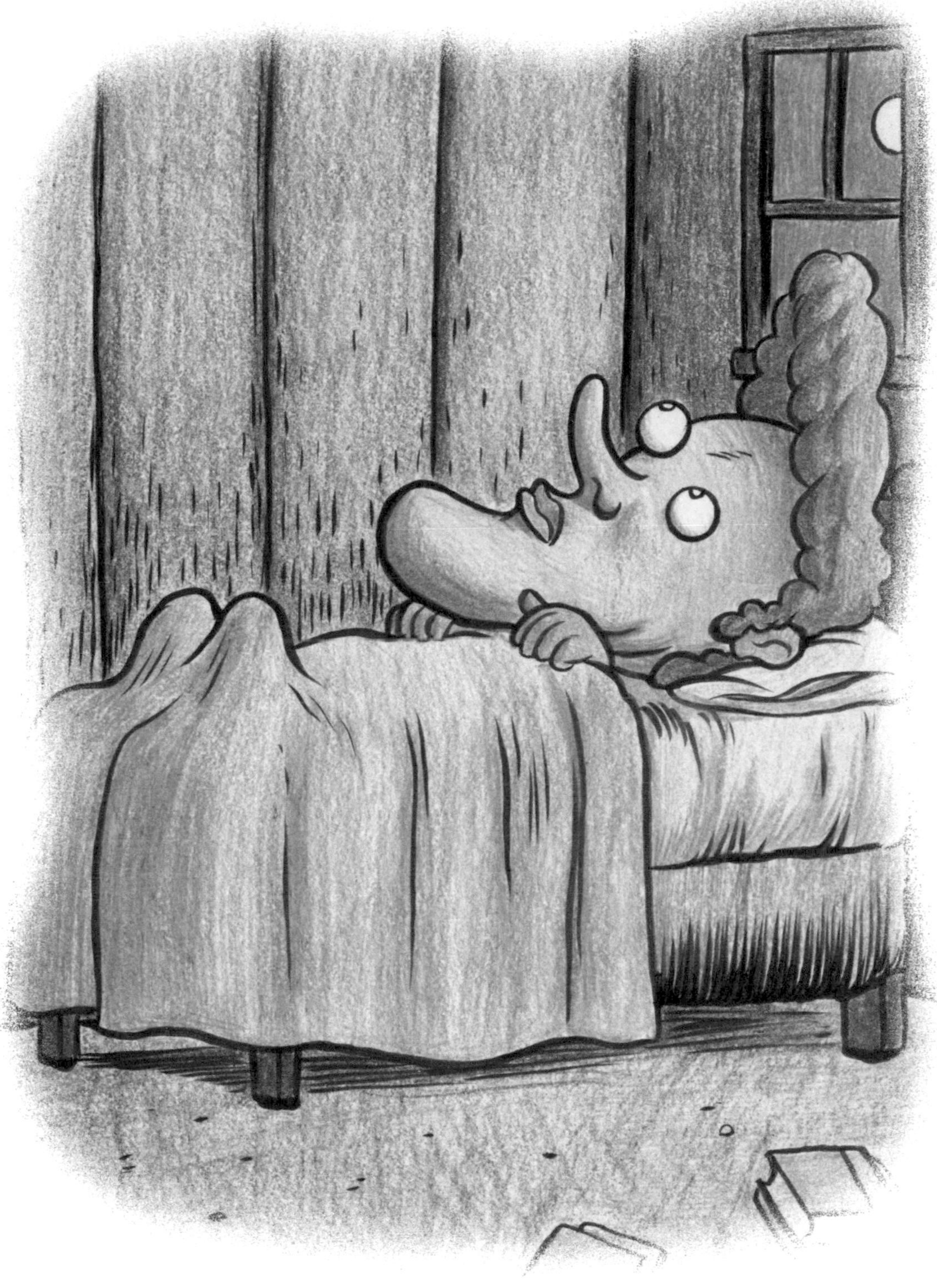

more MOME

$14.95 ea. Available in bookstores or at Fantagraphics.com.

NOW AVAILABLE!

MOME VOL. 1-10 MEGA-BUNDLE

Get the first ten volumes of MOME for one low price of $99.99 (retail value: $150) at www.fantagraphics.com.

MOME SUMMER 2005 (VOL. 1)

The debut issue, featuring Gabrielle Bell, Kurt Wolfgang, Martin Cendreda, Jeffrey Brown, Paul Hornschemeier, John Pham, David Heatley, Anders Nilsen, Jonathan Bennett, Sophie Crumb and Andrice Arp. Includes an interview with Paul Hornschemeier and covers by Gabrielle Bell.

MOME FALL 2005 (VOL. 2)

Tim Hensley makes his MOME debut. Also included: Nilsen, Bennett, Wolfgang, Cendreda, Hornschemeier, Crumb, Bell, Heatley, Pham, Brown and Arp. Plus: A Gabrielle Bell interview and covers by Jonathan Bennett.

MOME WINTER 2006 (VOL. 3)

Featuring Cendreda, Nilsen, Bennett, Heatley, Arp, Bell and Brown. Plus an interview with Kurt Wolfgang, as well as the debuts of David B. (contributing the 36-page "Armed Garden") and R. Kikuo Johnson. Covers by David B.

MOME SPRING/SUMMER 2006 (VOL. 4)

Featuring Heatley, Nilsen, Crumb, Cendreda, Bennett, Hornschemeier, Bell and Brown. Includes an interview with Jonathan Bennett, David B.'s 33-page "The Veiled Prophet," and R. Kikuo Johnson's "John James Audubon." Covers by John Pham.

MOME FALL 2006 (VOL. 5)

Featuring Arp, Nilsen, Crumb, Brown, Hornschemeier, Bell and Wolfgang. Hensley returns with his first "Wally Gropius" strips, Andrice Arp is interviewed, and Zak Sally and Robert Goodin make their MOME debuts. Covers by Tim Hensley.

MOME WINTER 2007 (VOL. 6)

Featuring Johnson, Hensley, Cendreda, Nilsen, Heatley, Brown, Hornschemeier, Crumb, Bennett, Bell and Wolfgang. Tim Hensley is interviewed, while French cartoonists Émile Bravo and Lewis Trondheim make their first appearances. Covers by Martin Cendreda.

MOME SPRING 2007 (VOL. 7)

Featuring the MOME debuts of Al Columbia, Eleanor Davis, and Tom Kaczynski, as well as returning artists Heatley, Hornschemeier, Bell, Crumb, Wolfgang, Trondheim, Arp, and Nilsen. Anders Nilsen is interviewed, under covers by Lewis Trondheim.

MOME SUMMER 2007 (VOL. 8)

Featuring the MOME debuts of Ray Fenwick and Joe Kimball, and sophomore stories by Kaczynski, Davis (who is cover-featured and interviewed), Columbia, and Émile Bravo, whose "Young Americans" in this issue is a 2008 Eisner Award Nominee for "Best Short Story." Plus regulars Crumb, Bennett, Hornschemeier, and the final chapter of Trondheim's "At Loose Ends," also nominated for said Eisner Award.

MOME FALL 2007 (VOL. 9)

Featuring return favorites Fenwick, Hensley, Columbia, Davis, Bell, Arp, Kimball, Kaczynski, Wolfgang, Hornschemeier, and Crumb. Also: a collaboration between O. Henry Prize-winning author Brian Evenson and Zak Sally; a ballpoint gallery from frequent Built to Spill album artist, Mike Scheer; the first part (of two) of a 45-page "Frank" story by Jim Woodring, "The Lute String," previously published only in Japan.

MOME WINTER/SPRING 2008 (VOL. 10)

Featuring original covers by Al Columbia, as well as returning favorites Crumb, Fenwick, Bravo, Goodin, Kaczynski, Wolfgang, Hornschemeier and Hensley. Also: the second and final chapter of Woodring's "The Lute String," as well as the debuts of Dash Shaw, John Hankiewicz, and Jeremy Eaton, and an interview with Tom Kaczynski.

MOME SUMMER 2008 (VOL. 11)

Featuring covers by and the MOME debut of French great Killoffer, as well as Mome familiars Columbia, Wolfgang, Fenwick, Davis, Shaw, Hankiewicz, Bravo, Arp, Kaczynski and Hornschemeier. Also: an interview with Ray Fenwick, and the debuts of Nate Neal and Conor O'Keefe.

SUBSCRIBE TO MOME

Save 10 dollars per year off the cover price. Rates for a four-issue subscription are as follows: $49.95 U.S. & Canada only, $54.95 for global surface mail, $69.95 for global air mail. Each issue is carefully boxed prior to being shipped. To subscribe using your Visa or MasterCard, call us toll-free at 1-800-657-1100 or visit our website: www.fantagraphics.com. Otherwise, send U.S. check or money order to: MOME Subscriptions, c/o Fantagraphics Books, 7563 Lake City Way NE, Seattle, WA 98115 USA.

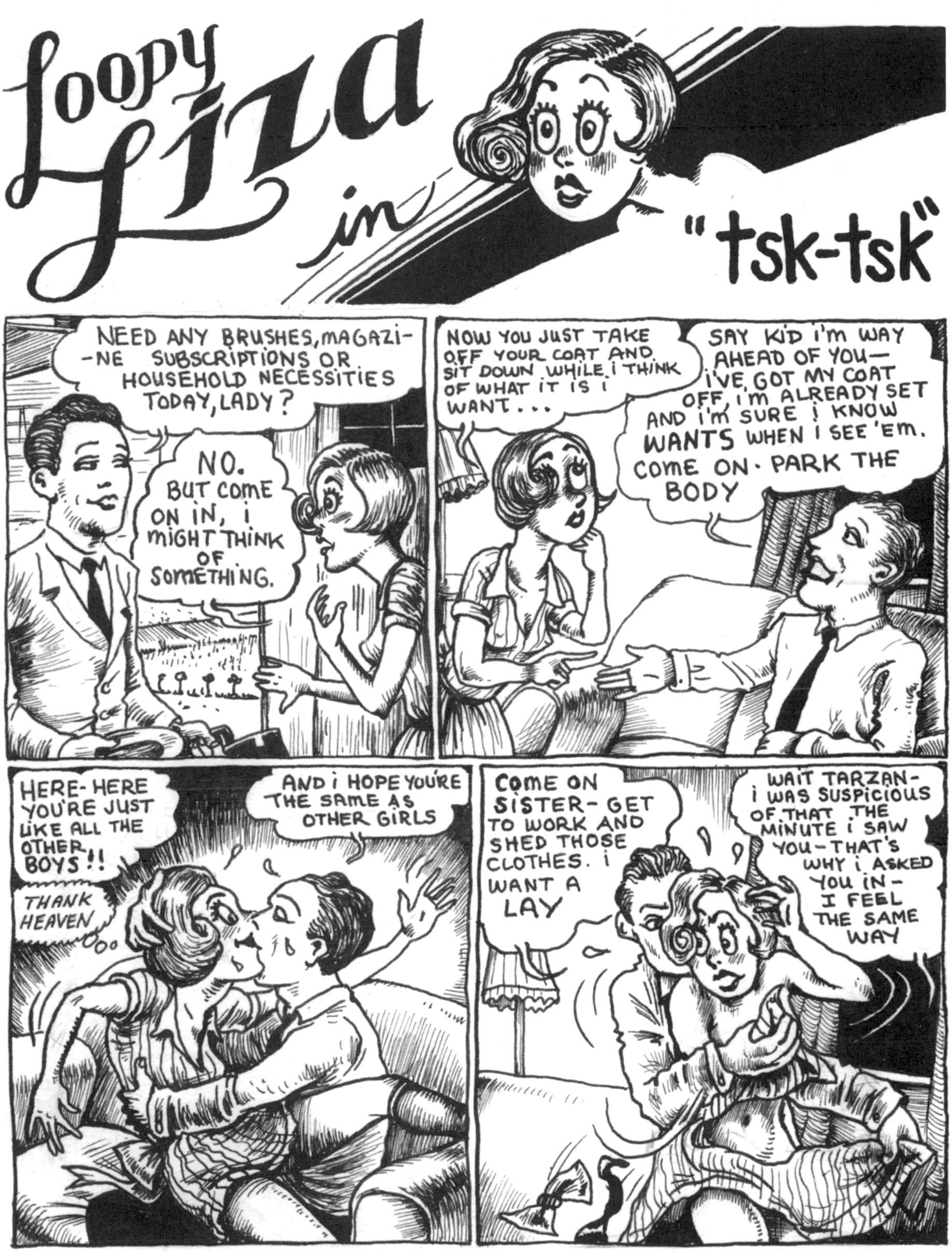
Loopy Liza in
"tsk-tsk"
NEED ANY BRUSHES, MAGAZI-NE SUBSCRIPTIONS OR HOUSEHOLD NECESSITIES TODAY, LADY?
NO. BUT COME ON IN, I MIGHT THINK OF SOMETHING.
NOW YOU JUST TAKE OFF YOUR COAT AND SIT DOWN WHILE I THINK OF WHAT IT IS I WANT...
SAY KID I'M WAY AHEAD OF YOU— I'VE GOT MY COAT OFF, I'M ALREADY SET AND I'M SURE I KNOW WANTS WHEN I SEE 'EM. COME ON · PARK THE BODY
HERE-HERE YOU'RE JUST LIKE ALL THE OTHER BOYS!!
THANK HEAVEN
AND I HOPE YOU'RE THE SAME AS OTHER GIRLS
COME ON SISTER- GET TO WORK AND SHED THOSE CLOTHES. I WANT A LAY
WAIT TARZAN- I WAS SUSPICIOUS OF THAT THE MINUTE I SAW YOU-THAT'S WHY I ASKED YOU IN- I FEEL THE SAME WAY

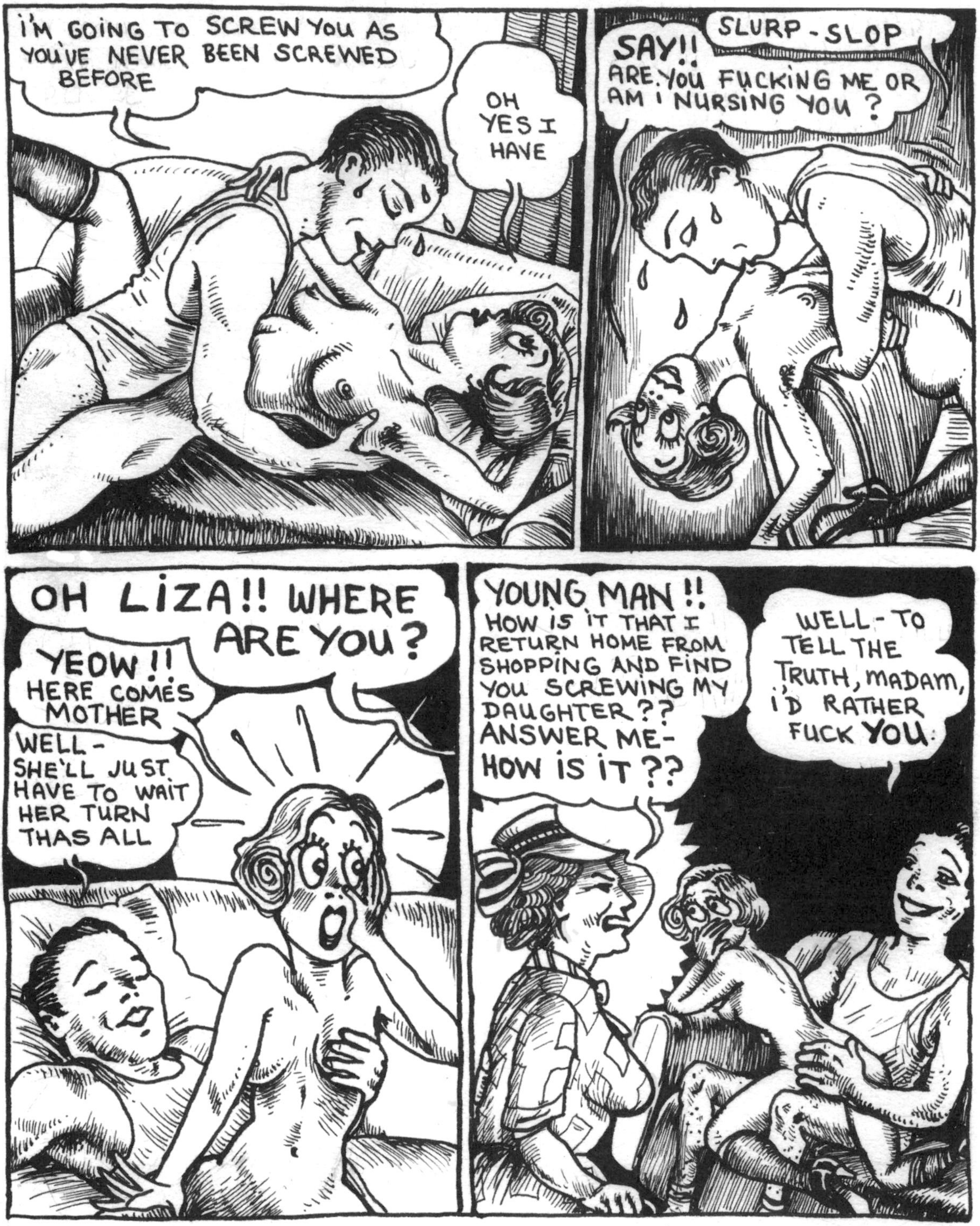
I'M GOING TO SCREW YOU AS YOU'VE NEVER BEEN SCREWED BEFORE
OH YES I HAVE
SLURP - SLOP
SAY!! ARE YOU FUCKING ME OR AM I NURSING YOU?
OH LIZA!! WHERE ARE YOU?
YEOW!! HERE COMES MOTHER
WELL - SHE'LL JUST HAVE TO WAIT HER TURN THAS ALL
YOUNG MAN!! HOW IS IT THAT I RETURN HOME FROM SHOPPING AND FIND YOU SCREWING MY DAUGHTER?? ANSWER ME - HOW IS IT??
WELL - TO TELL THE TRUTH, MADAM, I'D RATHER FUCK YOU.

ART BY SOPHIE CRUMB - WORDS BY UNKNOWN 1930'S PORNO FUNNIES. 04/08